LONDON,

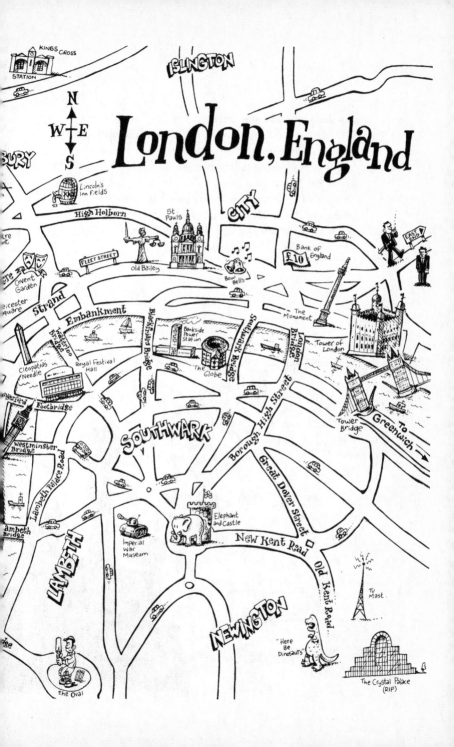

Derek Hammond was born in Leicester in 1962. In 1985 he was dubbed 'easily the best contemporary lyricist in Britain today' by the *New Musical Express* – but someone was sadly mistaken. As a freelance journalist he has since worked for BBC Radios 4 and 5 Live, and has written for a wide range of publications, including the *NME*, *Loaded* and *FourFourTwo*. He was recently co-author, with Jez Prins, of *The Space Cadets' Treasury of Football Nostalgia 2097*.

LONDON, ENGLAND

A DAY-TRIPPER'S TRAVELOGUE FROM THE COOLEST CITY IN THE WORLD

Derek Hammond

with illustrations by Simon Smith

First published in Great Britain in 1998 by
MAINSTREAM PUBLISHING COMPANY
(EDINBURGH) LTD
7 Albany Street
Edinburgh EH1 3UG

ISBN 1 85158 989 9

A catalogue record for this book is available from the British Library

Typeset in Bodoni Classic and Van Dijck MT
Printed and bound in Finland by WSOY

Contents

Introduction   I ♥ London   9

1   London Calling   13
King's Cross and Euston Arch; film-set London; the Post Office
Tower; *London on £1 a Day*; Madame Tussaud's and the Spirit of
London Ride; the real Sherlock Holmes

2   Hop-on Hop-off Glory   29
Trafalgar Square; National Portrait Gallery; Downing Street;
Scotland Yard and *The Sweeney*; talkin' *Cockney Wivout Tears*;
Houses of Parliament; Westminster Abbey

3   Leicester Square: Who, Me?   49
West End entertainment – and music hall, too; Cliff Richard and
the Birth of Cool; Soho spies; Carnaby Street; a 'Brief
Encounter'; Chinatown; Madame JoJo's

4   London: Zoo   67
Primrose Hill; London Zoo; Regent's Park; *On Her Majesty's Secret
Service*; Noel and Patsy's; Mary Poppins; Lord's cricket ground;
Abbey Road . . . and Paul Is Dead

5   EastEnders   81
Brick Lane bagels; Itchycoo Park; The Ten Bells; The Wonders of
Wapping Wharf; The Town of Ramsgate; Execution Dock; Cable
Street; the Krays; Jack the Ripper; jellied eels

6   The Stony-Hearted Stepmother   103
Dodgy old Oxford Street; Terry Venables' three-card trick;
Tyburn hangings; Selfridge's; Costa del Crime Bar; BBC Broad-
casting House; the British Museum in 23 minutes

7   In the City   119
The Museum of London; Newgate Prison and the Old Bailey;
Fleet Street; St Paul's – *Woo!* Serious *Height!*; the Square Mile;
The Monument; the Tower of London is a fake

8   **Walking Down the King's Road**   139
Quant and Westwood; mods, rockers, futurists and mockers; Sex
Pistols at World's End; Disco Chelsea FC; Sloane Rangers;
Cheyne Walk; Jim Bond's pad; Harrods

9   **Notting Hill Gate**   155
Typecast as Hugh Grant; Local Status; George and Van, Mick
and Marianne; Portobello Road; *London Fields*; Jimi Hendrix
hipster tea-towels; *Bedknobs and Broomsticks*; Carnival

10   **Bull and Bush**   169
Shepherd's Bush; *Steptoe and Son*; double pie, triple mash;
Quadrophenia; the Acton Hilton – London's Dream Factory;
Captain Peacock in the flesh; BBC TV Centre

11   **Hotel on Mayfair: £10,000!?!**   183
Tea at the Dorchester; infiltrating Gentlemen's Clubs; Beatles on
the roof; Piccadilly Circus; London Hilton – *The Stud* meets *The
Bitch*; Shepherd Market; *London Unexpurgated*

12   **Waterloo Sunset**   201
The London Nobody Knows; Bankside; South London is king!; Globe
Theatre; the George Inn; Borough Market; H.E. Popham's *Tavern
Frenzy* (1927); MOMI; Festival of Britain

13   **Park Life**   219
Marble Arch; Speakers' Corner; the *Changing* Guard at Bucking-
ham Palace?; St James's Park; Hyde Park; The Great Exhibition;
Albertopolis; Donovanopolis

14   **Near to the Theatre**   237
Covent Garden; London Transport Museum; Street Theatre and
Stringfellow's *v* Andrew Lloyd Webber; *Alternative London* and
Neal Street; Embankment; *The Mousetrap*

15   **Old Father Thames, Old Father Time, Inc.**   257
The *Royal Princess* to Greenwich; London Bridge; Docklands;
Canary Wharf; *The Sordid Side of London Town*; The Millennium
Starts Here; Nelson is Dead; the DianaDome

16   **Fantastic London**   279

Introduction: I ♥ London

Roll the titles: I LOVE LONDON splashed over Technicolor helicopter footage of Big Ben, shot from high over the river. Roll the soundtrack: a patriotic military march, just in case Betty Windsor's at home in Buckingham Palace. Zoom along Whitehall to Nelson's Column, and children playing on the lions in Trafalgar Square. Cut to stock shots of 'bustling' Carnaby Street; to lovers lazing in 'leafy' Hyde Park – and a busy, brassy slice of psychedelia that you just know was played by fifty-year-old men wearing pink ruffle shirts. And cravats.

Cue plummy actor's voiceover: 'Royal London. Swinging London! Theatreland. Gangland. Dickens' London; London at War. World capital of music, media and money; fashion, food and fiction. Centre of Empire. City of dreams. Shopping. Nightlife. Fame. Fortune. The most historical, mythological, phantasmagorical . . . *London!*'

This is the London I love: the picture-postcard images that have been shuffled together in multilingual guidebooks and self-important film documentaries for the past thirty or forty years, spawning a never-changing fantasy of London. But when the classic intro sequence is over, its reuse exposed as clever satire, am I the only one who feels let down by the unfolding history of yuppiedom? By *The Evils of the Tourist Trinket Trade*? By an intimate portrait of Lady Di's hairstylist? Far more sexy was the kaleidoscopic jumble of glorious cliché spliced together by dependable men in cravats. Nothing can live up to the promise of legendary London – to the *idea* of London.

This is the London I'm going in search of: the London that can somehow make you feel part of something glamorous; the London that exerts its magical magnetic influence all over Britain, Europe and the globe. London is the leader. The *biggest* and the *smelliest*. London means all things to all people. Freedom. Fog. Sex. Dick Van Dyke. Punk Rock. Cup Final day. Wren. Beatles. Pandas. *Cats.* Jellied eels.

Every London guide ever written threatens to lift up the petticoats of the city and expose the real London – *Smokers' London*; *Left-Handed London*; *London on Stilts*. But I don't want the *real* London.

I want to go day-tripping in *unreal* London. Sadly, I've never come across a guidebook leading the way into the avenues and alleyways of *Private Detectives' London*, or a copy of *Overfamiliar London in Unconvincing 3-D*. To search out the true Londoholic's London, I'll be following up leads in all the most tantalising guides ever to slip out of print without anyone noticing: Ian Fleming's *Thrilling Cities*, Anita Dobson's TV tie-in *My East End*, the indispensable *London on £1 a Day* . . .

I'll use the handy slang section in Len Deighton's *London Dossier* to converse with luvverly bosomy barmaids in dodgy jolly cockernee taverns. I'll patch together a history of the city exclusively from souvenir tea-towels. I'll ask directions from friendly London bobbies; walk the streets swinging my patent Londonometer and looking up at tall buildings. I'll visit all the very *Londonest* scenes of the past and present, judging them against expectations boosted sky-high by classic cinema, childhood TV and too much swinging spy fiction. Like Sherlock Holmes on the scent of cocaine, I'll track down those Perfect London Moments – when the unmistakable atmosphere, cutting-edge excitement and warped nostalgia combine . . . and you know you're standing in the Coolest City on the Planet.

In other words, I'm going to wander around London doing my best to have a good time. And if it's rubbish, I'll lie.

LONDON, ENGLAND

A DAY TRIPPER'S TRAVELOGUE FROM THE COOLEST CITY IN THE WORLD

Derek Hammond

LONDON England

1 London Calling

Adventures in fantasy London begin and end on the Euston Road. Every minute, hundreds of visitors pour onto the street from the three great rail stations, their InterCity seats and sticky toffee-wrappers already nestling beneath the bottoms of yesterday's visitors on the backwash to the North. One London story begins, another gets its final retouches on the journey home.

It's a grey February morning in King's Cross. One starry-eyed tourist turns her A–Z upside-down to get her bearings, and bravely strikes out for the Tube entrance, five yards away. Now for the ultimate test of those cherished images of London. A boy sits under a blanket on the pavement, his back to the railings, laughing at *The Big Issue*. NEW TO LONDON. SPANISH BEAUTY – just one of thirty calling cards Blu-tacked inside a telephone kiosk – HOTEL VISITS. 0171-XXX XXXX. How much does it take to dash anyone's London dreams on the rocks of reality?

By reputation, King's Cross is the seediest, most dangerous corner in all of London; but fortunately I'm far too busy day-tripping to notice any threat of impending brutality. I like it here. On the main drag outside the station, there's an electric potential in the air as people hurry in every direction, harried by weak neon temptations, hustled at every step for loose change. I cross the road for a peek, between the Great Northern and St Pancras hotels, at the gasometers by the tracks to the north, and the universally symbolic Sunday supplement experience costs me a grand total of £1.12. In the midst of Britain's first experiment with Bronx-style 'Zero Tolerance' of crime – and that means *any* crime, punk – luminous tank-topped RoboBobbies apply Instant Justice to help sort out four piss-artists' squabble over a can of Tennent's Super. Blanket boy gets told to 'move along', so he moves a few feet further down his railings. I feel the rumble of the Underground running deep beneath the gold-paved street, and think of all the landmark coming-to-London films – siren songs like *A Hard Day's Night*, *Georgy Girl*, *Smashing Time* – that still play a part in maintaining a flow of people into the city, each demanding a personalised fulfilment of London's unspoken promise.

Well, they did the trick for me, anyway.

Like everyone from Leicester, I grew up to accept the wisdom that London is a great place to visit, *but you wouldn't want to live there*. No one was talking about living in a cardboard box in London. They meant living in a house. In London. You wouldn't want to do it, me duck. For years I made regular trips, ostensibly on the business of writing rubbish or practising poses for useless LP covers, and all the while I secretly pitied my trailblazing friends for their obvious lifestyle gaffe of lining up endless amusement on tap. Then Lesley Wallace, my smashin' Sweaty Sock squeeze . . . my Chilly Jocko lovebird . . . my *delightful Scottish partner* got a job with Auntie Beeb, moved to London, and swiftly became the love of my life. She wasn't even suspicious.

Dick Whittington. The Beatles. Joe Orton. Oasis. Marx. Kylie Minogue. Freud. Dannii Minogue. Gaultier and Westwood. Hendrix and Hockney. Maxwell and Murdoch. Me and Lesley Wallace. We're all Londoners now.

But, after three years in The Smoke, the devastating truth has been revealed: London is, in fact, a great place to visit *and* a great place to live. Trouble is, when you *live* here, circumstances demand that you have to stop *visiting*. Londoners aren't really supposed to take any pleasure from bagging a front seat upstairs on an antique Routemaster bus, and pretending to drive. Buying the Sunday papers on Saturday night isn't generally regarded as miraculous. Yer gen-u-whine cockernee geezer would never deign to glance in the general direction of St Paul's or the Houses of Parliament. Not even if John Major were standing on a high ledge, threatening to jump. Not even if Her Royal Eminence Sarah Ferguson wobbled over the road from Westminster Abbey to tempt him back inside using *all her womanly wiles*. Nah, not interested, moy san. Sahnds like one o' vem tourist gimmicks to me.

Now it's time to crap or get off the pot. I need to wring more out of London than a weekly sherbet in Soho, and a few illicit hours snatched from beneath the noses of scornful fellow-citizens on the hop-on hop-off tourist bus circuit. I want to have my cake and eat it. With jam on it. Like a dog in a manger. As London's first and only Doorstep Day-tripper, I'm going out into the city *and I'm going to admit that it's not mediocre* . . .

In King's Cross, no one has fallen into the trap of taking London for granted. London is The Place To Be. The attraction of London seems to grow proportionally stronger in direct relation to ambition and greed, desperation and destitution — as if the unfathomable fortune of apparently hopeless cases made good (Kate Moss, Andrew Lloyd Webber, Peter Stringfellow . . .) might repeat, or somehow *rub off*. By turn, the energy and enthusiasm of all manner of recent arrivals bleeds into the atmosphere of the Euston Road. *Trainspotting*, in part a rewrite of *Smashing Time* for the hard-nosed '90s, features the Scotsmen who fly south 'with big dreams and small budgets' — the East Coast mainliners from Edinburgh via Newcastle and all stops to King's Cross, whose capital adventure never gets further than the station steps.

A low-rent to no-rent, fast-money community has built up around this permanently cracked Gateway to the North, with a version of all life's requirements laid out readily available for your fleeting gratification. You need look no further than Eddie's Kiosk for the basic NEWS CIGS SWEETS CRISPS DRINKS. For more substantial sources of grease, prepare to turn a blind eye to the Trade Descriptions Act at INCREDIBLE EDIBLES. Cheap hotels will sell you a bed for the night; some might negotiate a price for a shorter stay. One of Spanish Beauty's immediate neighbours offers CORRECTION DOMINATION TV WARDROBE RUBBER BONDAGE ELECTRICS.

Electrics?

Red neon blinks against the daylight, promising AMUSEMENTS at the optimistically named LEISURE CENTRE. A hand-chalked blackboard outside the Flying Scotsman pub advertises DANCERS DANCERS DANCERS. A couple of the BOOKS MAGS VIDEOS outlets actually stock old-style, specialist paperbacks — the ones with words, to be read with two hands. Bookies' shops and a snooker hall, the boarded-up Scala cinema and fluorescent-lit greasy spoons extend along the Pentonville Road, where Zero Tolerance has sent the few bored, tired-looking entrepreneurs who wait to serve up anything you can't find on the official menu. Charity flags? Smack? Their grannie?

And will that be *with* the optional electrics, sir?

Haughtily overshadowing the simple yellow-brick double arch of King's Cross station and all its grubby hinterland is the fantastic Gothic castle of St Pancras, a red-brick railway hotel and station frontage designed quite consciously to be mistaken for a cathedral. Built in the 1860s at the height of the railway boom, this wonder of its age shows what scale and grandeur can be achieved in architecture when money is simply no object: three hundred feet by six storeys of ornate arches, mouldings, balconies and turrets; an enormous frilly clock tower at the eastern end to sneer down on the Great Northern Railway's merely functional London terminus; and no less than seven weather-vanes to exclusively show Midland Railway's passengers which way the wind was blowing. The hotel was closed in 1935, hacked up into offices, and now stands empty.

On Pancras Road, tiny industrial units have burrowed into archways in the hulking station's side – dilapidated, patched-up, grimy behind metal grilles. Roads criss-cross haphazardly in the half-light under the diverging railway tracks. The empty iron gasometers stand in scrubland behind barbed wire, framing the entire shattered skyline. I cut down Weller's Court, a dead-end of damp black-brick tenements lifted straight out of Dickens' East End. Looking back

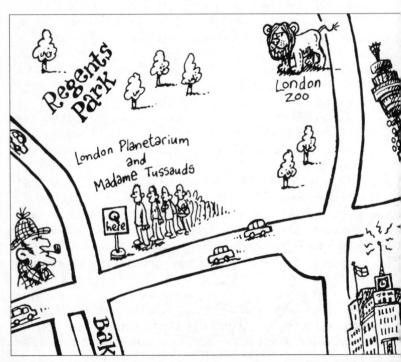

along the cobbled roadway, the great black roll of the St Pancras engine-shed has reared into view. No more than two hundred yards from the stew of the stations' platforms, and there can't be a lonelier, more claustrophobic spot in all London. Except at night, when the dark stretches between the streetlights cradle communities of blood and needles and bodily fluids.

In fact, the atmosphere around this tight quarter of squalid workers' hutches is so threatening, so perfectly grim, it has become one of the city's favourite film locations: a crack of light appears at the foot of the blank end wall, and around the tight corner is a lorry with an anti-aircraft searchlight slicing into the gloom of Cheney Road. All at once, we're back in Fantasy London – if you can use such a phrase in the same sentence as runaway children, *Mona Lisa* and prostitution for pennies. This is the south London street from *Chaplin*'s childhood in the 1880s; the scene of the bullion robbery in the Ealing comedy *The Ladykillers*; even home to Shakespeare's *Richard III* – the version set in the London of the 1930s, starring Ian

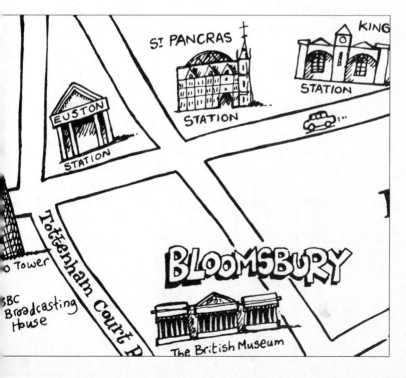

McKellen as the king, and St Pancras Hotel as his palace.

I climb up the steps from Pancras Road to relive my earliest London memory – of waiting with my parents to pick up my big sister from this lofty St Pancras forecourt. I remember looking down over the road at a Wimpy Bar, whose rubberised speciality dish seemed, at that moment, at once the most exciting, desirable and deliciously forbidden prospect. Ooh, we never had a Wimpy Bar in Leicester. At least if we did, I'd never seen it, much less sampled the authentic big-city wonder of junk food. I know this isn't necessarily the wildest first impression of London, but I was only five or six, and found myself in no position to choose. Would it make it seem any more vital and dangerous if I mentioned the Wimpy Bar is now a Burger King? On the London stage of this annual Whitsun trek to see my nanny and aunties and uncles in Bexhill-on-Sea, I would hang out of the car window in a pant-dampening state of euphoria, looking for famous people and football grounds and places to stop for a piss . . . in *London!* Even now, the intended cautious passage of our saluki bronze Vauxhall Victor is branded into my brain: *Turn right at the Blue Star garage . . . Baker Street, North Audley Street, South Audley Street . . .*

Every year, Uncle Cyril's foolproof directions would come out of their flap at the back of the *AA Book* and, every year, they would fool my mum. Every year, thanks to her high-pressure navigational skills, we would find ourselves safely delivered over Vauxhall Bridge. And then, without fail, a wrong turning left. Panic! (Mum). Confusion! (Dad). Tears! (me). Supreme teenage hippy boredom! (big sister Lynda). And back, in the wrong direction, over Lambeth Bridge.

Having scored myself a half-decent intro on the mean streets of King's X, I'm now tempted to hang about for nine minutes in the cavernous, iron-ribbed span of St Pancras, and catch the arrival of the 10.32 from Leicester. It's a tricky old business, the London Intro, especially when you can't afford a helicopter to fly under Tower Bridge, and describing a bunch of crumpled chancers rolling in from my neck of the East Midlands might just add a dash of romance. On the other hand I'm beginning to feel like a bit of a tosser, hanging around station platforms with no one to meet and no train to catch. I head out into the cold and light, and set out for a feast of wax-based London fun.

Passing by the black plastic office block which screens the equally disposable frontage of Euston Station from sight, I suffer a double pang of nostalgia for times past on the West Coast Mainline. Having moved to London from Birmingham, Euston is the station I associate most with that London feeling of endless possibility. Also, I've seen pictures of what was so casually demolished to make way for the 'faceless efficient' new. Of the original station's Great Hall, John Betjeman wrote, 'Never has there been since in England so magnificent a piece of railway architecture. To compare with Euston there is nothing.' At the front of the station once stood an awe-inspiring eighty-foot entrance archway, whose thick classical columns and portico looked as if they'd been carved from a single, colossal cube of granite – our own industrial Parthenon on the Euston Road. Betjeman called the arch 'the noblest thing in London, nobler even than the British Museum'. I once turned a corner into Curzon Street in the run-down, ex-industrial wasteland south of Birmingham city centre, and was struck dumb by the unexpected appearance of the Euston arch's baby brother which still stands, disused, at the old northern terminus of the original London–Birmingham trunk line – if you look, you can see it from the train. Birmingham's planners of the '60s may have spared their grand station entrance simply because it was out of the way, but in the Edwardian city centre they proved even worse vandals than their conspirators in London.

No one ever told me Birmingham was a great place to visit *or* a great place to live, so a higher logic dictated that I should end up staying there for eleven years. For old friends and baltis, Brum will always be unbeatable; but even a pamphlet on the mythology of the Second City might look a bit, well, *thin* – based around three mid-'70s hits by the Electric Light Orchestra, the Bull Ring shopping centre, and the superb, exclusively egg-based restaurant situated close by: at Mister Egg it is more than possible to 'Eat Like A King For Under A Pound'.

Some small echo of the impact of Euston arch can be gathered across the road at St Pancras New Church, which is immediately recognisable, even to non-students of architecture, as 'a cool-looking church'. This is a white-stone, controversially un-Christian example of the 'cool' school, so categorised because of its six great, fluted columns, the sorority toga party balancing the porch on their heads, and an elaborate spire which clearly foresaw Thunderbird One in the early years of the nineteenth century.

It only looks about four inches on the map, straight along Euston Road till it turns into Marylebone Road, then straight on to Madame Tussaud's, just short of Baker Street. But, hey, this map is four-and-a-half inches to the *mile*. No buses run the route. It's getting colder and it's starting to drizzle. I plod on, not bothering to try and describe any more of the old buildings along the way. I'm really more of a self-appointed expert on modern buildings: less technical terms, see. The new British Library, now running three times over its £160 million budget, still isn't open to the public five years after it was due for completion. It looks like a vast red-brick aircraft-carrier, and it's about as much use.

My favourite London building of all looms above me now as I trudge west. The Telecom Tower – or, as awkward fans of a certain age insist on referring to it (*quite correctly* as it happens, because who ever heard of anyone changing the name of a building once it's been built, just to score a cheap political point?), the *Post Office Tower* – dominates the skyline of central London, whether glimpsed between rooftops from the back-alleys of Soho or from miles out of town on Hampstead Heath. This futuristic, blue-glass rocket was thrown up in 1964, beaming out the message to the world: THIS IS LONDON. WE CAN DO ANYTHING. JUST WATCH US. They even installed a Tower-topping revolving restaurant, with the sole intention of forcing everyone who ever uttered the words *Post . . . Office . . . Tower* to follow them automatically and quite helplessly with the taboo London G-word: Grrr-*ooveh*!

Ever since I collected the stamps as a kid, and enjoyed a vicarious visit to the spinning, skyscraping summit of London courtesy of *John Craven's Newsround*, I always knew I'd make it to the restaurant myself, one day. When I was a big boy.

Gazing down each of the side-streets until I finally draw level with the monster mod monolith, I turn left without a conscious thought and step out in pursuit of my Big London Dream. I am as a moth – a large, flightless moth with an upside-down *A–Z* – drawn to the red light winking in the misty rain six hundred feet above the city. I am now that big boy, I tell myself. My time has come. I've been on Mission London for an hour and a half, and already my itinerary's gone to pot.

One unusual feature of the Post Office Tower is its groundbreaking, money-saving, rather confusing lack of a proper entrance. Before I can even attempt to book a table for two for next Friday, a security guard stationed inside what *looks* like an entrance tells me the Tower isn't open to the public, this *isn't* an entrance, and she only works here. I'm directed down an alleyway which passes by the very foot of the Tower, affording one of the finest views of London from one of the least promising standpoints, wedged tight between walls and wheelie-bins. The Tower thrusts proudly straight up into the sky, an array of buzzing kettle-drums strapped just beneath its bulbous, rotating upper section. When it comes to optional electrics, it's whatever turns you on, sir/madam.

Busy working out the length of rope you'd need to fire a grappling hook onto the flared third-floor concrete overhang, I almost miss the poky blue door with the intercom.

'It's not been open to ver public for ver parst twenty years,' larfs the guard behind the high-security screen in the tradesmen's entrance-burrow. 'Ve old restaurant still goes rahnd, vough. Twenty-two minutes, it takes to go *roight* rahnd,' he adds proprietorially, letting his high-security hat slip a fraction. 'Now vey just use it for fanctions to impress veir clients. Course, it's not for ver likes of ver poor sod wiv ver Telecom phone.'

Let me up let me up let me up let me up, I will him.

'Fanny fing is, it ain't even no good for fanctions, 'cos you can't see 'alf ver punters: vere's vis bloody big bit in ver middle where ver lift goes up.'

It's not fair. He hates it, and he can go up any time. I love it, and I'm stuck in the basement.

Then I'm back in the alley again, the phone number for BT's Stupid Enquiries Helpdesk secure in my pocket. The third floor overhang beckons. It'd take more than the absence of an entrance and a couple of security guards to keep your archetypal cravat-toting London secret agent from his ninety-ninth-floor earth-spinning dinner-date with Spanish Beauty. Me, I'll give the number a try before investing in five hundred feet of nylon rope and a set of rubber sucker-pads.

I'll be back.

I'm especially keen to visit Madame Tussaud's, largely on the strength of a back-handed recommendation from Betty James in her go-getter's gospel, *London on £1 a Day*. When it comes to day-tripping around the Londonest scenes, doing London things, London-style, there's no reason to assume a guidebook is useless just because it's slipped a little way past its sell-by date. Why put up with the ill-informed rambling of some pertinent teenage backpacker when you can tap into the ever in-form rambling of John Betjeman, Angie out of *EastEnders* or our Betty – the acknowledged greats? London may be at the cutting edge of culture, but one of its main attractions is that it never *really* changes. Unless you're picky and count little things like details.

Betty, the brilliantly chirpy, grumpy, semi-American cheapskate (maybe I'm being unfair – a quid would have bought more than five St Pancras toilet visits in her day) makes great play of forewarning us about the *funny joke attendants* at Madame Tussaud's. 'They are made of wax,' she says. 'They look as if they are made of wax. Their faces are too pink, their hair is too dry, and their eyes are too glassy.' Betty has made the mistake of earholing an attendant on the door, asking if they could waive the admission fee of four English bobs, seeing as how she's writing a guide for cheapskates. Only then does she notice the attendant seems curiously inattentive . . .

'Well, it *is* damned silly,' Betty huffs. 'I'm jolly glad I didn't go in now. And I'm jolly well not going to write about it either.'

In the modern-day entrance hall, Frank Bruno and Madame T greet visitors oh-so-very-naturalistically from small podiums in the middle of a fountain. A suspiciously pink-faced child sits on the barrier, and I can't resist giving him a playful slap. Luckily, his pink-faced, glassy-eyed, dry-haired parents see the funny side.

Although Madame Tussaud's reportedly sucks in and spits out 2.5 million visitors per year, I've never met one of them. I don't know what to expect. It makes the official Top Four London attractions in all the guidebooks, but even writers who have ventured inside think it's too obvious to elaborate on what's to be found inside a waxworks. The age and quality of the dummy mugshots posted to tempt you inside don't augur too well: I know Madame T has been showing off her gruesome guillotine death-masks on this very spot for 160 years, but that's no excuse for Kojak, let alone Mr T out of *The A-Team* . . .

In the case of Mr T, I suspect nepotism.

To be honest, my best hope at this point was for Madame T's to turn out to be simply, stupendously crap – stupendously crap being so much more enjoyable than your average, common-or-garden, *merely* crap. So imagine my surprise, after half an hour of giggling and poking and gatecrashing other people's snapshots, to be jolted by the unmistakable flashing and pinging of my patent Londonometer! What could the sensitive sensors have sniffed out? A real-life celebrity? A fashion alarm? Surely no one had ever been shot or filmed or accidentally stuffed alive on this spot? – but *something* was triggering an authentic LONDON MOMENT ALERT!?! in mauve and yellow neon letters.

Holding my breath, I follow the digital readings of the futuristic, computerised comic device, which lead me up to a modest sign on the wall: SPIRIT OF LONDON RIDE This Way . . .

Oh, yes indeedy. Here is every London cliché, myth and pipe-dream realised: four hundred years of history collapsed into two fantastic minutes. This is my kind of London: Instant London. Where a tape-loop of music-hall favourites leads the way to the thrills. Tears of joy, tears of larftah. *Let's all . . . go dahn ver Straand . . .*

I hop on board one of the miniature London cabs in the continuous rush-hour tailback whisking around the sights at a characteristic two miles-per-hour. A bar descends across my lap – a sound precaution to help prevent whiplash and squealing groups of Italian schoolchildren taking their place in the hallowed tableaux – and we're off! A robot voice in my ear announces: *Welcome! to the spirit of Londonlondonlondonlondon . . .*

First of all, way back in the mists of time, back in the olden days, there was this bird in a big frock by the name of Elizabeth I. She used to hang out with jesters and Roundheads and William Shakespeare. Then there was a plague of fluffy rats. *Bring out your dead. Bring out your dead.* A fireman squirts his hose over the procession of cabs and I catch his dribbles in my eye. Then we're on a cathedral building-site, and Christopher Wren is rebuilding London in stone. We're up at the top of Nelson's Column, and the voice of C3PO is tripping out his well-rehearsed 'eye' joke, which still needs work on the billionth time of telling. Queen Victoria is captured wearing authentic First World War flying goggles. Charles Dickens' arm is pushing on with its famous mechanised scribbling. We're getting bombed in the Blitz. And so is Winston Churchill. But that's his business.

Now for the crowning glory . . . *the sights, the sounds, the colours, the joy* . . . of the modern(ish) city. Twiggy is first up in this crammed thematic fairground, frugging in freeze-frame in a tinfoil mini-skirt. A dodgy cockernee teddy-boy spiv is trying to sell you the watch he just lifted off your wrist. A friendly London bobby has won a goldfish. There's a barrel-organ playing, a roundabout packed with lions and unicorns and pearly kings and queens. A yuppie in a pleasure-boat. A Chelsea Pensioner. A Beefeater. Benny Hill. It's *unbelievable* . . .

You could spend months in London and never come across one of these larger-than-life sights or sounds. If this stuff didn't exist, someone would have to go out and invent it.

Still reeling from the sugar high of SuperLondon, I shamelessly invade the personal space of a string of defenceless celebrities: the best of the models do have an undeniable physical presence captured in their stance or posture, which is most often transmitted by accidental eye-contact . . . with a block of wax. Personal highlights include Joanna Lumley's hands and Naomi Campbell's armpit. Very realistic, so far as I can judge. And in Naomi's case, probably more of a thrill than meeting the real person. What I mean is, you couldn't just walk up to Naomi on the street and check out the delicious fleshy fold of her underarm. I mean, it would be terribly sexist. And she might notice. Back on safer ground, I notice Kylie Minogue is *really tiny*. Marilyn Monroe bears a disturbing resemblance to Rosemary *Hip and Thigh Diet* Conley. Less flattering still is the hook-nosed Lady Di parked tactfully on the flank of the shifty royal team-shot: even the corgis are given a better deal.

Tussaud's seems to have suffered a slip in production values during the '70s and '80s, when dummies like Barbara Cartland and Kojak got their hot-wax treatment. Suffice to say they're back on form in the '90s; but it isn't nearly as much fun ticking off the triumphs as pillorying the decapitated losers on the shelves reserved for Last Year's Models. Or guessing which will be next to join them: *any year now*, Torvill and Dean, Jimmy Saville, Mr bloody T . . .

For just £3 extra on the price of my £9 waxworks ticket, I could have bought a combination deal that also covered entrance beneath the suggestive green dome of the Planetarium, next door; but I'm not in the mood for An Exciting Trip Through Time And Space. I haven't got the time. It says here it would take 341 years to get to the sun in a London taxi; but does that take into account the cabbie's secret short-cut via Jupiter? Another poster invites you in to touch the planets and check the weather live from a satellite; but you wouldn't catch me touching a planet, matey: I prefer to keep my feet on the ground. And it's easy enough to check the weather live outside, without the aid a satellite: it's still raining.

Ever since passing up my chance to exchange £3.99 for an official Chamber of Horrors severed-nose candle, I've been bursting to sift through the epicentre of shabby Londonobilia emporia between the Planetarium and Baker Street. In Fancy That of London, a plastic whalebone-effect Tower Bridge immediately catches my eye, but it's £9.95. They don't have a bobby's helmet in my size. Although I could use a stand-up bobby toothbrush for £2.99, it doesn't say *London* to me like a postcard of someone's breasts painted with amusing animal faces.

However, a quick Londonometer scan – DROP THAT BLEEDIN' CRAP – suggests my judgement may have suffered a temporary lapse, and reveals real hidden London treasure: CATCH THIS 'ERE BUS, SQUIRE!?!

Compared to the 94 notched up on my Londonometer by the Spirit of London ride, my sturdy cast-metal London bus keyring (£1.99) weighs in with a very credible reading of 91: that's great long-term value on a pence-per-point basis. This must be the very last of London's heavy-duty fancy goods. It's a throwback. An off-the-shelf antique. A prince among fobs. It's the kind of quality tourist tat that makes you think, I'll carry it with me forever, everywhere I go. Until I lose my keys again.

Baker Street was one of seven stations on the world's first stretch of urban underground railway, opened between Paddington and King's Cross in 1863, after three years of chaos on the surface as Marylebone Road and Euston Road were ripped up and filled in to make the cheapest possible tunnel. Baker Street is better known as the most annoying station on the entire Tube map, due to its un-failing ability to coerce passengers into whistling or humming the sax solo from Gerry Rafferty's piss-poor 1978 hit, 'Baker Street . . . mwa-mwa mwa-mwa-mwaaa'.

Just around the corner, at 221b Baker Street . . . *mwa-mwa mwa-mwa-mwaaa* . . . lived Sherlock Holmes, Victorian London's most celebrated snoop. And it was in the express direction of this self-same address that I was in the process of perambulating, my dear

Watson, when whom should I observe striding from the portals of said subterranean transport halt but *none other than the pre-eminent deductive detective himself!?!*

If it hadn't happened, I'd never have dared make it up: there I am weighing up the value of a visit to a museum devoted entirely to a fictional character, when he lopes right past me in the street, cape and deerstalker and funny bendy pipe to the fore, and disappears into 221b – presumably to pick up some of the five thousand letters he still receives every year at this address, from some of the world's most deluded day-dreamers.

Personally, I refuse to believe the man I saw was just an actor employed to drum up museum custom. Now I've seen the *real* Sherlock Holmes, the idea of mocked-up rooms with violins and oversize magnifying glasses and interactive touch-button pea-souper jets loses its appeal. I've already braved a completely (thankfully) unconvincing Jack the Ripper scene in Madame T's Chamber of Horrors – with Mitre Square and Catherine Eddowes' tomato-saucy body shifted half a mile to right outside the Ten Bells pub – and it would never do to get my historical facts too confused with fiction.

All the same, who can wonder that even the brilliant Holmes failed to collar the Ripper, with evidence-tampering on that kind of scale?

My own day's elementary detection is almost done. I turn on my heel and retrace my steps down Baker Street . . . *mwa-mwa mwa-mwa-mwaaargh* . . . in search of a welcoming lower-class hostelry in which to warm the heart of my cockles in the company of some bawdy songstress and a penn'orth of foaming ale.

'Driver, follow that cab to the most *typical* of taverns! A man's life may depend on it!'

2 Hop-on Hop-off Glory

Trafalgar Square is one of London's most symbolic sites, ever close to the heart of the nation – despite the fact that no one seems quite sure what it *means*. When Gazza's wonder-goal paved the way for England to beat Scotland in the Euro '96 football championship, English fans piled high in the fountains and provoked their own mini-Trafalgar against police baton squads. A week later, when England were knocked out of the same tournament by Germany, everyone went home peacefully. Members of the Great British public assemble in Trafalgar Square to cheer in the New Year; to march against Apartheid; to riot against the Poll Tax; to feed the pigeons we loathe; and whenever we win a war.

The heroic battle reliefs at the foot of Nelson's Column are cast from gun-metal captured in his victories. ENGLAND EXPECTS EVERY MAN WILL DO HIS DUTY, the inscription booms – and therein lies an explanation for the schizophrenic behaviour witnessed in the square. When this monument to Power and Glory was completed in the 1840s, the words clearly referred to every man's generous insistence on blindly following rich people's orders, and maintaining a nice shiny musket. A modern reading of Nelson's patriotic threat is more open to interpretation; but it's generally taken to demand grumbling support of the national football team, a willingness to get your round in, and don't kick up too much fuss when everyone else decides they want crisps. Incidentally, the same now goes for women, too.

Nelson's Column is guarded on four corners by brave British lions, long redundant. For a long time after the Second World War, Landseer's iron pussies formed a handy, helpless X at the centre of the world's juiciest atom bomb target; now they're demoted once again to mere toys for infants and tourists to clamber over in London's video playground. A ludicrous statue of the unpopular King George IV (previously known as *Black Adder*'s Prince Regent) riding bareback 'in his dressing-gown and drawers', was dumped by Parliament at the top of the square when the original plans for its perch (you'll never guess!) fell through. Two lesser (unscaleable) Raj

Generals were later augmented by busts of Jellicoe and Beatty, in order that 'their illustrious services to the State might never be forgotten' – but sadly someone forgot to attach a note to remind us exactly how those Brownie points were totted up. In the typing-pool? On the cricket field? Something to do with naval carnage? History has scarcely been kinder to Viscount Horatio himself: ossified in memory as seventeen feet of stone, he's best known for lending his name to a wrestling hold, and for offering one last snog to his first lieutenant in countless TV comedy sketches. The overall effect of his Column could have been a lot worse: the real Nelson was five foot four.

It's easy to take the piss – indeed, England and the English modestly expect it – but day-dreaming here at the balustrade above Trafalgar Square, there is still a sense of being at the centre of a rickety old empire. Every fixture in sight has stood here practically forever; it's just the world that's changed. Whitehall lies straight ahead, sloping away to Downing Street and Big Ben. Through the triumphal Roman office block of Admiralty Arch, The Mall runs direct to Buckingham Palace. The Strand leads off to the City. Canada House and the South African Embassy face each other across the square. Uganda House is here, too. Next-door to the Angus Steak House.

Columns of red buses putter clockwise around the white stone square, under a faded blue sky. Millions of people pass through Trafalgar Square every year, keen to hoover up the experiences those funny local people insist on taking so casually; happy just to play at being in London with a soya-goo hot-dog, a big-eyed caricature of the kids, a temporary tattoo, and feed the birds, tuppence a bag, guv'nor.

There's nowhere quite like an Angus Steak House to ground yourself in Englishness with a special blowout treat: Vic Reeves once nominated the chain as the venue for a fantasy dinner-date because of their monopoly on all the prime London locations, coupled with the apparent guarantee of a window seat. One day soon, I've promised myself, I'll become the first person I've actually ever known to go for a meal at a Steak House, where I'll order our unofficial national menu. Starter: prawn cocktail in small metal bowl, accompanied by a slice of lemon in a patent squeezing device. Main course: steak and chips, with peas and mushrooms and carefully counted allotment of fried onion rings. Pudding: Black Forest gâteau. Sorted.

According to the dodgy decimal ready-reckoner of LONDON'S ONE AND ONLY licensed birdseed seller, tuppence a bag equates to ONLY 25p A POT in the new money. Elsewhere in the city, polite notices warn of the plague-spreading propensity of rats-with-wings; but in Trafalgar Square it's traditional to HAVE FUN FEEDING THE FAMOUS LONDON PIGEONS. So that's all right, then.

'Ooh, they're fighting!' squeals one small child with a pigeon on his head, a pigeon on each shoulder and a seedy skirmish developing in his blood-specked hands. 'Ooh, they're pecking!'

Ooh, they're crapping. Ooh, in his hair.

Then something happens: it could have been a taxi revving at the pedestrian crossing outside St Martin-in-the-Fields, or a granny rustling a bag of stale sliced bread on the other side of the square, but they're off. The thick carpet of pigeons rises into the air in a single flapping wave and wheels around at head height. Then one of them realises it hasn't the faintest idea why it took off in the first place, and alights on somebody's cheese sandwich. Good idea: food. Six hundred pigeons resettle on two hundred lucky tourists. Well, they say bird crap is lucky. I'm not so sure it's lucky on your cheese sandwich. But look out. Wasn't that the sound of a granny rustling a bag of stale sliced bread on the other side of the square?

Interrupting my therapeutic study of the pigeons' regular two-minute cycle, a noisy guitar band strike up on the upper deck of a private charter bus circling to my right, weaving in and out of the regular services and the hop-on hop-off companies' movable grandstands. It's a brilliantly London publicity trick, straight out of *The Double Deckers* or the Beatles' *Magical Mystery Tour*; but unfortunately the driver catches the lights and the band are whisked away down Pall Mall before they've either chugged their way to a chorus or managed to get arrested. I suspect it may have been that Cliff Richard and his Shadows, rebelling again. I'd have to say the London bus gimmick worked better for Cliff in *Summer Holiday*; but he didn't half move those pigeons.

Standing raised across the northern side of the square is the National Gallery, with its delicate, too-small dome, and sheltering portico pressed full of visitors. Perhaps oddly, most of the British painters are not to be found in the Eurocentric National Gallery, but at the Tate. Either way, I'm hoping to see more of London reflected around the corner, in the separate east wing which houses the

National Portrait Gallery. I'm following up a tip-off from *Europe on $10 a Day*, in one of the more memorable sections where Arthur Frommer formally hands over the reins to Hope, his good lady wife. Mrs Frommer wastes no time in recommending the Portrait Gallery as 'a kind of picture book history', which sounds real neat to me; far preferable to that book-learning kinda history, with words. Apparently, 'there are paintings of everyone from the fifteenth century onwards, and while the paintings themselves are for the most part not worth mentioning, they are bound to appeal to the gossip in you' . . .

Bizarrely enough, Hope is dead right.

The Queen used to be quite a *sexpot*, didn't she? All Andy Warhol had to do was overlay four pairs of dilated pupils and four swathes of

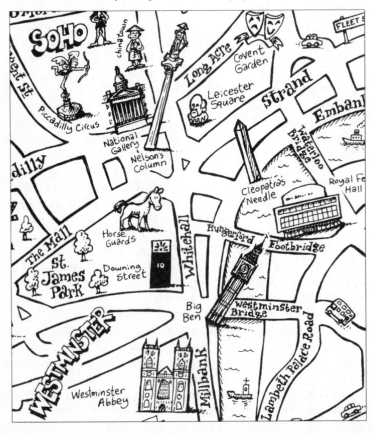

garish acid lipstick and eyeshadow, and Bob's yer uncle! – one demure old portrait, spectrally split into a quadrophonic splash of blue, purple, red and pink majesty. This psychedelic, swinging Queenie must be the ultimate art image for London. I'll never look at a first-class stamp the same way again. Let alone lick one.

Of all the actors, politicians, sportsmen, royals, academics and musicians who make an appearance in the late twentieth century, the most suitable mate for the acrylic Queen of London has to be a black-and-white photo of Georgie Best. What arrogance in his jutting, dimpled chin, in his arms folded across his chunky jumper. What a story: rags, riches, four Miss Worlds; the Fifth Beatle, the sixth bottle. What a *Londoner*. A couple of years ago, at a PR showing of the BBC's *Match of the Seventies*, I was offered a dream chance of interviewing Best, but declined out of a complicated mixture of reverence and pity. The Irishman quit Manchester United and top-class football at the age of twenty-six, when he was the greatest player in the world. I could only think of one question, and it didn't need a Perrier-sipping Best to supply an answer: you really blew it, didn't you, George?

So many essential London Faces: Christine Keeler, naked astride a reversed office chair, recalling *Scandal* and the disastrous (for the Conservative government, at least) Profumo Affair of 1963. Alfred Hitchcock in unmistakable profile. Pete 'n' Dud's cockney taproom philosophers supplanted by Smith and Jones. Lady Di vying with Margaret Thatcher on either side of the Queen. In Boozer's Corner, Oliver Reed looking surlier than Bill Sikes in *Oliver!*, and Soho socialiser Samuel Beckett, deep lines scoring his face, but with eyes as clear as the bottom of the bottle.

Just as illuminating as the pictures themselves are the way certain subjects have chosen to be presented. Alan Bennett with his mug of tea and a crumpled brown-paper bag, which could only possibly contain a curling cheese sandwich. Elton John with hair. Germaine Greer sitting with her legs hippily drawn up on her sofa – *so you can see the split in her shoe* . . . Times have moved on since the days when men yearned to be seventeen feet tall in a toga; but it's still easy to spot the subjects who had zero input on their image: cricketer Ian Botham (tiny head, massive neck); Stephen Fry (distorted beyond recognition); Salman Rushdie, whose daubed impression looks as though it might have been drawn from memory.

Upstairs in the past, Botham Syndrome is suspiciously rare: the Portrait Gallery's picture-book history has been carefully edited by the vain old Victorians paying the artists' fees – unless, of course, all politicians were *really* once this upright and sincere-looking, and women, no longer outnumbered by five hundred to one, have only recently lost the ability to fashionably bloat and contract every part of their bodies at will. The beautiful young Dickens, the frail Robert Louis Stevenson and gentle Thomas Hardy stand out like beacons in the dark galleries full of our courageous, stern, iron-jawed leaders. I've seen more honest likenesses produced by the caricaturists outside in Trafalgar Square . . . On the subject of which, *The Secret of England's Greatness* by Thomas Jones Barker (1865) features Queen Victoria presenting a bible to an 'unidentified' African king, kneeling before her in leopardskin and beads. *Some General Officers of the Great War* by John Singer Sargent (1922) features Major-General Sir, Field-Marshal The Earl, General Lord, General Sir and eighteen other handlebar moustaches, some of whom actually look pleased with themselves.

Outside the National Portrait Gallery, looking down the hill toward Nelson and his cohorts, stands Edith Cavell, the British nurse shot as a spy in 1914. Her riddle-me-ree epitaph, long the subject of whiskery debate, reads PATRIOTISM IS NOT ENOUGH.

Call me a gun-shy civvy, but it's *quite* enough for me, Edith.

Below Trafalgar Square, on the chiselling, windblown traffic island of Charing Cross, a mounted bronze statue of King Charles I looks down Whitehall toward the Banqueting House, where Britain temporarily parted company with his line of monarchy, by way of the executioner's axe. The stone plinth is weathered to Portland mush, but the statue is unscarred by its long and eventful history: cast before the outbreak of the Civil War, the proud king and his horse were subsequently passed to a dodgy Holborn brazier called Rivet, along with an order for their immediate meltdown. Having sold thousands of spoons as 'relics' to gloating Puritans and loyal Royalists, Rivet waited for the Restoration before producing the statue intact from its shallow temporary grave in his back yard. Ignoring a House of Lords decree that he should hand back the statue, the enterprising Rivet later sold it on to Charles II, and saw it erected here in 1675.

On the king's traffic island also lies the plaque from which all London mileages are measured. It's the kind of plaque you just can't resist standing on, looking all around, and mouthing *Woh*.

At the top of Whitehall, the fishy stallions on the Admiralty gate-posts, together with its rigged row of old-style radio masts, hint at its world-whipping nautical connection. In Whitehall lies all the rusty machinery of the British state. Passing by on the other side of the road, I'm not the first person to run into red tape at the Min. of Ag., Fish and Food.

'*Ban* the evil trade,' a man with a banner calls, although I was close enough to have heard if he'd spoken in a normal voice.

'*Ban* the evil and wicked trade,' his female accomplice hectors. '*Ban* the evil trade . . .'

It's something to do with cruelty and conservation, and feeding fruit to your cat.

On past the old War Office building, the Banqueting House hardly looks old enough or imposing enough to have played its peculiar part in history. That's because the simple stucco cube was London's first Italian-style building of the Renaissance, and influenced so much of what came later. It still provides a dizzying London sensation of *it happened here*. Inigo Jones built the Banqueting House as a ballroom and venue for Court masques in 1619, in the grounds of Henry VIII's Whitehall Palace residence, established on this site some eighty years before, when he made the short move from the old Westminster Palace. Although it sprawled ever closer to the city of London, Whitehall Palace maintained a suitable regal distance from the common hustle and bustle of the industrious port. Characteristically, Henry didn't go to the trouble of building his own palace; he simply asked his trusted first minister, Cardinal Wolsey, to sign over his own residence as a gift – and then sent a royal thank you note in the form of a warrant for the Cardinal's arrest and execution for treason. The low-rise, wooden palace once stretched for over half a mile down the Thames, and included residential buildings, the social centres of the king's Court, and administrative blocks. Today only the government offices remain in place, albeit in a slightly different form; sadly, Henry's jousting ground, orchards, bear-baiting pit and bowling alley have gone missing.

One cold January morning in 1649, a closely guarded King Charles I took the long walk across St James's Park, through Horse Guards, and into the midst of a chanting, baying crowd. Soon, they would watch him step onto a scaffold platform through a rough hole hewn in the Banqueting House wall, and go bravely to his death: 'Behold! the head of a traitor!' In the National Portrait Gallery, Charles looks a sympathetic figure, peeping out from his long, dark spaniel-ear curls. Ironically, he is shown in full, useless, parade armour, clinging to his commander's baton as a reminder of who's boss.

Like Nelson, King Charles I stood five foot four inches tall. They must have found him a seaside pony to pose on when he was modelling for his heroic statue, still clutching that baton.

Across the road at Horse Guards, the private who drew the Household Cavalry's shortest straw is strenuously guarding the Queen – who must have neglected to mention to his commanding officer that she's spending the month at home in Windsor. Even if she were in town, she'd be tucked safely away inside Buck House, a good ten minutes' charge away, and this soldier's job would be just as pointless. Or *ceremonial*, as they call it in the trade. He does look a picture, though, in his red Life Guards tunic and white, plumed helmet: a crowd of admirers is taking turns to blow on his face, whisper lewd suggestions and generally try to coax him into smiling for their videos. His two mates have got off lightly, guarding the gate from the safety of horseback.

On one side of Horse Guards Arch is posted a polite notice, warning that you can only drive through into the parade ground if you've got Queenie's permission. Of course, I'm paraphrasing. It actually takes a few more words to get the message across, because this is Britain, and this is Official. 'Such persons,' the notice eventually winds up, 'are required to show an ivory pass specially issued for this purpose.' On the opposite post of the arch, beneath the dinky clock-tower, hangs another notice – THE RIDING OF CYCLES THROUGH THIS ARCHWAY IS FORBIDDEN – a tragic reminder of the time some naïve holidaymaker dared imagine for one second that a purple-faced, pent-up Life Guard might not uphold the very letter of the law with his fully authorised degree of lethal force.

Through the arch, Horse Guards Parade is a large, understandably empty, carpark facing St James's Park. The contrast between Whitehall and the peaceful, willowy lake could hardly be more marked: the park seems more like a mirage than an oasis this close to the centre of the city. Back to the north, Churchill and his wartime cabinet's building-block bunker is now overgrown with thick ivy. And, underneath the regimented trees of the Mall, I catch a glimpse of the mocking, taunting façade of Carlton House Terrace . . . and the Institute of Contemporary Arts. My own memories of this area are every bit as fond as Charles I's. By now, I'm sure it'd be safe for me to take a peep in at the ICA and see what's cooking on the exciting interface between interpretive dance, shadow-puppetry, the slide-projector and the noseflute; but I don't think I'll ever overcome my deep, gnawing dread of the place.

In partial explanation, I was once invited to shout on an ICA bill as part of a week-long John Peel Festival – 'Putting The Fun Back Into Being Pretentious'. The banner title of the event is bottom-clenchingly awful enough, without the added embarrassment of it being the finest lyrical line you ever wrote.

Not content with being a weedy DIY Punk Rock band seven or eight years behind the times, I was a member of a weedy *cod-psychedelic* DIY Punk Rock band, missing that particular boat by more like twenty years. It gets worse: when we tumbled headlong into our first number on the wide ICA stage, none of us could hear what any of the others were up to. We kept stopping and starting. We sounded like a guitar, bass, toy drums and voicebox being kicked down a long flight of stairs. We panicked. We whinged. We were rubbish. Even worse than usual. And there's more. The BBC were taping the gig for posterity, and replayed the whole fiasco on Radio 1 a couple of weeks later.

So, for now, I think I'll steer clear of the ICA. I'm quite content to *imagine* London's foremost robotic mime-artists trapped behind their panes of glass.

Back on Whitehall, the Guardsman's eyes are still fixed dead ahead into the zoom lenses as he counts down the final minutes of his hour-long tourist duty. He's dying to move that tickly little strap off his bottom lip. He's dying to apprehend a cyclist and ask for their ivory token, in full knowledge that the last ivory token was issued some time in the *first* Elizabethan era. But if he moves a muscle without good reason, he'll be up before a firing-squad at dawn, facing a court-martial or toilet duty till 1999. And then, just when a nice little American lady is sidling in close, his time comes up: they call it *relief*, in the business. He stomps and clatters to attention, whisking his sword through the air, causing videos to jerk, mouths to loll open and pacemakers to strain in concave chests. Well, you would, wouldn't you?

The Brits seem to have a bit of a problem with heroic statuary, and it isn't confined to finding crates for our little big men to stand on. Lined up outside the MoD, as an example to the tens of thousands of Civil Service paper-clip counters and box-tickers who run the country, are a curious assortment of army generals, plus a ludicrously half-scale Walter Raleigh – the man who invented the fag-break. Field-Marshal the Viscount Slim's catchphrase was 'Defeat Into Victory': his sculptor could have done the decent thing and moved Defeat a couple of feet closer together. Field-Marshal the Viscount Alan Brooke is tagged as a 'Master of Strategy', which makes it all the more unlucky that he wasn't around to help put his head on straight. Monty looks like he's been freshly gouged out of plasticine by his attendant party of unruly French schoolchildren. Just as controversial in days gone by, the back legs of Earl Haig's mount are standing firmly planted, while its front legs are trotting happily to imminent disaster: an apt metaphor for a First World War general, if ever there was one. Singled out as doyens of Power and Glory, the dozen or so military men scattered around Trafalgar Square, Whitehall and Parliament Square stand for next to nothing in comparison with the Cenotaph, the stark stone pillar devoted to the dead of two wars.

Seeing a scuffle of activity at the security gates blocking off Downing Street, I hurry along to press my head to the bars, but the street is empty save for a couple of traffic bobbies. One of them must have moved. The blackened bricks of the familiar three-storey terrace are frankly out of keeping with the rest of the neighbourhood, the jazzy Italian palaces built for our good and faithful civil servants. Mrs Frommer is far from impressed with the house which 'serves as residence for the English Prime Minister', no matter how much the other guides stress its deceptive roominess inside, its extended kitchenette with serving hatch direct into the Cabinet Office, and sumptuous yellow lino throughout, as selected by Mrs Thatcher.

'Compare it to our White House!' gurgles the faithful Hope, none too charitably.

Stepping around the corner from Whitehall, the sheer enormity of Big Ben is always breathtaking – then your eyes refocus and you're astonished again by the splendour of the Gothic detail lavished over every square foot of its surface. Freshly buffed up and retouched last year, the Houses of Parliament – or the 'Palace of Westminster', as it's still called by those who didn't notice it burning down in the 1830s – positively drip with curlicues and filigree, microscopic chiselwork and vampirish possibilities. It's much more impressive in real life than on the side of an HP sauce bottle. Unless you're about to tuck into a bacon sandwich, in which case the sauce bottle wins every time.

The flow of pedestrians along the pavement towards Westminster Bridge is continually stemmed as tourists stop in wonderment to perform an HP video scan – left, up, along, down, right – or to find out they're standing too close to take a decent photograph. As any American tourist will tell you, this is a *mother* of a Parliament. Just one thing is needed to complete a Perfect London Moment: for Robert Powell to come crashing through the northern clockface of the tower and indulge in a spot of fisticuffs against a dirty-fighting German spy in a leather raincoat and steel-rimmed spectacles – all the while dangling by one arm from the minute hand. For both Powell's sake and our own, we should say our thanks that he was never called upon to defend the British Way at half past six. Or to try and explain why the film was called *The Thirty-Nine Steps*.

From the end of Westminster Bridge, I watch a pleasure-boat drift sideways into the pull of the dirty-green Thames. On the opposite bank, the grand old headquarters of the Greater London Council has met with an ignominious and wildly unpredictable fate: first put out of business by Margaret Thatcher, who decided London had no need of local government, County Hall has now been turned into . . . *an aquarium*. All change is the order of the day: master storyteller Jeffrey Archer has been mooted as a candidate in the battle to be new Lord Mayor of London. Ken Livingstone will soon be back in power. Dusty workmen sit all around, taking a break from their boarded-off Embankment building site, where they are excavating the new Jubilee Line Extension, on schedule to open some time before the next millennium, around the same time as the demolition of the new British Library. Even the river itself is getting a refit, with five spindly dredging platforms and cranes balanced among the eddies downstream.

The first-ever day-trip from Leicestershire to London is commemorated by the bronze Boadicea hurtling in her chariot along the

Embankment. History records the fearsome warrior queen sacking Roman London with her armies in AD62, burning the capital to the ground and slaughtering 80,000 Romans and Britons; but these reports are almost certain to have been exaggerated over time. Listening to the other side of the story, it seems the Iceni tribe may simply have cancelled their regular Bank Holiday outing to Skegness, opting for a change of scenery in London. Sandwiches for the journey were eaten before the tribe had even left the chariot-park, and after several refreshment stops at the M1 services, understandable high spirits ensued. Studying the statue closely, Boadicea is clearly driving her wild, unreined horses without due care and attention. A prematurely empty lunchbox is to be found on the back seat, where Boadicea's topless daughters are making inflammatory gestures at local charioteers. The scythes on the chariot wheels may well have added injury to insult. It seems likely the trip ended in tears, in a nasty traffic snarl-up, and London's first mass road-rage incident.

Take the facts as you find them, rule out the impossible, and what remains, however improbable, must be the truth.

Just as it has taken modern-day Londoners thirty years to come to terms with Scotland Yard's change of address to New Scotland Yard, so Sherlock Holmes' skills of logic and deduction would have been put to a similarly stiff test. At the beginning of Professor Moriarty's reign of nefarious insolence, Holmes would have called in to goad the ineffectual Inspector Lestrade at Great Scotland Yard, off Whitehall, just short of Trafalgar Square. Then, one pea-soupish afternoon in 1890, he would have found the Metropolitan Police HQ standing *mysteriously empty* . . .

New Scotland Yard, two squat fortresses separated by a heavy wrought-iron gate, was catapulted to fame after the war as a queue of British B-movie crews took it in turns to telephone Whitehall 1212, and capture the sight of a begoggled police motorcyclist racing out of the Yard gates, siren wailing and black-and-white light blinking. The stock shot offered three vital ingredients to the film-maker who was untroubled by an imagination: a) it was *exciting*, especially when the film was speeded up by a factor of three to make the cornering appear more daring; b) it was *atmospheric*, with Big Ben towering in the background (if anyone ever tells you Big Ben is the name of the *bell*, and *not* the clock-tower, kick them sharply in the shins); and c) it was *dirt cheap*. Indeed, such was the demand for shots of an intrepid motorised bluebottle buzzing out of the Yard, one brave bobby was put on permanent B-movie duty. PC Reg Tompkins, we salute you.

New Scotland Yard was in use by friendly London bobbies, bizzies and Peelers right up until 1967, when a New Age of police constable ('ver filf') demanded an expansion into modern offices more suited to the age of the hi-tech lapel CB-set rather than the trusty Sherlockian whistle. Just ten minutes' walk away up Victoria Street, New New Scotland Yard turns out to be the most faceless building imaginable: it's big and blank, just hundreds of square yards of reflecting glass for us typical light-fingered cockney tea-leaves to gaze into in all conscience. Not coincidentally, the mirror-effect also hides the high jinks inside – the card schools and the locker-room towel-flicking, the sexist badinage and the beatings casually handed out for sensible lapel crimes – as exposed in the 1970s' only 100 per cent realistic TV cop show, *The Professionals*.

Around the corner in Broadway, I find what I really came looking for. It's still here: the revolving triangular sign off *The Professionals*' thumping credits – NEW SCOTLAND YARD NEW SCOTLAND YARD NEW SCOTLAND YARD – as also featured in the background of every episode as Bodie (Lewis Collins) and Bubble-perm (Martin Shaw) came skidding out of the underground carpark, white Jag doors flapping open, siren wailing, coffee sloshing all over their leather upholstery, dashboard radio squawking VICTOR TANGO FOXTROT!?! OVER!?! Or when members of the rival *Sweeney* cast, Regan (Inspector Morse) and Carter (Minder) would drop by to challenge that '100 per cent authentic' tag; to compare shades of casual beigewear, illegal interrogation methods, and – the *Professionals*' final undoing – the vital approximation of gruff cockernee argot.

That's *Sweeney* as in Todd, as in Flying Squad, savvy? Well, you're *nicked*, you 'orrible little *toilet* . . .

Even today, when some sufficiently heinous crime has been perpetrated in or upon the capital, local and national TV news will dust off their two-second clip of the famous revolving sign to assure us all that Scotland Yard are on the case – and we're talkin' mob-'anded. For some reason, I never thought the sign would still be here in reality. I thought the news just ran the old clip from *The Professionals*' titles.

Heading back up Whitehall, I hop onto the platform of a crawling number 10 bus and cling to the pole on the platform as the driver accelerates wildly into the yawning void of open road. What a great transport system. It's unique, it's bright red, it's dangerous and it's free. Provided you're willing to jump and hit the middle of the road running at 25 m.p.h. when you hear the clippy coming down the stairs.

Following a cops 'n' robbers theme, there's only one place to drop in for afternoon refreshments: the Northumberland Hotel, on Northumberland Avenue – or the Sherlock Holmes pub, as it's now known. This was once Sir Arthur Conan-Doyle's local, and the very place he had Sir Henry stay when he came looking for help in *The Hound of the Baskervilles*. Conan-Doyle, Holmes and Watson are engraved on the windows, and upstairs lies a sealed study, complete with a wooden Holmes effigy positioned to shock as you peek in at the window. In the bar, glass cases preserve key clues from some of Holmes' best-known cases: a model of the remarkable red leech from *The Adventure of the Golden Pince-nez*. *Five Orange Pips*. *The Case of the Ancient Sandwiches*. Or maybe they're just the cheese-and-chutney ploughmans left over from lunchtime.

Finding my place in Len Deighton's *London Dossier*, I gain the barmaid's confidence by ordering in native rhyming slang. The slang section of the *Dossier* was chipped in by Frank Norman, the man who wrote 'Fings Ain't Wot They Used T'Be': impeccable credentials.

'Line us up a tiddly, luv. Forsyte Saga – sweet as a nut.' The barmaid gives me an encouraging look, but replies in an updated version of mangled, impenetrable cockney that doesn't seem to have been covered by the *Dossier*. 'Brighton, muvvah's ruin, pig's ear,' I recite slowly, pointing at the optics and taps to establish contact. 'Apple fritter, right? Gary Glitter? Forsyte *Saga*, gel.' It turns out the barmaid is Australian, and I'm getting on her West Ham reserves.

Reading past the first page, I find rhyming slang is full of subtleties and apposite phrases: 'Brighton' is a contraction of 'Brighton frisky': whisky. A 'tiddly-wink' is a drink, so if you have one too many, you get . . . 'tiddly'. Flicking on to advanced-level slang, it's not so easy to get your crust of bread around 'rouf' for 'four', or 'Charing' for 'horse' – and I ain't no Dunlop tyre. Also, if 'bottle of beer' is slang for 'fear', then could that be an ice-cool 'fear' I see in the Tower Bridge behind the Near and Far?

Considering where I'm sitting, it comes as something of a thrill to discover 'Conan-Doyle' is cockney slang for 'boil', and Scotland Yard is the 'bladder of lard'. Shame I'm all on me Tod Sloan, and there's no one around who looks like they might just need to know.

The Deighton *Dossier* is the kind of London book that I love: it's upbeat, and conveys an unbelievably infectious enthusiasm for its subject. It was bang up to date when it was published in 1967: the cover features a computer-style typeface, and a keyhole shape cut out of the cardboard, through which a girl's eye peers inquisitively. Open up the first page, and the girl is revealed as London's ace face, Twiggy. It's the kind of London book that everyone stopped writing in the '70s, when banging the London drum so quickly became passé, an embarrassment they were keen to confine to the previous, positive decade. The Queen's Silver Jubilee of 1977 was a watershed, when London actually became anti-fashionable: good news for scruffy music, but hardly inspirational of a buzzing London Guide scene. Few people now bother to dust off and replay their *25 Years of Pomp and Pageantry* video. And few will look back on London's Thatcher years with any passion or pride: a few people got rich, and there was some privatised flagwaving, but on TV it always looked eerily like somebody else's flag. Call me a party-pooper, but neither *The Sloane Ranger's Handbook* nor *Asset-Stripper's London* appear in my Top 2000 London books: not enough free love, or people referring to one other as toilets.

In the '80s, London was most famously referred to as 'that great cesspool into which all the loungers and idlers of the Empire are irresistibly drained' by one John H. Watson, MD.

But hold on. That was the *1880s*.

Now London is once again 'the coolest city in the world': I know it must be true because they said so in *Newsweek* and *Vanity Fair*. We don't need faddish American fashion-writers to tell us we're at the top of the heap, with expectations and confidence soaring . . . but isn't it great when they have to admit London is number one? It's *Time* and 'Swinging London' all over again, with a tangible tabloid feelgood factor rising to match the promise of a fresh political era. Even *The Sun* has swapped sides: ENGLAND WINS WORLD CUPS UNDER LABOUR. Not to mention the Eurovision Song Contest. Union Jacks are flying on Oasis guitars. Not to mention Spice Girls' knickers.

Time Out and the *Standard* are perpetually stocked with articles on *unbeatable* London. Even the funny old *Express* has caught up with the mood and tried to prove its finger is on the pulse: ALL ABOARD THE GROOVY TRAIN TO HIP LONDON. London fashion and films leading the way. Booming industry. The Love Generation sweeping to power. Peace and Profit. The Post Office Tower to be reopened to the public. Well, you never know.

The time is ripe for a rash of new London literature: I've already got my advance orders in for *London's Real Neato*; for *Millennial Nostalgia on £500 a Day* and Tony Blair's *Hopelessly Idealistic Plans for Westminster* . . .

There's a skinny new barmaid on duty, with seven-inch wedge heels and a Dusty Springfield beehive hairdon't. On the way out, I tell her how much I enjoyed her 'boil' display.

She says, 'Sahnd as a pahnd', 'Look arfter yerself,' and 'Don't be a Glarsgow Ranger.'

If there's one place in London proportionally lacking in feelgood factor, it's the Houses of Parliament, where the Commons is on the verge of collapse under the combined weight of governmental corruption, deception, arrogance and sleaze. 'Business as usual,' the culprits argue – and that's supposed to be their *defence*. In Parliament Square, Winston Churchill could be hunkered down in drizzle in his concrete overcoat, but he still looks stubborn and oddly dependable. Likewise the leather-clad Oliver Cromwell standing outside Parliament clutching his bible and his sword; but don't tell the Queen I said so – Cromwell took a cheap pop at royalty, and ended up being disinterred and gibbeted at Tyburn. All the surviving Cavaliers who signed Charles I's death warrant were later hung, drawn and quartered on the site of the martyr's traffic island. So, just in case Queenie gets the wrong end of the stick, I'd just like to say I'm really pleased the pious Lord Protector put down the republicans involved in his military *coup d'état*, so we had to wait another three hundred years for the vote. Parliamentary democracy isn't everything it's cracked up to be, ma'am.

As for old Sir Winston, he's looking remarkably chipper, considering the debilitating injury inflicted on his statue by Joe Orton, in his final play *What the Butler Saw*. In the early stage productions, in the last months of the '60s, the killer appendage blown off the statue in a gas explosion was changed to Churchill's 'cigar'; but the offensive weapon quickly reverted to the uncensored original.

Is there no respect left for traditional values, for our great national leaders and institutions?

Before he was bludgeoned to death, Orton even had the temerity to write a film script for the Beatles which, if produced, would have seen our most fabulous foursome seriously compromised. *Up Against It* went so far as to describe the Kennedy-style assassination of 'Lilian Corbett', a jackbooted female Prime Minister – morally reprehensible in its own right; but at the Royal Albert Hall, of all places . . . The producer of *Help!* and *A Hard Day's Night* went out of his way to explain how the boys should not be made to do anything that might reflect badly on them, for fear of imitation.

'I hadn't the heart to tell him,' Orton wrote in his *Diaries*, 'that the boys, in my script, have been caught *in flagrante*, become involved in dubious political activity, dressed as women, committed murder, been put in prison and committed adultery. And the script isn't finished yet.'

Standing in a sentry-box outside the HP is another speciality bobby – not, this time, a motorcycle stunt-rider, nor one of Orton's thuggish cross-dressers, but a tactically posted mine of information. Completely at ease with the regular fielding of stupid questions, he confirms once and for all that the Victoria Tower is taller than Big Ben – *impossible!* – and breaks the bad news that I'm not going to be allowed in for a squat on the vacant front benches. When the new parliament is elected, I can call in and watch from the public gallery, so long as I promise not to abseil into Edwina Currie's lap; or I can get in touch with my MP and gain entry that way. The bobby's accent is pure Officious Londoner: why use five words when fifty will do?

'You could always go on a guided tour about the labyrinthine historic structure of the, ah, edifice,' he says. 'It's not called a guided tour, mind,' he bristles. 'Here at the *Palace of Westminster*, we call it a *line of route* . . . which is, as a matter of fact' – he struggles manfully for another synonym – 'a *guided tour*.'

Unknown to the friendly bobby, I'm thinking of gate-crashing a Guildhall University walkabout organised by my old schoolmate Simon, who Teaches English as a Foreign Language. He comes here every year, because it's an insight into the workings of democracy for his students, and a day off for Si. Last year, he was waiting outside when another teacher sidled up and asked if he knew which one of the guides was Norman Porch. She showed him her official itinerary: 'Meet Norman Porch, 11 a.m.' . . . Another woman asked him if he was waiting for Glenda Jackson, which is the kind of London experience money simply can't buy.

Robbed of my appointment with Guy Fawkes' Gunpowder Plot cellars and a laze on the woolsack, I resign myself to five minutes in the company of an unseasonal 99 ice-cream cornet, and Emily Pankhurst's railings.

Over the road at Westminster Abbey, I find a big old church.

I don't make a habit of visiting churches when I'm doorstep day-tripping in London. They tend not to be too much fun, especially when it isn't possible to *climb* them – as in the case of the Abbey – and indulge that classic sense of *conquering* a tourist target for your four and a half English pounds. I'm not a real tourist, after all – I'm not obliged to be interested in buildings just because they're nine hundred years old. And you never know when these modern vicars might start asking awkward questions.

No such problems at Westminster Abbey, which is hardly a church at all – no jumble sales or coffee mornings here – more a royal mausoleum; royal weddings and coronations a speciality, with long-term parking space available for all the old crowd from the National Portrait Gallery, a few years further down the line. I know the Church of England only came about with Henry VIII's opportunistic merger of Church and State, but the Abbey is really no great advert for *balance*: poor old Jesus can hardly get a look in for the cluttered statues of ghostly Great Britons. When Henry organised the dissolution and demolition of the monasteries, Westminster was even spared on the strength of his vested interest. Frozen rows of soldiers, politicians, titles and letters reach out reasonably, or clasp their heavenly accessories. And thousands of others crowd for space, willing in life to hand over a fortune to be buried on their heads in half a square yard, and all to register their names alongside the worthy, and rub shoulders with kings at the great garden party in the sky.

Westminster Abbey inspires precious few thoughts of Eternal Life, packed as it is with these desperate monuments to the very, very Dead. The Abbey does have a pageantry and a power all of its own, but it is royal rather than spiritual, with the Nation neatly salted into the equation as an Englishman's short-cut to God.

So *that's* what Trafalgar Square was all about: the lump in your throat when the English football team lines up to be dutifully slaughtered by Brazil; the perfect fizzy head on someone else's round of lager . . . It's as close as we come to religion. And I think that's official.

In Poets' Corner, a coach-party shyster is herding his bored multinational flock into a tatty U-shape around a grave.

'Yeah, vis one's D.H. Lawrence, 'oo some of you will be surprised to find in 'ere. Highly controversial, vough I say so myself. What you might call a very *descriptive* writer. Bordering on pornography, actually . . .

'Vis 'ere's a memorial to ver War Poets. Vey put old Robert Graves' name on 'ere and 'e weren't even dead! No problem – *'e is now!*

''Ere's Tom Parr, 'oo died in 1635 at ver ripe old age of 152 . . . and 'ere's 'Andel. *Right!* – if you want to get in ver gift shop you better step on it 'cos ver coach leaves fer ver Tower in . . . two minutes. Parkin' aht vere's a nightmare. Very strict. Cheers, fanks, ta.'

3 Leicester Square: Who, Me?

Up until the age of twelve I only had one LP in my record collection, a scratchy copy of *The Legend of . . . Dave Dee, Dozy, Beaky, Mick and Tich*, which I inherited from my cousin, Peter. Ah, 'The Wreck of the *Antoinette*'; 'Mrs Thursday Came to Tea', and, most crucially of all, 'Last Night in Soho' . . . The legacy of spinning that one record every few hours for three years remains with me to this day: I have great taste in music. The effect of the cover alone (a bowl-cut DDDBM+T variously sporting ruffle shirts, tight flares, stripy blazers and cravats) was a psychological time-bomb. Tragically, misguided attempts at mind-expansion and a downward spiral into swinging sex-addiction were never part of my problem. Instead, I fell in love with the '60s soft-sell of psychedelic London, and soon devoted myself to a sadly outdated version of *modernism*. I would move to Soho as soon as I had left school and secured a job as a sophisticated spy. In the meantime, I started to wear my dad's old shoes, and Adrian Bartlett's dad's all-crimplene suit. The condition worsened: one week to the day after I first spotted it leaning at the back of Julie Hawes' garage, I 'persuaded' her dad to take fifty quid for his purple C-reg Vespa 150 motor-scooter, which weighed a fraction under a ton, and had a top speed of 29 mph, downhill.

Heck, I was young and stupid.

But here's a strange thing. Springing up the steps of the Leicester Square Oxo-cube today, I'm prone to much the same boundless expectations as when I made my first school-trip pilgrimage to Soho. Of course, I now know that David Bowie doesn't spend all of his time loitering in phone-boxes like on the cover of *Ziggy Stardust*, and that a crimplene suit is the only 100 per cent safe contraceptive known to man. I now recognise the unlikelihood of an overfriendly local plying me with drinks (even using my money), inviting me back to her flat, and turning out to be an advocate of Free Love. But if it's going to happen *anywhere in the world*, it'll happen *here*.

If London promises all things to all people, then nowhere delivers like Soho. A warped, selective history oozes from almost every brick in this tight-packed square half-mile. It's impossible to have a drink without sitting in the fireside seat still reserved for George Orwell or Dylan Thomas, or else blocking the light still reserved for Canaletto or William Blake. This is where the teenage Paul Weller used to come and *tape London*; to record the sounds of the streets on a portable cassette-player, and stare into vacant buildings for a line in on pop history. Teenagers were *invented* in Soho, along with striptease, television and the discotheque. Musicians who couldn't even play guitar – Wagner, Liszt, Mozart – still jostle for attention along with the ghosts of the most celebrated London penpushers that no one ever reads: Johnson and Boswell, Shelley, Marx. In Soho, a sense of Time and Place is tangible: virtually every building here could be fitted with *layers* of blue plaques. And, for those unaffected by the sheer density of historical, nostalgic triggers, Soho also happens to be Britain's *real life*, *modern-day* gay capital, red-light and porn capital, restaurant and clubbing capital, media capital, and home to our film and music industries . . .

They say everyone finds what they're looking for on the streets of Soho. French schoolchildren, too young to have heard of the Beatles, don't see an overdeveloped tourist trap in Carnaby Street; just for this week, they see the home of the Spice Girls. On one of his strictly constitutional walking tours, Ian Norrie in *A Celebration of London* warns his gentle readers not to venture *near* Soho's porn-infested alleyways: '. . . and *certainly not* at night. I don't wish to exaggerate its reputation,' he stresses, 'but it is a district harbouring low-life nightclubs, brothels and criminals' hideouts.' Hence the happy tradition of theatregoers dipping their big toes into Soho for a pre-*Misérables* dinner, and long remembering their evening for the agreeably appalling antics of a strip-club doorgirl.

Soho's schizophrenic state – simultaneously cosmopolitan, bohemian and more than slightly seedy – is firmly rooted in its distant past: since the 1700s, waves of outcast French artisans, Italian, Greek and Jewish (and, more recently, Chinese) tradesmen have funnelled into its narrow streets. By the mid-nineteenth century, the aristocrats and bohemians had been forced out of what had become a seething slum area, cursed with cholera, crime, open prostitution and a fondness for music hall. By the late Victorian age, the wealthy were back, lured by the development of Leicester Square as a centre of entertainment, and an unhygienic bit on the side. Before the turn of the century, Shaftesbury Avenue was sliced out of the slums, and its burgeoning theatreland soon spawned the trend for eating out in late-night Continental restaurants. Throw in a dash of jazz, a handful of slimming pills and white lipstick to taste, and bingo. Soho.

The benches in Leicester Square are full of people watching Charlie Chaplin and Shakespeare for signs of movement. I'd love to conduct a straw poll to see if anyone actually thinks the statue of Shakespeare is 'Albert Grant MP' – that's the only name that appears on the plinth, as the man responsible for saving the garden from ruin in the 1870s. Who cares if 'Baron' Grant was really born Abraham Gottheimer, and was more of a con-man than a tycoon-benefactor? The man who planted these superb shady plane trees in the square deserves to be remembered, and, after all, no one's going to forget the name of history's greatest playwright – even if he did himself spell it no less than nineteen different ways throughout his lifetime. I'll bet that's why they left his name off the statue. It's almost certainly how Shakkkspeare gained an unenviable reputation as a Scrabble cheat.

In each corner of the garden is the bust of an illustrious past resident, including the artists Hogarth and Reynolds, and a posted copy of the Open Spaces Act, which forbids 'verminous or offensively filthy' day-trippers from lying on or about any seat. No cattle, prayers or whippet-training either. And as for 'beating, shaking, sweeping, brushing or cleansing any carpet, drugget, rug or mat', don't even think about it, slum-dwellers.

The black granite Odeon, to the east of the square, looks like a spaceport control tower left over from a *Flash Gordon* matinee of the 1930s, when cinema boomed, and the outlandish *Arabian Nights*-style Alhambra variety theatre was in the wrong place at the wrong time. All that remains from the Victorian birth of the West End is the name of the Empire Cinema, which replaced the Empire Theatre in the '20s, and the Hippodrome, now a tourist rock venue, still spectacularly surmounted by its heavy metal Roman charioteer. The Warner West End cinema stands on the site of Daly's variety palace. Crowds once flocked to Leicester Square to see Little Titch perform his hilarious comedy leaning, wearing those funny, funny long shoes of his. Risqué cockney songbird Marie Lloyd shocked audiences with the sheer sauciness of her wink, and her triple-X-rated playground dittie, 'A Little Bit of Wot Yer Fancy'.

My wife went to Jamaica.

The West Indies?

Most certainly!?!

The thing about music hall was, you really had to *be there*.

Almost as great an attraction as the stage acts themselves were the saloon-bars and promenades at the back of the stalls at the Empire, the Alhambra and the Pavilion on Piccadilly Circus. They must have been fun, because they attracted the attention of the puritanical anti-vice campaigner Mrs Ormiston Chant, and these unofficial added attractions were quietly closed down during the First World War.

At the basement Café de Paris on Coventry Street, the Prince of Wales (later Edward VIII), Noel Coward and 'the Crowned Heads of Europe' used to dance and smooch to Dietrich and wave their ciggie-holders in the air – until fashions shifted, and they moved on to Mrs Simpson and *Flash Gordon*.

Also just off the north of the square, London's first real discotheque, the Ad Lib, used to strut its stuff above what is now the Prince Charles Cinema. One of the club's owners, almost incredibly a PR man by trade, once boasted that it was the only place in town where you might find a Lord of the realm dancing alongside Diana Dors, a pool of typists, a fashion photographer and 'the occasional highly paid young docker'. Just as well the Beatles and the Stones became regulars and the media caught on, otherwise that quality of sales patter could have killed off the disco long before 'Hi-Ho Silver Lining' was ever written. Even the Comedy Store, recently removed around the corner from its original burrow between the Odeon and Capital Radio, would struggle to book a bill with the comic potential of the old Ad Lib crowd. The great Alexei Sayle may no longer be resident compère at the Comedy Store, and the original '80s crop of alternative venom-spitters have all moved on to bigger and better things, but I'm still amazed the club manage to sell tickets for tables within five yards of the stage.

The main attraction of Leicester Square – more alluring than cinema, comedy or even Ms Dors – is a tantalising eating option: here, you can take your choice between the Aberdeen Steak House and the Angus Steak House. To a novice, their menus, decor and big red signs are practically indistinguishable, but I'm sure there's a world of individual flourishes to be found on the Black Forest gâteau trolleys alone. In case of emergency, six more spillover branches are to be found within a stone's throw in Shaftesbury Avenue, Charing Cross Road and Coventry Street.

I walk up Charing Cross Road as far as Cambridge Circus – headquarters of George Smiley's MI6, if John le Carré's information is to be believed; but there is some question of him being a Circus double agent, or even a pedlar of eminently credible fiction. Sidling into the backstreets of Soho proper, today's 'typical' sights include a full rack of newspapers in every language except English (unless you count *USA Today*), pavement cafés doing brisk business at 12 degrees centigrade, and one Italian waiter gesticulating wildly over a seated customer, presumably explaining how his forming one mountainous blob of pasta into green tubes, pink sheets or white strings gives rise to a culinary choice any wider than steak, steak or steak. Ignoring the cosmopolitan cuisines of Greece, France, Indonesia, Russia, Japan and Hare Krishnaland, I take a seat just off the pavement in Greek Street, look up the page in my *London Dossier* and start ticking off the tasks set by Len Deighton, my Soho spymaster:

'Buy some pâté and ogle the photos of backsides . . . smell the fresh bread and sip the fresh coffee . . . argue with the barrow-boys and buy a flower for your buttonhole . . . whistle at the girls and listen to the street musicians, for this is Soho where anything goes, and just make sure it's not your wallet . . .'

Ronnie Scott's club in Frith Street dates back to the 1950s, when the explosive combination of American jazz and blues, Caribbean

social habits and Italian coffee somehow gave birth to the pheno-
menon known as the Great British teenager. Almost unbelievably,
top of the bill tonight is the legendary jazzer Jimmy McGriff, one of
Blue Note's original cheesy organ tinklers, who must have played
here in the days of the Moca Bar and the 2i's; when Colin MacInnes
was still writing *Absolute Beginners*; when George Melly was *young*;
when recreational drugs found their first use in late-nite dance-clubs,
and in the invention of finger-poppingly triple-hip teen lingo.
Straight from the fridge, daddy-o. Jimmy McGriff only has to walk
out into Frith Street and the memories, the faces, the mood must
come flooding back. The rest of us have to satisfy ourselves watching
Cliff Richard relive his past as a 2i's skiffler in *Expresso Bongo*.

More layers of history stack up across the street. At number 20,
large-screen satellite Italian TV flickers out over the polished coffee
machines of Bar Italia where, seventy years before, John Logie Baird
first demonstrated the wonders of his newfangled electrical
television contraption. At number 22, the stage-door of the Prince
Edward Theatre, a placard boasts: 'The world's greatest artistes have
passed and will pass through these doors.' Not such an idle boast,
either, for at this address the musical talents of the infant Mozart
and his little sister (er, Mozart) were shown off and cashed in for
hard currency in by their father, Mr Mozart.

Never mind the exploitation of child-prodigy labour in the 1760s
– Karl Marx would be far more horrified to find the Sunset Strip
parlour, right next door to his old Dean Street lodgings, staging the
ritual degradation of its labour force in the final years of the
twentieth century. 'Workers of the world unite, you have nothing to
lose but your . . . *tassles*'? Meanwhile, the restaurant immediately
downstairs from Marx's blue plaque offers Iranian caviar at £250 for
250 grammes. There's *clarse* for you.

As to today's prospects for revolution, Karl Marx is currently
spinning in his grave in Highgate Cemetery at a steady 33⅓ r.p.m.

Anti-establishment activities continue around the corner on
Carlisle Street, where a poster sellotaped in a downstairs window
announces the offices of *Private Eye*. Since 1961, Lord Gnome's organ
has been busy exposing the hilarious hypocrisy and double-dealing
expected of our media and government – which lapses they might
otherwise have expected to *get away with*. Sued for millions by the
high-placed crooks (and, of course, the blameless innocents) who can

afford to hide behind our archaic libel laws, the *Eye* has regularly been brought to its knees by judges' outlandish awards for printing sentences like 'Robert Maxwell is a bloated liar and a thief'. The comedian Peter Cook ploughed money into the mag in its early days, when he also opened the first modern comedy club, The Establishment, on Greek Street. Under its 'nightclub' licence, the likes of Lenny Bruce and Barry Humphreys (not forgetting Cook and his *Beyond the Fringe* partners, Jonathan Miller, Alan Bennett and Dudley Moore) were first able to circumvent the theatre's strict official censorship, and satirically suggest that neither every public figure nor every private individual was managing to live up to the high moral standards of the Lord Chamberlain's Office.

As I'm walking by the exclusive media-biz Groucho Club on Dean Street, a group of four revellers spills out onto the pavement in front of me, shouting and sniffing and compulsively straightening their suits and ties. Some time later, another member follows them out of the club, looking at me slyly, as if I should recognise him – and, yes, it's that little bald bloke with bags under his eyes and a hangdog expression. I can't remember which TV sitcom or advert he was in. He's the sort of actor who might have appeared in the sketch sections of someone else's comedy show. You'd know him if you saw him, but you wouldn't want his autograph.

On Old Compton Street the two-way shop-windows of the cafés and bars are in perpetual use. Nothing catches my eye at Swank, Clone Zone or the Gay and Lesbian Video Centre, but I'm forced to stop for a closer look at Paradiso Bodyworks: firstly, the girls' window-display features a pair of female mannequins draped in drastically immodest chain-mail dresses, which bring to mind all the obvious questions of underwear etiquette, and a list of potential *pros* and *cons* quite apt for Soho. In the boys' window is a rubber one-piece swimsuit and a plastic posing-pouch with industrial-strength fasteners – surely a practical feature. More sensible still is a wide leather collar studded with four-inch nails to keep at neck's length the threat of those theatrical, European butterfly kisses, widely adopted as a greeting by all friendly, outgoing Londoners. Mwa! Nice to see you. Argh!

Got it: the bloke coming out of the Groucho was none other than *Jonesy*, the little Welsh whinger out of *Porridge*. At last, I'm moving in stellar circles.

Len Deighton tells of groups of men loitering on the various corners of Old Compton Street, which apparently once served as unofficial labour exchanges. Nearby Archer Street was the traditional spot for out-of-work musicians to congregate on a Monday morning: that's where Dozy, Beaky, Mick and Tich would have wound up when the big, big hand ticked upright and signalled the beginning of the '70s. The corner of Compton and Dean was reserved for waiters. Len warns us not to dawdle too long near Compton and Frith in case we're picked up for a spot of rubber-glove slavery in a local hotel. I guess much the same rule still applies.

I turn right out of Old Compton Street into Wardour Street, the centre of the resurgent British film industry. Warner Brothers and Rank Film Distributors are located here, alongside various film service industries, editing suites and agents' offices. In the immediate vicinity are George Harrison's Handmade Films (*Monty Python's Life of Brian*), Working Title Films (*Four Weddings and a Funeral*) and Merchant Ivory Productions (*A Room With a View*). Walking past Rank, the sight of its famous gong-banging logo gives me a warm, proprietorial feeling: my family has enjoyed a long and intimate involvement in the film industry. When he was evacuated to Leicester during the war, my dad moved into the same street as Trev Billson, whose second cousin was none other than Bombardier Billy Wells – the bloke who got to bang the gong before the titles of every Rank film. In its day, that kind of star connection was every bit as impressive as spotting Jonesy out of *Porridge*.

Setting aside my natural bias, I'd say the building second most worthy of attention must be Hammer House, once the home of Hammer Films, and the origin of 90 per cent of all popular historical knowledge of London. Hammer Films' East End, invariably swirling with dry ice, was peopled exclusively by slow-witted bobbies-on-the-beat, mysterious antique-shop owners, Sherlock Holmes, and an endless supply of golden-hearted, ample-bosomed cockney wenches destined to fall victim to Jack the Ripper. Or else some evil-hearted, ample-bosomed vampiress. Often both.

How long can it be before one of our slick new breed of production companies takes up the Hammer mantle and introduces a new generation to the horrific possibilities of a Hansom cab, darkened Pinewood cobbles, a fog machine . . . and a blood-curdling scream?

On the glorious day that Hammer remake *Jill the Ripper Meets Dr Hyde*, the cheeky cockney barrow-boys in the squalid Dickensian market scene will be played by themselves: the stallholders from Berwick Street market. The rickety wooden barrows and wiry street people have been here forever. Only the custard-apples and the currency betray the date: the rich market smells, the traders' banter and their friendly mock-skirmishes have been the same since long before Marc Bolan worked here on his family's stall . . . ever since the flower-seller last washed his apron.

'Aye, aye! *Strawbs* free fer one-twenny, your best buy!

'Fanking you, young sir. You got ver twenny, sir? Fanking you, sir. *Strawbs* free fer one-twenny!'

And ten yards down the street: '*Strawbs* free a pahnd.'

Behind the market stands a bland tower-block, left over from a '60s scheme to repopulate Soho. At the time of my day-trip its most celebrated tenant was Jeffrey Bernard, the professional drunkard who made his name writing a wonderfully melancholic, alcoholic column for the *Spectator*, but whose legendary status was sealed by Keith Waterhouse's hit play *Jeffrey Bernard is Unwell* – named for the euphemistic tagline employed when he was too sozzled to type. In the Soho of the '50s, Jeff fell in with the private drinking-den demimonde at the Colony Club, along with his buddies George Melly, the artists Lucien Freud and Francis Bacon. Jeff spent his last years drinking and smoking with abandon, despite the amputation of a gangrenous leg. He would cheerfully admit he was 'waiting to die' – his only wish being to avoid a clash of dates with the Queen Mother – and what better place to wait than balanced precariously on 'his' barstool of thirty years at the Coach and Horses on Greek Street, being insulted or ignored or further pickled in vodka and lime by Norman Balon, 'the rudest landlord in London'? The *Private Eye* strip, *The Regulars*, followed the story for longer than anyone could remember. Especially Jeff.

As fate would have it, his death slipped by virtually unnoticed on the same day as Princess Diana's.

Further up Berwick Street, the haberdashers', costumiers' and showbiz tailors' quarter directly overlays the second-hand music market, with a scattering of gay and straight sex shops spilling over from Brewer Street to the south. Bona Books. Soho Silks. Reckless Records. There's little chance of confusion if you're ducking into a shop called Stallion Videos; but do they sell anything seedy at Mr CD? Simply Sausages, anyone?

And how about that Canadian Muffin Company?

On Carnaby Street it's possible to watch the potent mythology of London working its magic first hand. Expectations are cranked so high by ancient stories of the in-crowd shopping for luminous kaftans and flower power fingernail stickers, no one seems to notice that there's no longer anything here of any value or interest. Of course, there are the ubiquitous tourist T-shirts, baseball caps, sunglasses and beads: Carnaby Street reminds me most of Amsterdam, with Tower Bridge steins and one rather tempting pie-and-mash shop teapot taking the place of the clog-shaped dope pipes in the souvenir shop windows. Even my patent Londonometer is momentarily caught off-guard, its hopes raised by the weak background readings of Beatles and better times:

FASHION ALERT! it flashes excitedly, 3-INCH PLASTIC MINI-SKIRT AT 12 O'CLOCK!!! – when, in fact, all its scanners have picked up is a girl wearing pink jeans with a wide belt.

IS THAT A MINI-SKIRT? the next printout reads. OR IS IT A TOPLESS DRESS!?!

My own image of Carnaby Street was formed at an impressionable age by one passage in a classically bad, Bonding-by-numbers spy novel. In recent months, I've tried to locate it by buying up all the vaguely familiar works by Adam Diment, James Mayo, Peter O'Donnell and company; but no luck so far. Actually, Adam Diment has been something of a rediscovery: his particular Bond substitute is called Philip McAlpine (as opposed to Charles Hood, Philip Driver, Matt Helm); his gimmick is driving everywhere too fast, and saying things like 'pot parties' and 'swinging on the up curve'. According to the *Daily Mirror*, McAlpine is 'the most modern hero in years . . . He's hip, he's hard, he likes birds, and, sometimes, marijuana': worth 20p of anybody's money. Anyway, my character-forming memory is of one of these jetsetting wisecracking playboy spies swinging into his secret hi-tech undercover base – cleverly concealed *behind the full-length mirror at the rear of a Carnaby Street boutique* – and sniggering at the state of a spotty young mod trying on a hairy pink mohair jumper. At the time, I thought pink mohair would look a treat with my navy-blue crimplene suit. Albeit subconsciously, I've been on the lookout ever since.

There's precious little point searching for anything that is, or has ever been, remotely fashionable in Carnaby Street. Carnaby Street is out of fashion. One or two individual shops cling to their addresses in the face of the deluge of T-shirts, bum-bags, spray-painted Doctor Martens and yet more T-shirts. When the *New Musical Express* was based at 5–7 Carnaby Street, I spent the three most fulfilling minutes of my young life spouting the usual risible nonsense (but this time someone was being paid to listen) in a band interview made triply climactic by its very location. Years later, as the *NME*'s unofficial freelance Crap Correspondent, I used to post off reviews of LPs that no one else would touch with a fluffy needle; but by that time the offices had moved to Bloomsbury . . . and Bloomsbury has never enjoyed anything like the literary caché of *Carnaby Street* . . .

Anything calling itself a 'boutique' closed down well over one hundred years ago, fashionably speaking, since which time the designers have shipped out of Carnaby Street *en masse*. Crumbs of consolation can be found in Newburgh Street, an equally long-established centre for overpriced, smart, ironic clothing – *fashion* – which runs parallel to the ravaged skeleton of its celebrity sister. This is much more like it: just the kind of gear dismissed in the '60s by the Menswear Association of Great Britain as 'codswallop fashions for perverted peacocks'. I don't know if the pinstripers have turned soft or simply gone smart-but-casual, but I don't hear any lofty proclamations on the evils of a deafening green shirt with gull-wing collars, and no price-tag. The next window display is a beige nylon car-coat, also missing a price-tag. Next door is a plain black school dress, no price-tag. I go back and check for belly-laugh T-shirts.

The most fun to be had in Carnaby Street is halfway up a wall, technically in Broadwick Street. The bright, witty street-map mural of Soho is packed with symbols, famous faces and landmarks in 3-D relief. Karl Marx swigs Coca-Cola behind a copy of *Das Kapital*. The mural clock incorporates a Regency fop and his painted lady, rigged up to kiss and wink on the hour. In the foreground is a crowd of Sohoites, not all recognisable due to the effects of rain, weathering and copious amounts of alcohol: Jeffrey Bernard was meant to feature on the mural, but fell off his barstool at the vital moment. Thomas de Quincey, the Regency-era author of *Confessions of an Opium-Eater*, is the one who looks a bit queasy. Fruit and veg pour out of the sky into Berwick Street; tiny *azzurri* footballers limber up in Little Italy, and saucy *folies* high kick at the Windmill Theatre, where Britain's first almost-nude revues wiggled into motion in 1932, gyrating non-stop throughout the Blitz. 'We never close' was the Windmill's catch-phrase, until it did.

BEAUTIFUL GIRLS FROM ALL AROUND THE WORLD achieve a state of FULL NUDITY in the strip-clubs and cinemas of Walker's Court. BLUE POLE DANCING is the latest unlikely-sounding attraction imported from the USA. The Sunday tabloids have repeatedly warned that once inside certain of these strip-joints, the eager flesh-spotter is brainwashed into buying a toothglass of lemonade for a peaky girl in a dressing-gown; at this point, burly enforcers burst in, frogmarch their victim to the cashpoint and force him to withdraw his life savings. Hence the recurrent promise of NO HOSTESSES NO DRINKS, but I'm taking no chances. No need:

'On my left was a room with about sixty seats and a stage as big as a fireplace . . . a slum in total darkness . . . I'd hate to see it with a window open . . . girls thin, fat, tall and short . . . clad in a handful of sequins . . . her lipstick was lop-sided . . . she seemed to have very little skill at putting things on . . .'

Len Deighton has beaten me to it, sending out another of his operatives – Michael Caine in *The Ipcress File* – on the strip-club reconnaissance job, armed only with a service revolver and Len's *I-Spy* checklist:

THE GIRLS ARE NAKED: score 10 points . . . AND THEY DANCE: score 20.

The woman on the poster outside the Raymond Revuebar's Festival of Erotica indeed ROCKS THE STANDARDS OF ACCEPTABILITY, but only because she seems to have smeared her torso with lard and her face with plum jam: score zero points.

Shop doorways in the busy alleyway are hung with plastic ribbons to guarantee the privacy of sex-aid shoppers, and to preserve the innocence of small boys, who cluster around the windows, pointing and pushing and shouting out video titles like *Rude Girl in Plastic (and Other Uniforms)*. Inside the shop, there are thousands of magazines and videos on the popular subject of Full Nudity, plus hints on how to attain Full Nudity (stockings and sequins can make it tricky), and helpful suggestions of what to do once Fully Nude.

Silky magazine stands out, all too literally, like a pair of underpants at a nudist convention. For starters, it's shot in black-and-white; it's only A5 size, but it's still fifteen quid for fifty pages.

Seeing me fingering his merchandise, the burly black security man saunters over for a word in my ear: 'Nice one, mate,' he acknowledges a fellow connoisseur. 'Now *that's* what I like.' He nods appreciatively at the centrespread of a woman reclining in gigantic knickers, pyramidal bra, thick stockings and a complex suspender belt arrangement. This is quite clearly *somebody's mum*.

If he fancies women who wear clothes, I have to ask, isn't he in the wrong line of business?

He nods wistfully and saunters back to his stool.

Outside a cinema club in Brewer Street stands a machine which rates your sexuality on a scale running from Maggot to Superstud, or from Shy to Nymphomaniac. All you have to do is Insert Coin Press Button Of Your Sex. Before I can find out whether I'm a Mummy's Boy or a Stallion – or whether the machine would know if I pressed the wrong button and shot up the Bitch-Slut-Teaser scale – I am approached from the rear, and importuned . . .

'You lookin' fer a girl?'

The woman is chubby, about twenty, dressed in shredded jeans and a bomber jacket. I wonder if she's the girl she has in mind, but it seems rude to ask. Strictly speaking, it's irrelevant. Shouldn't she at least be wearing stiletto heels, or flashing a block of lard?

'You gay?' she presses on with the interview. 'You from ver church?

'Wotchoo doin' ven?

'You from ver *San*? Betchoo get paid good money, eh?'

Er, no.

'So, you lookin' for a girl, or *wot*?'

Having convinced her that I'm not looking for a girl; that I'm just a puzzled under-cover Mummy's Boy, she trails away, giving me the chance to slip off and spend two pounds on an entertainment advertised as a 'Brief Encounter'. Having changed a fiver into pound coins, I shuffle into a small wooden cubicle, being careful not to touch the walls. Two pounds disappear into the slot, and a steel shutter slams open. A skinny girl in a sky-blue bikini stands up in her narrow corridor, shouts 'full strip?' and performs a surprising star-jump as the shutter slides back into place. Was it supposed to happen like that? In a spirit of enquiry, I feed in two more pound coins and enjoy another six seconds of pop-mobility.

Emerging from my dingy trap, the proprietor gives me a look as if to say 'that didn't take long'. I'd complain, but he'd only smirk and point at his sign: 'Brief Encounter'. Also, I'm scared he might hit me. Or call the police.

I only know of one man who admits to scaling the stairs at one of the propped-open doorways advertising 'Model third floor' or 'French Lessons': Barry Clarke's little brother. In town for Leicester City's glorious 1997 Coca-Cola Cup final appearance against Middlesbrough, Barry's brother and his nine compatriots embarked on a night of premature celebration, not only forcing down ten gallons of refreshments and paying a visit to the Trafalgar Square fountains, but ditching their hired mini-van and jemmying a slot-machine along the way. Any club's Wembley awayday is something special – the hallowed twin towers; the wide-open spaces; 1966 and all that – but this was our first major final in twenty-eight years, so high spirits were only to be expected, ossifer . . .

At four in the morning, Blonde Student Very Patient peered out of her cupboard door to explain, very patiently, that her all-night rate was prohibitive, and she could never consider conducting business ten-at-a-time, anyway. Especially with boys who dripped puddles of water on her lino.

'How about forty quid each?' Barry's brother bartered, hoisting his carrier-bag full of change. 'Four hundred quid till morning. You can have the night off, me duck. We just want to get us heads down . . .'

I'm in good time to meet Lesley Wallace in Chinatown, and take the chance to fully explore the location of my favourite Jack Nicholson film. Chinatown isn't really a town. The Chinese name for the strip between Leicester Square and Soho proper is more realistic – *Tong Yan Kai*, or 'Chinese street'. Road access into Gerrard Street (excuse my English) is blocked by ornamental arches, creating a pleasant marketplace atmosphere for visitors to stroll in, taking in the pagoda-style phone-boxes and looking for esoteric gifts. When you reach the end of the street, you turn around and walk back. Apart from a branch of the Hong Kong Bank, a supermarket and three or four gift shops, every other establishment is a Chinese restaurant, with squashed Peking ducks hanging in the window.

The pattern of the average tourist's stroll works very much to the advantage of the gift shops. On the first pass, your attention is drawn to the pile of cassette-tapes in the window at Sounds of China; on the way back, you realise they're not just full of clinking washing-up sounds, and you just can't resist. The same goes for the street entertainment, a synthesiser-backed duo on two-string fiddle and Chinese autoharp, whose approximate rendition of 'Boiled Beef 'n' Carrots' could only be described as a grower. On my first sweep, I was very much taken by a basket of large, prickly green vegetables; on my return I spotted an even larger, not-so-prickly green vegetable priced reasonably at £1.10 per portion. I resisted, but you get my point. I found the Chinese Medical Centre on Little Newport Street, too, selling powdered duckling for overindulgence, small phials of panda-fluff for impotence, and dried strips of prickly green vegetable just for the hell of it. Well, at that price just around the corner, who can blame them?

Lesley Wallace and I first ventured into the Kowloon restaurant because it was the only restaurant in Chinatown with donuts in the window alongside the flat ducks. Having tasted his duck and slurped on his excellent noodles, it has always seemed pointless to take umbrage at the attitude of the Kowloon's waiter, Mr Yip, and take our trade elsewhere. Mr Yip is not a happy camper. This evening, I manage to provoke his trademark blank glare by asking for chilli oil with my fried beef and green pepper noodles. Just for a laugh, Lesley Wallace leaves the lid open on the pot of jasmine tea: now Mr Yip is duty-bound to give us a refill. How did we find out about *that* old Chinese custom?, Mr Yip asks with a glance. Making conversation, I ask Mr Yip if the name of the British-Chinese newspaper, *Sing Tao*, has a similar meaning to that of our Chinese beer, *Tsing Tao*.

'Tcch,' says Mr Yip. '*Different name.*'

Over Mr Yip's shoulder, the restaurant's patriarch, Mr Tao, catches our eye. I wouldn't like to guess how old Mr Tao is; he wears wispy snow-white whiskers, and speaks about as much English as I speak Cantonese. But Mr Yip's cartoon grumpiness transcends language, and works direct on the smirking glands.

At the French House pub, Lesley Wallace sits on the very barstool that acted as General de Gaulle's Free French operations centre during the Second World War, and I accidentally block the light (or should that be the fish?) reserved for one-time local Salvador Dalí. At the Bear and Staff, a sign in the window reads, 'Staff Required': I must remember that one for Mr Yip. The Dog and Duck on Bateman Street wins the prize as both the smallest and most unspoilt pub in Soho. A tiny toy bar is wedged into the corner by the window; the cramped twist of the staircase cuts through the limited airspace of the bar below, tiled two hundred years ago in claustrophobic green and brown patterns. The Coffee House on Beak Street is another pub that has resisted the slide into wine-bardom, with generations of stout-hearted managers swiftly returning to sender their well-intentioned brewery parcels of random old things for the top shelf. In the Coffee House, the light is orange and the air is brown, nicotine coating the chocolate-brown ceiling and clogging the pores of the fairly old masters stacked four high on every wall. There are stuffed foxes and fish in glass cases, too – pub pets of a bygone era. No need to ask how they died.

Clubbing in Soho: the choice is legendary, reverberating with historical glories; but it would be pointless choosing a club night solely on the basis of its past clientèle. Jimmy McGriff at Ronnie Scott's would be an obvious choice – too obvious. It's time to break free from this cloying Soho nostalgia and head somewhere young and fresh and vital. There are plenty of techno ambient jungle nights up and running; but that percussion-drill music gives me a headache, and nowadays you can never hear the words . . . There's a funk night at the WAG Club, where Boy George and Wham! and Limahl out of Kajagoogoo used to primp and pose back in the '80s. There's cool, poppy soul tonight at the 100 Club; but nothing to compare with The Who's Maximum R&B at the Marquee – when it was in Wardour Street, of course, not the place that's just been closed down in Charing Cross Road. As for the Flamingo, the All-Nighter and UFO on Tottenham Court Road . . . well, they all closed down when I was still in infant school.

Luckily, Lesley Wallace has already decided where we're going, to meet up with a couple of her friends at a club they've described as (I'm paraphrasing) the newest, nowest scene in London: Club Indigo at Madame JoJo's.

Back in the heart of the red-light district – right opposite my Sexy-ometer, in fact – we pay the entrance fee and descend into the unknown down a steep flight of steps.

Madame JoJo's hasn't had a refit since 1964. Red and yellow lights are let into the ceiling. A mirror-ball spins over the tiny wooden dancefloor. Flitting between the miniature chromium tables are gorgeous waitresses in bunny costumes . . . who turn out to be gorgeous transvestites in bunny costumes. Men wearing *cardigans* are dancing to the organ-and-brass theme-tune to *that* London documentary.

I never realised I was so with-it.

4 London: Zoo

Primrose Hill isn't steep and, at 206 feet, is barely more than a slope with good PR. Nevertheless, in the warm morning sunshine, it comes as a relief to flop on the grass near the summit, to take in the spectacular view of London and a deserved draught of ginger ale. Two women have beaten me to the top of the broad, southern face of the Primrose: one is busily sketching the panorama; the other is wrapped in a maroon robe, sitting cross-legged in the lotus position, meditating on the silence, the heat of the sun and the crispness of the air.

The long, low London skyline is lorded over by the Post Office Tower at centre stage, well over a mile distant, but you still have to look up to see the top. Canary Wharf shows up as a blunt stud to the far east, with the dome of St Paul's midway between the highpoints of the '60s and '90s. Overshadowed by a thicket of anonymous skyscrapers, the cathedral still catches the eye against the faint outline of the North Downs. Centre Point sits in the slot between the Post Office Tower and an office block of stunning indescribability, lent a flattering prominence by its thoughtless positioning, and perspective. Scanning west, the tops of the twin towers of the Houses of Parliament are visible, lower than you might expect, at the river's edge. The chimneys of Battersea Power Station follow, well to the west, and partially obscured by the flats at the bottom of the hill. And that's all I recognise, apart from churches, which are the little pointy things. The view doesn't bear much resemblance at all to those artfully concertina'd silhouettes of the skyline familiar from London guidebooks, maps and tourist leaflets, where Tower Bridge is shown more-or-less correctly in relation to St Paul's, with Big Ben and Nelson's Column sandwiched in between. Without a copy of *Long-Range London* to hand, I can't begin to fill in the daunting number of blanks pushing up between the trees of this green garden city.

Spread in the foreground is Regent's Park, and its curious collection of zoo buildings: artificial outcrops of rock, concrete wigwams and a large net stretched around splayed poles. Then the gentle gradient of Primrose Hill, criss-crossed with footpaths, slopes up to where I sit, culminating in a scattering of pistachio nutshells at a range of three yards, and, too close for comfort to my Hush Puppies, the casually discarded home-made filter ('roach') from a marijuana ('Bob Hope') cigarette ('Just Say No'). It's the kind of view that lends itself to meditation and profundity of thought, or just gazing dopily into space.

When I look again, the artist has put down her sketch-pad and is now also meditating, on what looks like a cheese-and-onion pasty. Away behind me, a family group has climbed to the summit of the hill, and dad is doing an impressive job of reading the skyline. 'Westminster Cathedral'? – where's that, then? 'The Danish Church'? – how can he tell them all apart? Aha. By skilful use of the viewpoint plaque. For the record, the brutal oblong block is called Euston House; the tallest tree in the downtown jungle is the NatWest Tower, and the spindly spike furthest west is the Hilton Hotel. I was right about the churches.

Walking to the Zoo, I cross a footbridge over the Regent's Canal, once the busiest stretch of canal in Britain, linking the Grand Union Canal to the Limehouse Basin and the East London Docks on the Thames. Populated primarily by pleasure barges, the canal now links Little Venice (well, it is a *little* like Venice, if you squint and really want to believe) to the market cafés and record shops of jazzy Camden.

The Zoo is one of my very favourite London attractions. Where else can offer all the guilty pleasures of a Victorian freak show, an opportunity to learn, even a rare opportunity to *do good* – and all in such fantastic surroundings? Architects of every period have been let off their leashes at the Zoo; allowed to let their imaginations run wild to create outlandish habitats far in advance of anything designed for humans: in short, the animals have been used as guinea-pigs. The legacy of the Zoo's futurist policy is a fabulous film-set world full of archetypal London shots just waiting for a director, a camera and a private-eye chase plot. Gunplay amid the steel-frame prisms of the Snowdon Aviary! Romance, leaning against the clean white curve of the art deco penguin pool! Social comment, shot against the windowless concrete of the elephant house! It's hard to believe the Zoo has never featured in a trademark London film – one of the Ealing comedies, or a Bond blockbuster. A few indistinct cages did make it into *An American Werewolf in London*; but wouldn't the Zoo have been great for a smoochy date in *101 Dalmatians* or, even better, as a one-off location for *Men Behaving Badly*? If this were Hollywood, the Zoo would long have been enshrined in film history as a stock setting for illicit californication. If *The Prisoner* hadn't been set among the follies of Portmeirion, London Zoo would have worked just as well. What a waste.

Zoos across the world have had to reinvent themselves in recent times, playing down their circus sideshow past and stressing their role in conservation. Promoting the Zoo as a centre of learning and Green awareness, no mention is made of the low-level thrills it affords the merely inquisitive browser. No matter what it tells its visitors in the glossy souvenir family brochure, London Zoo remains a voyeuristic treat. You've chipped in eight quid towards a saucer of fishy slivers for the gentle keeper to feed to the tiny, quivering jackass penguin chick, so now it's *okay* to stare, just as the Zoo's first visitors stared, and indulge your childish fascination for the unusual, the bizarre, and the intriguingly *different*.

'Dad, look at this over 'ere,' a small boy shouts across the primate section. '*Well* good. It's got a bum like plastic.'

'*Robin!*' the child's father scolds. 'Look at this one 'ere then – its bum's *blue*.'

Television now forewarns us roughly what to expect of a camel or a monkey, but there's no mistaking the wonderment of seeing something new and exotic and *alive*. In the 1830s, when the royal menagerie first arrived here from Windsor, and the royal zoo was moved from the Tower, visitors were able to have a good poke at the animals, too. One keen zoo-goer took home a memento of his experience on the human-animal interface: Alice the elephant's trunk was later discovered to be shorter by a foot. Hands-on learning opportunities are now limited to the children's petting zoo, and encounters with giant centipedes' piercing and sucking mouth-parts in the creepy-crawly pavilion: Alice's Revenge.

A reptile keeper of 1840 made an early contribution to public enlightenment when he attempted to charm a cobra out of its basket. It bit him. He died. The keeper at the questions table in today's reptile house is confidently stationed to field any possible enquiry. A schoolgirl tentatively touches his contraband snakeskin, as invited. 'What's the *difference*,' she asks, 'between a *snake* and a *lizard*?'

It's almost feeding-time at the penguin pool. I stand for ten minutes in a crowd of face-painted children, who smell of crisps, and wait for a man in wellies. Excitement rises to fever pitch when he arrives, throws half his bucket of fish in the water and starts to hand individual morsels to the lazier birds, who bump and shove mildly on the upper slopes of one of their concrete spirals. It isn't really that exciting at all until a posse of seagulls intervenes (the penguins ignore them – they can't even swim), closely followed by a wild heron swooping like a pterodactyl from a tree in the tiger compound (the unflappable penguins have seen it all before). The groundbreaking penguin pool, with its arctic-white, stepped sides and interlocking

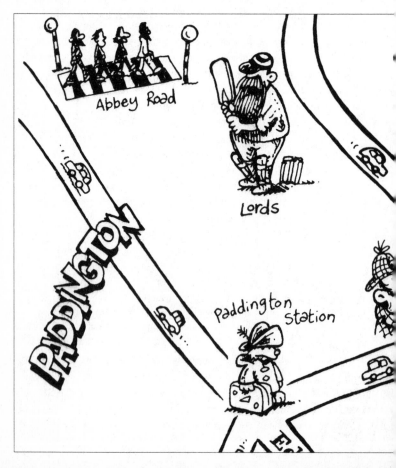

concrete coils, is great to visit, but you wouldn't want to live there.

I buy an ice-cream and follow the smell of crisps to the zoo shop. The Londonometer bucks excitedly in my pocket, sensing London nick-nacks of quality and distinction. A life-size rubber rat (£2.50) really says 'London' to me, but I'm not sure what I'd do with one. I know perfectly well what I'd do with a lion in a snowstorm (£2.50). No, you're wrong. I'd put it at the back of the kitchen drawer, and forget it. For sheer *Londonosity*, it's got to be a panda-face baseball cap, a panda pill-box or a 100 per cent impractical panda thimble (£11.99). I settle on a pair of panda earrings (£2.50) for Lesley Wallace, and set off to see the panda.

I'd been putting off my greatest Zoo treat – going to tap on the panda's glass, and being disappointed when the small ball of black-and-white fur doesn't stir from its corner. The panda is my pet favourite, and now it's time to make my call. Past the tamarins and the chimps into the bamboo-screened pandarium. Not much of a crowd here, but that just means there'll be all the more panda for me. Perhaps it'll move, and only I'll see it. But wait a minute.

The Londonometer lets off an alarming buzz, and breaks the bad news as gently as it is able: THAT'S NO XXXXIN' PANDA-BEAR. The bamboo is still painted on the back wall to make the panda feel at home. The panda's unused climbing-frame is still in place. But there's an imposter sitting on it. THAT'S A CAMPBELL'S GUINON.

WHATEVER ONE OF THEM IS.

The Zoo has had a panda since 1938. Sometimes two. Suddenly, I realise the panda is missing from the cover of the Zoo guide, replaced with a menagerie of less-than-giant beasts, all lapsed bambootarians, and so predictably Good In Bed. London Zoo without a panda is like the Tower of London without the Crown Jewels; like a copy of the *Evening Standard* without a photo of someone called Tamara Palmer-Farquharson out on the lig. The Zoo has always had a star turn, a celebrity as a symbol, ever since Jumbo and the ill-fated Alice. Guy the Gorilla. Victor the Giraffe. Goldie the Eagle. The original Winnie the Pooh. The nutty tiger. Ming-Ming, Chia-Chia, Zen-Zen, Goo-Goo.

The Londonometer goes into a sulk and scores the Zoo 14 out of 100, and that despite the guide's assurance that the absence of a panda is something to do with conservation or cruelty.

Empty cages seem to have taken over as an unwelcome feature of the Zoo. Too many animals and birds have either gone missing or put their cage on the market for redevelopment. Today the 'must-see' pygmy hippos, the tapirs and lion cubs are apparently out to lunch. The elephants' ceremonial three o'clock weighing is cancelled, with no reason given. The orang-utan has gone, and not been replaced. I don't even get to see any zoo-staple kangaroos or zebras.

As fashions fluctuate and funds shrink, the crumbling infrastructure of the Zoo is obviously a problem. The art deco beaver-dam is uninhabited, and looks ready to collapse. The monkey hill is another goner. The aquarium is one quarter depleted due to

construction work, but will hopefully be ready for the summer
season.

Walking through the aquarium, the final leg of the Zoo tour, it's
a struggle to summon much enthusiasm for any fish that couldn't
capsize a fishing boat or strip the flesh off a horse inside 30 seconds.
At least it's clear how the less exciting fish get their names. The
rainbow fish. The zebrafish. The spotted pufferfish. The toothbrush-
wedged-sideways-in-mouthfish.

Ah yes, I think to myself, a fine example of a big-nosed baldiefish.
Only then do I realise I'm looking at my own reflection in one of the
empty tanks.

More building-site cordons surround the Grade-II listed Mappin
Terraces, a range of *Star Trek*-style mini-mountains fanned out before
a wonderful Edwardian tea-room. Closed years ago, on the strength
of the blatant perils facing the bears and goats, it is now reportedly
set to be repeopled with 'sloth bears' – creatures which move very
slowly, and which actually quite enjoy falling thirty feet onto their
arses.

All day long I've been working on a complex yet stubbornly weak
zoo allegory for London as a whole. London as a zoo. London *is* a zoo.
London: Zoo.

Starting out, as ever, with the big picture: London Zoo looks
amazing but, on closer inspection, you can see where the cracks have
been papered over. The Zoo is an anachronism. The Zoo is largely
dysfunctional. The Zoo reinvents itself, and people are ever-willing
to believe. People love the Zoo.

And then there are the London animals. The star attractions and
the small fry. The bad neighbours. The sloths. The chameleons. The
mad tigers. The fish with the missing tail, once mistakenly
imprisoned along with a predator. Hey, not all of the animals in the
Zoo even know they're in cages. Some of the animals might think
about leaving the Zoo, but where would they have a better time?
Dudley? I don't think so.

As you can tell, *London: Zoo* isn't exactly *Animal Farm*; but as an
allegory it's still only on the drawing-board. Problems arise as soon
as I try and shoehorn the slender lorises and the blue-crowned
hanging parrot into the scheme.

I can't help wondering how it would feel to suspect you'd been
caged along with a potential tail-gnawer. And how I'm going to

explain away my preference for all the cuddliest, most showily superficial animals.

Regent's Park was not originally planned as a public park at all, but rather as a grandiose park-city containing fifty-six villas for the super-rich; a picturesque playground complete with a pleasure palace for the scheme's patron, the Prince Regent (later King Georgy Porgy IV). The architect John Nash was enlisted in 1810 to create a lake from a stream; to enclose the whole area in magnificent terraces; to somehow work a canal into the plan, and carve a direct path – Regent Street – to link the Prince's residence in St James's to the park on the northern boundary of the city. In the twenty or so years it took to complete this sizeable portion of the grand Regency design, some simplifications were considered. The majority of the park was eventually left open as public space, gardens were landscaped, and the Zoo set in the northern corner.

A stroll down Broad Walk comes regularly recommended as a suitable Sunday afternoon London pleasure. I have to report it works pretty well on a Friday, too; but for me the walk offers more than the beauty of the trees racing each other into leaf, glimpses of endless colonnaded terraces, and their statues set against the skyline: I happen to know the headquarters of the Secret Service overlooks Regent's Park . . .

There's no telling *exactly* which building James Bond goes to work in when he isn't on one of his deadly assignments. Ian Fleming never let on. It isn't called the Secret Service for nothing. The fact remains: behind one of these windows lies the broad mahogany desk of M, the primly flirtatious Miss Moneypenny and – who knows? – maybe even the firm, dry handshake of the man himself.

In *You Only Live Twice*, 'James Bond strolled off in the direction of the tall grey building whose upper storeys showed themselves above the trees', while 008 and 003 'finished their picnic lunches in the Prince Edward cactus garden.' *Dr No* lets slip that M's office is on the eighth floor. In *Thunderball*, Bond hears 'the eerie cackling of a spiky pangolin' from M's office window . . .

Putting two and two together, and triangulating from the upper levels of the listed bakelite pangolin shelves, the Secret Service HQ must be approximately . . . here: hidden away behind the outwardly innocuous nameplate of 'Universal Exports Ltd' . . .

The north of the park is given over to a desert of football pitches, whose goalposts provide an embarrassment of easy targets for two young bluntshooters. The park is wooded and built up in an area to the south, although a women's college and a couple of villas cradled in the long arms of the lake hardly qualify the Inner Circle road as a typical slice of inner city. Birds outnumber dog-walkers by hundreds to one, with geese and ducks kicking up a fuss at the water's edge and a variety of curious calls coming from the treetops. A birdwatchers' log lists woodpeckers, chiffchaffs and blackcaps among the local population, incredibly less than a quarter of a mile from the mayhem of the Marylebone Road, as the chiffchaff flies. In the cool of late afternoon, just two hardy souls are holding out for their full half-hours on the boating lake.

The golden dome of the London Central Mosque appears over the weeping willows like a hovering UFO. Behind the mosque, in St John's Wood, lie three of the very *Londonest* locations (four, if you include the house where Mary Poppins worked as a nanny, when she wasn't cruising over the Houses of Parliament beneath her anti-gravity umbrella). First is Lord's – the Home of Cricket. Then, a London image even more instantly recognisable around the world: an outwardly unremarkable level crossing in Abbey Road. And just around the corner, permanently besieged by a pack of hopeful paparazzi, groupies and drug-dealers, is Liam and Patsy's pad.

Back at the boating lake, seven shades of pink blossom presage the variously singed blubber in the stands at Lord's: next week sees the start of the cricket season. On the inner side of the lake, abandoned deck-chairs are still clustered on the lawn around the bandstand. Purple pansies and red and yellow tulips blaze in their beds. I'm surprised to find I remember the names of grape hyacinth, azalea, polyanthus – even polyanthi.

Inside the Inner Circle there are more surprises. It's like *Tom's Midnight Garden* hidden away behind the wrought-iron royal gates: sculpted hedges and clipped lawns; squirting fountains and and double-take statues; a tinkling mountain stream; a hexagonal-block tea-room with a hexagonal-block patio; even an open-air theatre nestling under blossoming chestnut trees. I've missed out on culture by less than six weeks: the theatre hasn't yet reopened for its revolving summer season of *All's Well That Ends Well*, *A Midsummer Night's Dream* and *Kiss Me Kate* (the fall-back option for those of us who are scared to admit we can't make head nor tail of live Shakespeer). In the maze of rose gardens, every plant is individually pampered and nameplated: 'Tower Bridge'; 'James Mason'; 'Princess Royal', the most fragrant of them all; and, screening the countrified toilet block, a little rose-grower's joke, 'Golden Showers'.

In June, when the roses bloom and the Secret Service lovers aren't shivering on the benches in chubby Cupid's range, this must be London's ultimate tranquil retreat. In any year, they must spend more money on the upkeep of Queen Mary's Gardens than on all the city's roads – and they're worth every penny.

The wide white arc of Park Crescent still forms a grand southern entrance to the Park. In retrospect, it can only be good news that the Prince Regent's privatised country park was never realised. Still, it's difficult not to imagine how it might have looked if the other half of the Crescent's circus had been constructed; or if Nash's dream of a palace of national heroes had been built, as planned, on the high land of the Inner Circle.

As for the Prince's pleasure palace, who can resist wondering what outrageously overblown design he might have sanctioned – or how the tour-guides of today would begin to explain away the mirrored ceilings in the servants' quarters.

I walk back around the park on the Outer Circle road, past the complementary stucco backdrops of York Terrace, Cornwall Terrace and Clarence Terrace to Nash's Sussex Place, the most flamboyant of his boundary designs. Its pointed domes and Anglicised eastern ambience were a practice-run for Nash's Brighton Pavilion, the truly eccentric holiday hideaway he later fashioned for the Prince Regent's hard-earned seaside breaks.

Opposite Lord's cricket ground in St John's Wood are a couple of standard-issue '60s blocks of flats with a very special place in my heart. From the balconies of Lord's View One and Lord's View Two, it's possible to watch Test cricket for free. Having seen the flats' cocktail-toting residents picked out by zoom lens year after year during lulls in the excitement of England's latest humbling, it seemed to me the definitive London place to live – and so the sardonic, battle-hardened *yet seductively quirky* hero of fifteen swiftly abandoned teenage espionage novels was duly installed here. In some of the later, angrier abandoned chapter-plans, my self-styled sex-spy grew a chip on his shoulder and made the symbolic move to a flat on the wrong, south-facing side of the block. His quirky gimmicks, undeniably rare in the genre, were spottiness and sulkiness, which proved a surprising hit with his kung-fu detective sidekick chicks.

I'd love to drop in for a sophisticated Martini with Vernon Swathe/Napoleon Visage/Garrison Homer, and have a listen to his Joy Division bootleg cassettes – only it turns out both blocks are only one flat deep, and there's no such thing as a south-facing address. None of the names on the security intercoms ring a bell. Knowing old Vernon, he's probably off on some secret sex mission.

As I'm passing by W.G. Grace's gates, there floats from the other side of the old, brick-vaulted grandstand the odd cry and scuffling applause of cricketers hard at practice. The satisfying *thonk* of leather on willow. Grown men wearing red-and-yellow stripy ties. A straight bat, a prod to leg, a captain's innings. This is invariably the most enjoyable phase of the cricket season – when English batsmen only have to contend with English bowlers (and vice versa), and optimism for the summer's Test matches is still running high.

Ten minutes away, through a quiet suburbia of rustling trees and damp Victorian town-houses, is Abbey Road. And Abbey Road Studios. Where the Beatles recorded *Abbey Road*.

Under the guidance and tutelage of producer George Martin – the Fifth Beatle – the band in fact committed their entire catalogue to tape in Studio Two, the rear extension of this unassuming stuccoed villa. Recording history was revolutionised at Abbey Road; the Beatles' seventeen number-one singles and twelve albums changed the world, or at least mirrored the changes of the '60s with unerring accuracy. Rock 'n' roll. Mod. Psychedelic. Hippy. Screams were screamed and panties were flung. In 1971, the band walked in procession over the zebra-crossing outside the studio, and when they reached the other side, they went their separate ways.

The Beatles' crossing is an unbelievably popular tourist attraction. That said, it is only a five-minute walk from the Tube, and it is free. A kind of fleeting immortality springs from finding a space on the wall and linking your own name to that of a latterday saint, in fairly-waterproof marker. Of course, it isn't only the Beatles who recorded at Abbey Road: all of EMI and Parlophone's top acts have sweated here in the glow of the red light. We're talking T Rex. Pink Floyd. Gracie Fields. Odd snippets of wilfully obscurist graffiti make claims like THE QUEEN ARE GOD OF MUSIC; but the vast majority who call in to pay homage are Fab Four freaks. JOHN LIVES 1996. PAUL, YOU HAVE MY NUMBER. GEORGE PEACE TATTVA. RINGO WAS QUITE GOOD TOO.

You can tell a lot about a person by their favourite Beatle, not to mention the size and neatness of their carving, the colour of their felt-pen, their idiosyncratic inclusion of personal details and the date. Fans who aren't so smart deface paving slabs with their full names and postal addresses: the council should deliver, and charge accordingly. Edward James Anderson of Baltimore, Maryland, was thoughtful enough to leave a personalised change-of-address sticker on one belisha beacon. The bad drawings, spookily apposite song-titles, gooey lyrics and international messages of goodwill make for a solid three minutes' entertainment.

L + K FROM FINLAND – WE ENJOY
DANCING YOUR MUSIC.
IN THE NETHERLANDS WE ALSO LIKE THE
BEATLES.
BEATLES BEST BAND IN THE EARTH.

After all, there's precious little else here to see or do.

Representatives from all nations hang around for a respectful period, then trail back to the Tube, or on to the lesser-known but attractively multi-purpose shrine on the other side of Maida Vale. The BBC Studios on Delaware Road have played host to just about every artiste in pop music history: this is where the BBC records its specially commissioned radio sessions. Everybody who has ever been anybody has recorded a Peel Session, a Radcliffe Session, a Wogan Session; and, of course, millions of forgotten nobodies have been given a chance to play primadonna, too. Young men in leather trousers are often to be sniffed out in the pubs on neighbouring street corners, passing the hours while cooped-up engineers twiddle and pan their spam-fisted guitar-bashing into a broadcastable shape. At BBC Maida Vale, I was myself once privileged to work alongside Dale 'Buffin' Griffin, one-time drummer with '70s glam popsters Mott the Hoople (although, sadly, by this time he'd traded in his shoulder-pads and glitter mascara for a pair of producer's earphones. He called them 'cans').

Enjoined to fashion a listenable sound from sixteen tracks of off-key grating, legendary sessions sound-man Mike 'Megawatts'

Robinson delivered a telling judgement on our own sub-glam stab at pop superstardom: 'You can't polish a turd.'

Back at Abbey Road, it's hard to credit the fact that so few Beatles fans have come to terms with Paul McCartney's tragic death by moped-crash in the late 1960s. At the time, an extreme inner sanctum of Maccaholics were genuinely convinced of his premature demise – although only a few persist in their campaign to expose the cynical record company cover-up. Desperate not to rock the Beatle boat in the wake of the 'accident', it seems the powers-that-be ordered a body-double to replace Paul in photo-shoots. The band had already given up playing live, so problems inherent in any public appearance were luckily reduced. But soon the rest of the band tired of the deceit, and started to leak hints in their music and on their LP sleeves: among the many giveaways are John Lennon's slurred 'I buried Paul' in the final run-out grooves of 'Strawberry Fields Forever', and the even more blatant confessions which reach out and box you in the ears when you play the *White Album* backwards at 17 r.p.m.

By 1971, and the release of *Abbey Road*, the Beatles had decided to come clean: on the album sleeve, 'Paul' is tellingly *out of step* with John, George and Ringo in a shot reminiscent of a *funeral procession*; Paul never smoked, *but he's smoking on the crossing*; he's also barefoot, and *corpses were always buried barefoot in ancient Greece*. A black maria police van – *just like the one that would have attended Paul's car-crash* – is in the background of the shot and, most impressively of all, the number-plate of the Volkswagen on the other side of the road is LMW 281F: Paul would have been *28 IF* he hadn't been killed!?!

Paul *is* dead. What more proof could you possibly want?

The last time I dropped by to renew my homage to Ringo, a group of fanatical Japanese tourists had their shoes and socks off and had sparked their ciggies in authentic fashion, but were sadly rotating their posing and snapping duties on the wrong Abbey Road crossing – the one a hundred yards down the road from the studios.

It seemed a shame to interrupt their industrious Beatling.

I've still got the photos.

5 EastEnders

Inescapable poverty forms the backdrop to every aspect of the East End story, even if most of the cockney celebrities hammering on about the place do now live in Virginia Water. As the tearfully nostalgic picture-books continually remind us, life in Hell's Kitchen ain't never been no bowl of cherries.

Successive waves of immigrants have rolled into London's Promised Land, often fleeing persecution or squalor in their native countries, only to end up working for scraps in an East End sweat-shop, or holed up in some fauna-infested dosshouse, sleeping on the floor under someone else's bed. If they were lucky.

Always at the front-line of the war against British bigotry, and even longer a *breeding-ground of vice and crime*, the East End survived its first real crisis in Victorian times, when the area became known as a *cradle of philanthropy*. Hence the origins of the locals' legendary luvverly sensayooma, a vital weapon in the face of the reformers' soupy piety. The East End suffered further during its phase as a *hotbed of radicalism*, when it was actually made illegal to wonder whether beds of radicalism had ever been available at any other temperature. And yet darker days were to come during the Second World War, when a third of the East End was buzz-bombed to brick-dust, and a desperate population turned in droves to the consolatory cult of Miss Vera Lynn . . .

Consider for one moment the East Ender's historical lot: the horrors of endemic disease, extortion and the rub-a-dub singalong. Thievery. Prostitution. Murder. Whelks.

But first things first: breakfast at the Beigel Bake on Brick Lane.

Embraced by the ruins of the Jolly Butchers pub, the busiest bakery this side of Beirut promises HOT BEIGELS ALL NIGHT, so I'm expecting a price reduction for eleven o'clock in the morning. In the window, thick slabs of salt-beef are sizzling on a hotplate. Breads of every size and shape are stacked neatly on shelves behind the counter. Chola, black bread, platzels. Don't ask which is which. Since the local Jewish community of Spitalfields and Whitechapel moved *en masse* to the suburbs, bagels have been baked twenty-four hours a day to meet a new demand from – so far as I can tell – dispatch riders, student ravers, electricity board skivers and City office juniors carrying sticky wads of Post-It orders.

I scoop up my generous half-pound of brisket, mustard and bagel and lean at the stainless-steel shelf on the opposite wall. The hot salt-beef is hot, salty and difficult to control, the bagel deliciously sweet. Looking into the bakery through the open end of the shop, fresh batches of fragrant breads and Danish pastries flow from the batteries of ovens. The Danish pastries are the ones with cherries on top.

This far northern end of Brick Lane borders on Bethnal Green, and desolation. Tin cans and tumbleweed blow along the pavements. Sidestreet terraces have been sheared off, leaving chimney-places and wallpaper patterns suspended in mid-air over wasteground dumped with old cookers and bin-bags. Further south, by the shell of Truman's Brewery, the street cobbles have been smashed and only half-heartedly repaired. Once the largest beer-producer in the world, the Black Eagle Brewery dates from 1705, although Truman's were brewing in London as early as the 1380s. The flaking golden eagle still glares down into the road from the top of its solid, portholed wall, where it nestles now among the weedy twigs of an opportunist shrub. Behind the plaster bird, the towering chimney-stack survives, with the brewer's name picked out in white bricks among the red. I don't find any sign of the old-time music hall which thrived for a while in the ruins. On the other side of Brick Lane is the glassy new Truman's factory, now also closed down.

It's a shame about the music hall finally slipping into extinction forty years after it officially bit the dust, mainly because I wanted to soak up some of the atmosphere of *What a Crazy World* – without doubt the most curious film ever to be nominally set in the East End. Ignoring all American influences and any approximation of reality, the film contrives to tell the story of a uniquely English version of pop, spawned from the demon seed of music hall. Never mind Elvis and the Beatles and R&B – in a *Crazy World*, cockney rockers Joe Brown and Marty Wilde set the kids' feet tapping with some hot licks borrowed from Harry Champion, London's rightful King of Pop. According to the hard sell in the BFI's *Celluloid Jukebox*, Joe and Marty play 'streetwise London lads, carving out a space for fun and frolics in a world of street markets, council estates and dole offices'.

The pair don comedy leaning-boots to encore with Champion's barnstorming 'I'm 'Enery ve Eightf I Am', while forty-year-old teenage girls squeal in delight, making RADA-tinged comments along the lines of 'Aren't vey ve bee's knees, or wot?'.

I've never actually seen the film, but don't it sound a proper corker?

Bengali Brick Lane is a highly specialised shopping area, split equally between curry houses, cheap leather jacket boutiques and textile outlets, the latter doing big business this season in thick nylon fur printed up with *101 Dalmatian* spots, leopard spots or pink-and-yellow psychedelic tiger stripes. Most of the leather and fabric shops also sell fruit and veg, hookah pipes and banghra tapes as sidelines: if you haven't cornered the market in at least four diverse lines, you're not really trying. Above the first storey, Brick Lane is a crumbling Georgian slum; below the level of the multilingual street-names it's a frenetic Bangladeshi bazaar, seven feet of cobbles choked with badly parked cars and intoxicating spice fumes, tinkling with tinny bassbeats, bustling with barter. Twentieth-century slums rise to the east, all streaked concrete and uninviting walkways. The East End is overpopulated to bursting point, and this frenetic hive of industry is all about making good, making an escape, making room for the next wave of ground-level Londoners. Personally, I wish I had some room left for fresh samosas, or a greasy takeaway bag of pakora with raw onion and minty dip: the ideal pudding for brunch.

On the corner of Fournier Street, the Jamme Masjid mosque provides a thumbnail history of Spitalfields: originally a French Huguenot church in the mid-eighteenth century, it later served as a Wesleyan chapel and a synagogue before conversion to Islam in the '70s. On Woodseer Street and Fournier Street itself, the terraces retain their letterbox-shaped attic windows, which shed light on the work of the French weavers and silkworkers who first established the rag trade around Fashion Street, later taken up by Jewish tailors, leather outfitters and pre-nylon furriers. Today, the controversial artists Gilbert and George live in a distinctly gentrified Fournier Street alongside bankers and architects. Controversially, G and G don't have a kitchen in their house. It's another great advert for those Brick Lane bagels and samosas.

Each side of the Spitalfields Market building is designed to resemble a Victorian high street terrace from some pretty, fictitious, country town. Only when you venture beyond the green gables, through one of the entrances, do you find the façade is just a stage-set, and the quaint shopping streets all back onto a vast open area the size of a football pitch. The fruit and veg market was moved away east in 1991, and now Spitalfields is occupied by temporary shops, cafés, a flea-market and, fittingly enough, a row of astroturf football pitches. A few reminders of the East End's own Covent Garden can still be found painted up on the walls surrounding the market: PERCY DALTON LONDON LTD – NUT IMPORTERS AND ROASTERS. And a flaking advert for wrapping paper and florist's packing tissue which covers the front of one tiny shop: DONOVAN BROS – THE NOTED HOUSE FOR PAPER BAGS.

Just south of the market stands the imposing Crispin Street Night Shelter, just one survivor of the dismal Victorian workhouses and dosshouses which were run like open prisons for the destitute. One of my first days out as a native Londoner involved dragging Lesley Wallace into the East End backstreets for an organised Ripper walk. Our guide was none other than Donald Rumbelow, author of *The Complete Jack the Ripper*, a copy of which he kindly flogged to Lesley Wallace for a quid off the cover price, even inscribing it 'To Del-Boy, best wishes', to make sure I couldn't go and exchange it at Waterstone's. Don proved to be quite a trouper, leading his group of fifty excited gore-tourists around the key Ripper sites, bantering with winos, pitching in local colour by the vatful, and drawing many a gasp of appalled glee. For all the detail and proximity of the five gruesome murders spread over six weeks in the autumn of 1888, nothing brought home the atmosphere of the Victorian East End so much as Don's dosshouse exposé, performed with relish outside Crispin Street: fourpence would once have bought you a bed for the night, twopence an area of floorspace; while if only a penny could be raised, you were ushered into a dormitory strung from wall to wall with lengths of rope, which you were invited to twist around your outstretched arms, and sleep standing up in your clothes. That's Livin' Orlright.

The first two victims of Jack the Ripper, Polly Nichols and Annie Chapman, were both murdered and mutilated after being turned away from dosshouses in the middle of the night, and died trying to raise the money for a bed.

Today there are three young down-and-outs camping outside Crispin Street under the gaze of a plaster Jesus. Empty cans of Special Brew and Skol Super-Strength are spiked along the railings. The side door is posted with two printed signs: PROVIDENCE ROW COLD WEATHER SHELTER and CLOSED.

Nicholas Hawksmoor, Wren's brightest pupil, built his great Christ Church overlooking Spitalfields as a beacon of godliness in the already anarchic boom-town of the 1720s – where two pints of gin was the average weekly consumption for every man, woman and child. Today its white Portland stone may be blackened with years of soot and grime, but workmen are carrying out repairs behind a green scaffold screen, and this is still a church that commands respect. Its spire reaches up undaunted into the empty white sky, while masons tinker blindly down on the launch-pad: 'Tuscan portico' just doesn't do justice to the power of this giant-colonnaded, vaulted entrance. Some 67,000 people are buried in the churchyard – unless that's a typo in my *Virgin Insider's Guide*. And the small park at the side of Christ Church – nicknamed 'Itchy Park' for the flea-ridden dossers who huddled here until last year – entered pop mythology with the Small Faces' 1967 number one, 'Itchycoo Park'.

That's when Ronnie Laine, Steve Marriott and Co were well on their way to establishing a wholly un-American Britpop, based loosely around pub singalongs, traditional folkie forms, copious quantities of mind-altering drugs . . . and music hall. Joe and Marty's *Crazy World* wasn't so crazy after all. The Kinks, Madness, Blur – they're all the wayward offspring of only the chirpiest cockney journeymen. Now is the time for a reappraisal of Arthur Askey's gifts; of Bernard Cribbins winking his way through 'My Old Man's a Dustman'. Chas 'n' Dave revival, anyone?

In *My EastEnd*, Anita Dobson – for years better known as Angie, long-suffering wife of Dirty Den, and brassy barmaid extraordinaire – provides an exhaustive list of East End entertainers whose impact on pop culture is impossible to exaggerate. Jack 'Evenin' All' Warner out of *Dixon of Dock Green*. Bernard Bresslaw, Sid James's big, bald sidekick in the *Carry On* films. Des O'Connor. Harry Pinter. And then there were the music hall artistes: Marie Lloyd, Tommy Trinder, Stanley Holloway . . .

But what's this? I think I've just put my finger on the elusive attraction of the East End music halls. According to Angie, most of them doubled up as brothels, full of drunken sailors, bawdy tarts and temperance activists. West End theatregoers came 'slumming it' in the East, to the palatial Wilton's music hall, off Cable Street, where they were routinely robbed as soon as their trousers hit the floor, knocked on the head, dropped through a trapdoor and dragged out into the neighbouring streets.

Now that's what I call the thrill of Variety.

I would drop into Itchycoo Park for a nostalgic groove about under dreaming spires – at very least some streetwise fun and frolics – only there's a builder's fence blocking the way, and it isn't all too beautiful. On the corner of Fournier Street, opposite Christ Church and the market, the Ten Bells pub presents a likely alternative. For years the pub was known as the Jack the Ripper, staking a proud claim to have once been the preferred pick-up spot of local prostitutes, including the Ripper's victims. In deference to the wishes of feminists, the pub reverted to its original name a few years back, and removed its grisly checklist of victims, dates and details from public display outside. Goodness knows what kind of clientèle would be drawn to a pub revelling in such a history. I make it my business to find out.

As I pole through the door, I'm met by the unexpected sight of a young woman wiggling naked on the floor at my feet. I must admit it isn't the type of pub welcome that's often extended my way, but I'm sure it could catch on. I gulp a cartoon gulp, and try to think of something to say. The jukebox tune is 'Wannabe'. 'Spice Girls, eh?' I comment stupidly to a hypnotised neighbour, who replies, 'Yeah.' There are thirty or forty men, mainly suited City-types, already at home in the bar, spaced out along the walls around the carpeted pallet in the centre of the floor. It's hard to know where to look, although everyone seems to have reached an agreement. The song grinds to a halt, as does my new intimate acquaintance. She gathers up her bra and knickers and totters off behind the bar, clutching them to her chest in a belated attempt to save my blushes.

I buy a half of lager from the suddenly crowded bar and take in some of the Ripperabilia tacked up over the walls. The list of victims, taken down from outside. JACK'S LONDON in poster form. Old copies of the *Police News*, showing the discovery of mutilated bodies on damp, gaslit cobbles. MURDER MOST FOUL. I don't want to make too much of a show of being interested in the yellowed newspaper clippings, because it must look like the worst imaginable excuse for being here: Oh no, I'm only interested in the original Georgian decor, me. I'm a staunch supporter of the Women's Movement. And I don't just mean pelvic gyrations.

Another teenager in high-heels and a scrap of nylon negligee stands on tiptoes and larfs up into the perplexed face of one of the suits who followed me inside: 'Give us 50p, luv,' she explains, 'and I'll show yer me fanny!'

When her pint pot is an inch full of loose change, she reinvests 50p in the jukebox. It's a smoochy one, by someone I'm afraid might be Michael Bolton. Baby Barbawa Windsor swings artistically round her scratching post and gets on with her dance of the one-and-a-bit veils.

In cockney rhyming slang, strippers are 'Jack the Rippers'. Confusing, that.

But this will never do – hanging around in seedy East End pubs when I've got an top-level luncheon meeting in Wapping with a representative of Rupert Murdoch's News International. By the time I've discovered the East London Tube line is out of service, and have been zigzagged through the Shadwell badlands by the replacement mini-bus service, my mate Gavin is already halfway down his second pint at the Town of Ramsgate. I'm all of five minutes late.

I've been drawn to ver Tahn (as us locals call it) by the amazing write-up in my *Alka-Seltzer Guide to the Pubs of London*, an invaluable crawl around the refreshment high-spots of 1976, and a master-stroke of complementary marketing. I'm chuffed to say I picked it up from the 10p junk basement at the Notting Hill Book Exchange, where it had been flung mistakenly with the pre-war chemistry textbooks and Jeffrey Archer novels. Experts have estimated its true value, for insurance purposes, at something approaching 15p.

Gav is alone in the bar with his complimentary copy of *The Times*, a thicket of skinheads and a twittering Shadwellian hen-party making an early start. The chemistry at work in the narrow, dark corridor of the pub is authentically medieval. I point out a passage in the *Alka-Seltzer* lowdown – 'in the cellar of the pub are the dungeons where convicts were chained and grappled before deportation to Australia' – and Gav chuckles nervously. He thought this was just a tourist pub, and didn't know about the early-morning licences granted in these parts 'to cater for the early shifts of dockers'. We take our beers out the back into the light, and pull up damp metal chairs on the raised patio, just feet from the quiet slopping of the khaki Thames. The river is at high tide, reaching up to ankle-height on the other side of the pub wall. For an open river, it feels oddly claustrophobic. The view is blinkered by the wharf and pier on either side of the pub, but in the segment that is visible, the odd tug sputters by against the tumbledown waterfront of the south bank.

Before their little disagreement over *The Mutiny on the Bounty*, Fletcher Christian (who looked a lot like Marlon Brando) and Captain Bligh (Trevor Howard) used to sup rum and porter together at the Town of Ramsgate. A worn flight of steps leads creepily into the water a few yards down from the patio: Wapping Old Stairs, where Colonel Blood (Errol Flynn) was apprehended with the Crown Jewels tucked under his cloak. Judge Jeffries, the murderous 'Hanging Judge' of the Bloody Assizes, was caught in the pub dressed as a sailor, as he tried to escape the mob. It's all in the *Alka-Seltzer*.

And 'the hanging dock where petty criminals were tried was situated where the riverside bar now exists'.

Right here.

If I'm ever tried for any 'petty' misdemeanour, I trust it won't be somewhere called 'the hanging dock'.

Before secure docks were built, around 1800, the Port of London was already the busiest in the world, but there was nothing like enough space for every ship to moor at the bank: they were unloaded by lightermen with long poles, and their cargoes rowed ashore. Now, what percentage of any shipment do you think might have 'gone missing' during unloading? Do I hear 10 per cent? Am I arskin' 20 per cent? Nah. Between them, the luvverly light-fingered lightermen and the gangs of cut-throats who habitually plundered the craft 'alf-inched an outrageous *50 per cent* of all cargoes: tea and butter for the table; ivory to be fenced off at cut-price; dodgy Lacoste knitwear to be sold out of boxes around the pubs.

That's one for vem . . . and one for us. Fair's fair, arfter all.

The 'River Pirates' specialised in cutting merchantmen adrift at night, running them aground and helping themselves. Dodgy porters and labourers, known for 'taxing' any goods that passed through their hands, were called 'Heavy Horsemen': they used to throw goods overboard to be collected at low tide by 'Mudlarks'. I'm not sure what the 'Scuffle Hunters' did, but they had the best team name, and were as crooked as a dog's back leg.

When the West India Dock Company mobilised the world's first police force on the river, the cockney tea-leaves were up in arms, incensed at the denial of their 'right to plunder'. They suffered the indignity of being searched when they finished work, and were even made to wear a special tight uniform, making it difficult to conceal their knock-off hundredweights of coal, and the more substantial flaggons of wine. Then the inland docks were cut, fortified and defended by cannon. East End dockers found out what it was like to be *really* poor; but they never lost the habit of ducking and diving, wheeling and dodgy dealing.

Gav is a West Ham United fan. Upminster, Essex, might be on the edge of the Hammers' catchment area, but he's a bit of a Scuffle Hunter himself. He recommends a visit to Bermondsey Market, over on the south bank, if I'm on the lookout for goods of a certain nature. Farcically, Bermondsey's Friday-morning free-for-all is still covered by a Royal Decree of 1314 (or something), which means if you buy any goods from the market, you become their legal owner – no matter what their history; whether they're name-tagged, security-coded or whatever. A nod's as good as a wink to a blind man, and you don't look a gift horse in the north and south. Last week, Gav snapped up a couple of still-damp Old Masters and a 'shopsoiled' car stereo. Unfortunately, while he was there, one of the less scrupulous dealers sold Gav's parked car to a Shadwellian for two hundred pounds cash-in-hand, as-seen. Gav says it's a case of swings and roundabouts. You win some, you lose some.

When the tide is out and the Mudlarks are on duty, Wapping Old Stairs lead down to the shallow beach of Execution Dock, where pirates and smugglers were tried and hanged, their bodies left dangling as an example until the tide had washed over them three times. We slip past the modern-day descendants of Captain Kidd, all tattoos and earrings and eye-patches – nice girls – and wander down to Wapping Pier Head looking, without much luck, for a wharf that's supposedly marked with an 'E' for Execution. The entrance to the old London Docks has been filled in and grassed over – which has done nothing for local trade figures, but what a pleasant view from the windows of Michael Crawford's riverside gaff. Cher's London bolt-hole is balanced on top of the wharf buildings looking out over the river towards Tower Bridge, a world away, not half a mile upriver.

Back in the '60s, the area had its share of showbiz names to drop, only then they were all locals: the Small Faces were known as 'The Wonders of Wapping Wharf'. Anita Dobson still lives in Wapping, Gawd bless 'er.

We walk back along Wapping High Street in the deep, curving trench between the waterfront Gun Wharves and their twins opposite, all now converted into yuppie flats. At lunchtime, none of the workers from Fortress Wapping wander down through the Wapping Lane estates to the superb old riverside pubs; they stay within the fortified walls of Tobacco Dock. Redeveloped in the '80s to cash in on the arrival of New Money and Rupert Murdoch's all-new, non-union workforce, the vaulted brick honeycomb of Tobacco Wharf was split into prestige retail space. Only the sandwich shop and the wine-bar remain, with names like the Body Shop, Our Price and Next all felt-penned carefully out of the floor-plan. It turns out journos and printworkers only want to spend money on lager during their lunchbreaks, and waterfront wharf-dwellers only ever lift their electric garage barricades to zoom straight into the City. It's nice to be able to have a poke around a couple of dry-docked clippers without interruption by swarming tourists, but it's hardly what the developers must have had in mind.

If Tobacco Dock had taken off, it would only have made the contrast between the New Money and the local population all the more discomfiting. I leave Gavin at the site of the Siege of Wapping and trail back through the council flats and bomb-site playgrounds, walking in a mile loop to Cable Street. Wapping smells of drains. Run-down launderettes and community centres rub shoulders with smart new estate agents. The Three Suns pub has been converted into a wine merchant's. Other pubs are bricked up, boarded up or broken down. The streets are all but deserted in the middle of the afternoon, as lonely as the Bronx. Kids kick a punctured football against a graffitied courtyard wall. Generations of cheap housing are piled up between the Tube line and the docks, each of them another crime against the past. Hundred-yard-long blocks of pre-war red-brick balconies. Nineteen storeys of streaky '60s concrete. '70s low-rise hutches with slitty windows – too high for a man to climb in, a smaller target for stones, and cheap to replace. Shame they don't let in any light, but beggars can't be choosers.

In *Full Metal Jacket*, Stanley Kubrick substituted London

Docklands for a Vietnam war-zone, and no one noticed.

Cable Street was once the most notorious thoroughfare in Whitechapel, the only beat in London where the police patrolled in twos. 'Cable Street, the whore's retreat'. Where seventeen-hour days stuffing mattresses or making matchboxes were common in Dickens' day; where baby-selling was rife among starving women, who knew that children of the East End stood worse than a 50 per cent chance of living past the age of five. Cable Street, where in 1936 Oswald Mosley, Britain's own crappy little would-be Hitler, led a march of three thousand Blackshirts. Protected by seven thousand policemen. Repelled by a united East End.

On the surface, Cable Street is still a poverty-stricken ghetto, worn down by years of neglect and unemployment; but that legendary, embattled East End spirit must still exist just to put up with this ugly boredom year after year. Since the '70s the East End has had to organise every few years to kick Alf Garnett and his racist gangs off the streets. Sadly, it's nothing new for London: the baker who started the Great Fire was forced to admit he was an 'agent of the Pope' before he was executed. The fire that razed Whitehall Palace was blamed on a Dutch linen-maid. The Gordon Rioters of 1780 attacked the Bank of England, the Theatre Royal and the city's prisons; but their initial motivation had not been anti-wealth, but anti-Catholic. Post-Notting Hill, even *Sidney Poitier* had to win over a bunch of tough East End yooves (including a suspiciously over-age Lulu) in *To Sir, With Love*. Black and Asian East Enders are still routinely blamed for unemployment, crime and the erosion of the British Way of Life, much like their Jewish, Irish and French fore-runners.

The safety-net of the welfare state suspends the whole area below the poverty line, just short of the old degradations – but necessity is the mother of invention.

Ironically, the Ripper murders (first suspect: a mad Polish Jew) served to draw attention to the state of the East End. Respectable Londoners in the west were shocked to find there were forbidden stretches of the Jago where the police would only venture to retrieve a murdered corpse; where Dr Jekyll could turn into Mr Hyde without attracting a second glance. The idea of a forty-five-year-old, tooth-less prostitute being disembowelled was upsetting enough, but the revelation that she was at the time wearing five petticoats and carrying with her *all her worldly possessions* hit home in a different way. One of the more imaginative theories on the identity of Jack the Ripper casts the killer as an unhinged social reformer, unconventional, uncompromising but undoubtedly effective.

Whitechapel Market is the poorest I've seen anywhere in London, a string of stalls set out along the gutter, selling thin T-shirts and windcheaters, fishheads and chicken feet. Toynbee Hall, further down the Whitechapel Road, was built at the turn of the century as a hall of residence for all the middle-class mercy-missionaries. The Salvation Army was founded on this very spot, as soon as William Booth set eyes on those chickens feet; and the first pub crowd to dodge the rattle of a Sallies' tin was at the notorious Blind Beggar. The London Hospital on Whitechapel Road, once the largest hospital in the world, became the refuge of John Merrick, ex-freak show Elephant Man and one-time door-to-door salesman. Ragged Schools and the first Doctor Barnardo children's home sprang up to save homeless orphans from a life of crime, while public parks were sliced out of the rookeries. Which is all very well, but Victorian good works don't exactly set the old Londonometer pinging like stories including words like 'crossfire' and 'anarchy'.

East End conditions not only attracted Victorian philanthropists, but political radicals, too. One Communist Party meeting on a corner of Whitechapel Road in pre-revolutionary 1900 was attended by Lenin, Trotsky and Stalin. Second only to Jack the Ripper in East End criminal mythology is the anarchist anti-hero Peter the Painter. In January 1912, a couple of weeks after an interrupted jewel robbery had resulted in 'the Houndsditch Murders' of two policemen, the boys in blue paid heed to a tip-off and laid siege to a lodging-house in Sidney Street. A fierce gun battle ensued, lasting all morning, and two squads of Scots Guards were called in as reinforcements. The Home Secretary, young Winston Churchill, arrived to take command of the operation, and the house was soon mysteriously set ablaze . . .

The charred bodies of two of the Houndsditch Murderers were found inside the barricaded house, but Peter Piatkov, the brains behind the gang of desperadoes, was missing, and was never seen again. Today, it's sad to say that not a single brick remains of pre-war Sidney Street, although myths and rumours still abound on the fate of Peter the Painter. The latest conspiracy theory, linking him to Queen Victoria and the cupboard under the stairs at Buckingham

Palace, made an entry into the betting at odds of 200,000-to-1, approximately five seconds ago.

Even by the time of the Second World War, many East Enders had not forgotten the firepower and ferocity of the troops sent into the docks to break the General Strike of 1926. Or the *carte blanche* given to them by the then Chancellor of the Exchequer, Winston Churchill, who declared that any shootings or beatings administered by the forces of law and order 'will receive, both now and afterwards, the full support of His Majesty's government'.

Set about by British Nazis and Russian anarchists, by Downing Street and the British Army, by Jack the Ripper and all four Horsemen of the Apocalypse (update: they've got guns and drugs and bombs), life out east ain't never been no bowl of cherries.

Still, mustn't grumble. Have a nice cuppa char.

Luvverly jubbly.

Before risking my reputation in another East End boozer, I check with my local bibles for an overview of the scene. I don't want to be pressganged or challenged to a bout of Russian shove-ha'penny. I don't want to have to sing (or strip) for my supper . . . although I wouldn't mind being called a *slaaag* by a traditional TV landlord.

Somewhat disappointingly, the *Alka-Seltzer Guide* points out that pubs now 'provide the background to family and friendly gatherings, and social events'. Apparently the era of the gin palace is long past, when 'the high ceilings, ornate decorations and cut glass of these Victorian pubs witnessed the fights, the murders, loves and jealousies' of local roughnecks with nowhere else to turn for entertainment.

And so it must surely follow that TV's *EastEnders* is set in some mythical, composite era some time between the strike of the Match Girls and the Blitz.

Not so, says Anita 'Angie' Dobson, brassily. 'Living in the East End, I know people like the characters in *EastEnders*': unhinged laudromat assistants, mainly. 'There is an authenticity about the way in which the programme reflects contemporary developments': love and hate, crime and disease, going to the dogs. Ange assures us Albert Square and the Queen Vic are based on yer actual East End architecture, lovingly recreated in period chipboard. And 'when the series started, researchers even went to the trouble of visiting East

End markets to ensure that the actors were wearing the right clothes'.

Lesley Wallace's friend, Chris, used to be a camerawoman on *EastEnders* out at Elstree Studios. She says look out for Pauline Fowler's disguised designer-label clobber.

Having established beyond reasonable doubt that I won't be dropping in for a pint with Nick Cotton, Dirty Den or the Mitchell brothers, the Kray twins seem almost an easy option. I wonder whether the Blind Beggar will be one of the 'easy-to-find musical pubs of Whitechapel', boosted up to sound so very thrilling in my *Alka-Seltzer Guide*: 'Some provide live groups ranging from pop to jazz to folk,' R.M. Smith (ed.) generalises unashamedly. 'Some are pub discos; still others provide professional cabaret or organise talent contests for local hopefuls.'

So *that's* what must have been going on at the Ten Bells: I must have stumbled in on a good old-fashioned *talent contest* . . .

Three years ago, stand-up comedy was hailed as 'the new rock 'n' roll', a reputation which stuck for as long as three whole weeks, before food, and then British and Commonwealth philately temporarily took over the title. Two weeks was plenty of time for me to write an entire set of side-splitting material, to arrange a world tour of two 'new talent' nights, practise for twenty minutes in front of the mirror, and sit back and wait for the groupies and heli-pads. Coincidentally, both of my three-minute 'open-spots' were at pubs on the fringes of the East End – one at the Eagle in Stratford (where David Essex was discovered!), and the other on Hackney high street. Not the Hackney Empire, mind – I took my bow out of the big-time at the grubby little pub next door, having explained my joke about the big-nosed baldiefish twice too often.

Naturally, I lay the blame for my stupidly high hopes on London, the city itself: you know the old line about every waitress and barman in LA being an actress, a writer or the next Divine Brown-in-waiting; well, things aren't so very different here, with endlessly ambitious, multi-, semi- and not-really-very talented individuals pouring into Dreamsville at a staggering daily rate. In the cut-throat world of the Millennium City, you ain't nobody if you ain't a Wannabe. Or a Could've-Done-That, a Turned-It-Down, or a Choosing-Not-To-Be, Honest. Or, at least, that's how it seemed to me, for two weeks, three years ago.

I walk through the doors of the Blind Beggar confident that I won't interrupt another compromised cabaret hopeful. Confident that there won't be a broken microphone set up on a pallet in the corner. Confident that the Salvation Army will have found other pubs to visit in the past 130 years. And fairly confident that I'm not going to get a bullet lodged in the back of my skull, courtesy of Reggie Kray. That was George Cornell. That was 1966. That's what you got for calling Reggie a 'fat poof'. And that was that for the Kray twins' East End reign of terror.

A gruff voice floats over my shoulder: 'Wot you comin' rahnd 'ere lookin' for, you *slaaag*?'

It isn't Reggie Kray, or even 'Mad' Frankie Fraser – it's my old schoolmate, Simon. He's knocked off work at the Guildhall University and dropped by to show me the ropes at his local. Si is another graduate of Miss Glover's English class who now suffers strange Londoholic fantasies about geezers with shooters and girls with spectacularly false eyelashes.

'I've gone on my toes, squire,' I reply in kind. 'I went down for a carpet thanks to a gentleman with a long tail. I bet your bottle wouldn't fall out if you blew me a peter . . .' Then I notice the barmaid has wandered over within earshot, and almost certainly thinks we're taking the piss. 'Er, two pints of lager, please.' Tales of Reggie's bullet-holes lovingly preserved in the wall are exaggerated, but this barmaid is *brassy*.

We take a table by the window while the renovated family fun emporium fills up with after-work trade, mercifully adding to the row of solitary oldsters at the bar, and one sinister youth on the bandit who doesn't seem to like the idea of us having Angie's bumper picture-book open on the table. 'Cos books is for poofs. No disrespect meant to Reggie. And none taken.

Now Si is excited because he's noticed a sheet of paper tacked to the wall by our escape-route:

TORTOISE
stolen from Stepney area
Large crack in shell
Have you been offered a tortoise or
do you know of someone who has recently acquired one?
Any information, call 0171-XXX XXXX

Of course, this is anything but a polite community enquiry about a missing pet. This is the Blind Beggar. The message is a veiled threat. When we find out 'oo's nicked our Reginald, we'll *do veir knees*, is the unwritten suggestion. The pet's owners are tortured by the image of a greasy spiv sidling up to loners in the snug-bar, a large, wriggling lump in his jacket lining. It's the classic Scuffle Hunter mentality captured in a cracked carapace: screw it down or wave goodbye. Finders keepers. Watch yer back. Keep yer nose clean. Yer Gotta Pick a Sky-Rocket or Two.

I once bought a two-day-old labrador from a bloke in an East End juicer. It turned out to be a hamster.

Armed criminal gangs have a long history in the East End: razor-slashing mob warfare once raged up and down cramped Dickensian courts; only the spray-can territories and mobile phones are new. Extortion, robbery, counterfeiting and poncing were once commonly regarded as honourable family trades, with tricks and tools passed down from father to son. *Oliver!*'s armies of guttersnipes were organised to roam the city, relieving the unwary of their 'surplus' money and goods, graduating from 'kynchin' lay' (stealing laundry from delivery boys), to be a 'mutcher' (robbing helpless drunks), a 'shootflyer' (snatching gold watch-chains) or a skilled 'whizzer' (the Artful Dodger himself).

Here we sit at the heart of historical gangland; the brassy barmaid is almost certainly telling all the Krays' old henchmen about me and my schoopid mouf; at any minute a Great Train Robber or some fictional nutter from *The Long Good Friday* could drop in for old times' sake – and Si's dropped into cockney nostalgia mode: 'Ronnie 'n' Reggie, vey was luvverly boys,' he tells me, wiping a tear from his eye. 'Vey was so close, vey used to wear a pair of tights over bofe of veir 'eads aht on a rumble. We didn't need no police when vey was abaht. Vey only ever coshed veir own. Very polite wiv ver ladies.' And all that old bollocks. You must have seen the film, starring the Kemp brothers out of Spandau Ballet, and Boy George as Jack 'The Hat' McVitie.

It seems to me Si is veering onto dangerous ground, daring to doubt there was ever such thing as a respectful code of villainry; honour amongst extortionists, a *criminal nobility*. Just because the thousands who lined the route of Ron's funeral procession were only really interested in gatecrashing the *Six O'clock News*. Just because

Reggie is certified barking mad. Just because Charlie Kray was recently arrested for his part in a would-be drug-smuggling racket, and the police who set him up called him a 'pathetic old man'. Just because 'Mad' Frankie Fraser has given up slicing villains for a living, and runs a guided tour around the Krays' Vallance Road birthplace, the Blind Beggar and Turnmills club. And the price of a ticket includes a meal on a boat-trip, where 'Mad' tells jokes about concrete boots.

That's no reason to doubt the dignity, the *chivalry* of old-style thuggery.

Back in 1963, top Londonologist Daniel Farson was drinking with some noisy West End friends in a newly opened East End club, the glitzy Kentucky on the Mile End Road. He'd never even heard of the Krays. Until a burly gentleman in an immaculately shiny suit took one of them aside, and respectfully asked: 'Mind your language, moy san. Ladies present.'

An hour later he was back, eyes like pissholes in snow, for a word with an unfortunate youth chatting to a woman at the bar. 'That's *moy* little lady you're talkin' to. *Step ahtside.*'

Ronnie leads the transgressor into the back yard. They take off their jackets and ties, and they *box*, Queensberry Rules. Ronnie knocks the boy to the cobbles three or four times and bloodies his nose – then helps him to his feet and gives him his handkerchief. They shake hands, put on their jackets and return to the club.

Buoyed by a misguided yearning for the days of honourable coshings, and several pints of gassy refreshment, we retire to Brick Lane for a plateful of those samosas and a steaming Ruby Murray.

Dan Farson, who brushed lightly up against Mr Kray in *Limehouse Days*, is best known for swanning about *Soho in the Fifties* with Jeffrey Bernard, George Melly and his Colony Club cohorts, although he does have a far more impressive claim to fame, Londonologically speaking: he (re)discovered the identity of Jack the Ripper. Probably.

And no, it wasn't Queen Victoria's nephew, the Duke of Clarence.

Montague Druitt was a struggling barrister, the cricket-loving son of a Dorset surgeon. He knew the East End well and, according to Farson, lodged and possibly assisted at his cousin's surgery on the Minories, on the eastern boundary of the City. The Whitechapel Murders – and police vigilance in the East End – came to a mysteriously abrupt halt when Druitt's weighted body was fished out of the Thames, off Thorneycroft's Torpedo Works in Chiswick. He had been in the water for four weeks, his death coinciding with the time the Ripper might have been expected to kill again, given the broken cycle of his increasingly frenzied attacks. Druitt had lived in fear of following his mother into insanity, but still visited her regularly in a private mental home – in Chiswick. At the coroner's inquest, Druitt's brother 'accidentally' described himself as the only surviving kin: had he been given an inkling of Montague's ghastly secret; and was he trying to shield his mother, brother and three sisters from an impending scandal? Finally, Sir Melville Macnaghten, Scotland Yard's chief Ripperologist, admitted just one regret over the case: that he'd become 'a detective officer six months after Jack the Ripper had committed suicide'.

The inference is clear: Druitt had emerged as a prime Ripper suspect, but seeing as he'd done the decent thing, a cover-up was ordered to protect his wealthy, professional family.

And one more irresistible shard of circumstantial evidence: Montague Druitt was the spitting image of young Prince Eddy, the Duke of Clarence.

One hundred and nine years ago, with two Ripper victims already dead, and the East End in paranoid tatters, desperate prostitutes kept up their slow circling of St Botolph's Church, on the lookout for business. If they paused, they could be arrested for soliciting, so they walked slowly by the front of the church . . . and then ran smartly around the back.

Catherine Eddowes – only just released from Whitechapel Police Station, where she had been held for drunkenness – left the crawling parade of ragged women and entered into brief negotiations with a man. At one o'clock, as Eddowes was led across the Minories to Mitre Square, waves of a police manhunt bore down along the Whitechapel Road: just fifteen minutes before, the steward of a Working Men's Club on Berners Street (now renamed Henriques Street) had driven his horse and cart into the pitch-dark club yard. When the horse shied from trotting on, he dismounted to discover the body of Elizabeth Stride, a well-known local prostitute. Her throat had been cut so recently, blood was still pumping from the wound. The Ripper had been disturbed in his work, but had escaped unnoticed in the dark, amid the clatter of hooves.

Today, the cobbles are the only remaining original feature of Mitre Square. This was where Donald Rumbelow, origin of all my Ripper clues and several thousand others, showed us exactly where the luckless Eddowes was found by PC 'Steve' White — whose notebook describes the 'sallow' man with brilliant eyes and 'long, tapering fingers' he had just passed in the alley leading into the square.

'In the East End we are used to shocking sights, but the sight I saw made the blood in my veins turn to ice. At the end of the cul-de-sac, huddled against the wall, there was the body of a woman, and a pool of blood was streaming along the gutter from her body . . .'

This time, the Ripper had had sufficient time to vent his pent-up, psychopathic lust. Eddowes lay broken on her back, her face smashed, her throat cut, her belly ripped open from rectum to breastbone.

'It was clearly another of those terrible murders. I remembered the man I had seen, and I started after him as fast as I could run, but he was lost to sight in the dark labyrinth of the East End mean streets.'

Following the footsteps of the Ripper, I now double back to the east, past St Botolph's churchyard, which is scattered with prone bodies and discarded beer-cans.

By now, the Metropolitan Police manhunt was almost upon the Ripper, combing down the Whitechapel Road from the east. The hastily assembled City Police dragnet following from the west had him all but surrounded.

The Aldgate subway emerges at the end of Middlesex Street, better known by the name it enjoyed before the Victorian authorities decided it was unseemly for an item of women's underwear to appear in a street name: THIS IS THE WORLD-RENOWNED PETTICOAT LANE SUNDAY MARKET. Tubby Isaac's eel stand is a throwback to the days when East End streets were full of vendors dishing up muffins, hot potatoes, pies and winkles. Of course, there's no historical evidence to suggest that the Ripper stopped off here for jellied eels, but I did: £1.70 entitles any Tubby customer to an earthenware bowlful of fishy segments suspended in thin yellow jelly. The kind of jelly you find between the meat and the pastry in a pork pie. The part of the pork pie that always makes me want to gag.

A couple of elderly vaseline junkies are already scooping the goo into their mouths. My dapper neighbour along the metal counter spits a bone into the cardboard box within leaning-and-dribbling distance of his size 4s, and pauses in his shovelling. He shows me how to prepare the glop for human consumption: black pepper first, then a good sprinkling of chilli vinegar 'to wash it all frough'. He can only be about four foot ten, in his miniature double-breasted whistle and flute, and those spic-and-span slip-ons.

'It's 'is fird time 'ere today,' says Tubby Jr of his slurping regular. 'Can't get enough, can yer?'

Jellied eels, though: not so much of an *acquired taste* as I'd been led to fear. It's a very delicate fish, not at all tough or rubbery as you might imagine. As a loyal cockney, I'd describe the taste as *subtle* – not unlike slightly fishy pepper and chilli. Chewing the jellyish meat off its spiky bone is the really fun part.

Properly refreshed, I turn off Petticoat Lane into Wentworth Street, back on the trail of the Ripper. Among the blowing litter and stripped stall frames from the daily market on Goulston Street, I find the passageway by the Happy Days kebab shop where the Ripper dropped a torn, blood-soaked strip of Catherine Eddowes' apron. Surely a false trail, reckons Donald Rumbelow (likewise the chalk-scrawled message found in the alley: *The Juwes are The men That Will not be Blamed for nothing*) but a trail to lead the police away from *where*?

Further up Goulston Street stood a public drinking-fountain, which constables on the manhunt found still swirling with blood, just after the Ripper had used it to wash his hands, before he disappeared into the black maze of alleyways and lodging-houses.

At the top of Goulston Street lies the Crispin Street Night Shelter, opposite a multi-storey carpark built on the site of a squalid tenement called Miller's Court. Here, after the passage of nine more nights, the Ripper would claim his fifth victim, whose murder marked a final escalation in the frenzied savagery of the attacks. Mary Kelly, an Irish prostitute aged just twenty-five, was heard singing 'Only a Violet I Plucked from My Mother's Grave' at around eleven o'clock on the night of 9 November 1888. Later, a cry of 'Oh! murder' was routinely ignored: Miller's Court was that kind of neighbourhood.

Mary Kelly was found not so much mutilated as mechanically dismantled, with organs and body-parts left draped all over the bed and about her single room. She was the last person to know with absolute certainty the identity of Jack the Ripper.

Back on Commercial Street, outside the Ten Bells pub, prostitutes still patrol, ducking and bobbing in stockings and hot-pants, to catch the eye of passing motorists.

6 The Stony-Hearted Stepmother

Oxford Street isn't really so different from the main shopping street in any British city; it's just twenty times longer. The shops are the standard-issue high street chains – M&S, C&A, BHS, KFC, HMV – offloading wares from the same production lines that serve branches in Leicester, Leeds and Limerick (probably). The flagship branches just tend to be a floor or two more expansive, a penny or two more expensive . . . and fifty times busier. This is London.

Many of the more restrained London guides don't exactly approve of shopping. '*Cross* Oxford Street – and for my money that is what I always do,' barks Ian Norrie, on one of his admirably upright, lust-free walks around the capital. Then, a few pages later: 'Cross abominable Oxford Street once again' – and this is from *A Celebration of London*!

David Piper's scholarly *Companion Guide to London* is hardly more charitable: 'Crowds eddy into voracious grottoes of chromium, neon and glass . . . the principles of window-dressing are quantity and glitter – hynotise your customer . . . people seem to float, slow and turgid with the swaying drift of jellyfish in the doldrums . . .'

Steady on, Dave. It's only a *street*.

Even on a Thursday morning, the endless procession of red buses can only inch along in the fume-belching traffic. It's overcast but warm for the time of year – perfect weather to enjoy a brisk walk to hospital with carbon monoxide poisoning. The wide pavements are clogged with shoppers swinging large carrier-bags emblazoned with only the most famous names: Dickins and Jones; Harvey Nicks; even Sotheby's, the auctioneers. I can't help suspecting some of these characters of dropping into Liberty's for a packet of tissues or a Lion Bar for their elevenses, and tipping the till assistant a pathetic wink – 'Go on, stick it in a big bag for us, luv' – then transferring all their shopping from their Mister Byrite carrier, and stepping out transformed into these fully fledged, card-carrying London jellyfish. Can the street really be awash with so much casually disposable income? I get the sudden urge to apply for a job as a shop security guard, so I can peek inside all these huge olive-green and yellow bags and check for phoneys; at least get some insight into the troublesome question of what all these people *do*. I mean for a living. There can't be this many people on holiday in May, even in London.

At least I'd make a *thorough* security guard: 'Excuse me, sir/madam, but shouldn't you be at work, earning some *money* so you can *afford* to swan around Selfridge's on a Thursday morning?'

And women love a man in uniform.

As I've said, apart from the odd tat 'n' T-shirt motto grotto ('Good Girls Go To Heaven, Bad Girls Go To London' – *hmm*) Oxford Street is wall-to-wall with just the same shoe shops, fashion chains and burger bars as you'd find anywhere else. Selfridge's is the one notable exception to the rule, a block-long temple to conspicuous consumption that would pass for a presidential palace in any other capital city. A national flag flutters above each of the façade's two-dozen fluted columns. Over the main entrance, a bulky art-deco clock, 'The Queen of Time', features an eleven-foot statue of Britannia on her day off, slumming with a couple of exhibitionist mermaids. Selfridge's was never meant to be subtle, and subtle it ain't. Gordon Selfridge was American. Completed in 1928, his 130-department store was originally intended to have a skyscraping phallic tower sprouting from its roof: the planning authorities just laughed. Elsewhere on the self-publicity trail, Selfridge was the first store-owner to keep his window displays floodlit all night; he invented the 'bargain basement', 'spending a day at Selfridge's' and 'only 268 shopping days to Christmas'.

Selfridge was eventually voted off his own board in 1939, aged eighty-two, having run up debts of more than £370,000, allegedly largely through his habit of befriending nubile young actresses, parading them through the store, and letting them have their pick of the goodies. The store's current advertising slogan is 'It's worth living in London' – an admirable sentiment, even if they did modestly leave out the proviso, 'especially if you're Gordon Selfridge'.

I haven't got time to 'spend the day at Selfridge's', but I can appreciate how it might well be possible to move in full-time: there are four bars, six cafés and three restaurants in-store, including one ('Gordon's') that's 'trendy' and 'lively' (you betcha). Unfortunately, I haven't arranged the mortgage necessary to go shopping at any of the checklist of designer departments. I haven't even got the guts to go and buy a Lion Bar and plead for a bag.

John Lewis is more my kind of department store: maybe I feel a kinship because it looks like it's roughly my vintage – furiously modern on the outside, but emanating a lovable lived-in quality. Even the store's motto is applicable: 'Never Knowingly Understated'. Strangely, the store's critics call it shabby, outdated and reminiscent of a bad '70s sitcom; but what does Lesley Wallace know about shopping, anyway?

JL's reminds me of those identikit mid-size Woolworth's stores that only seem to have survived in run-down English seaside towns, with their pick 'n' mix counters ideally placed for petty theft just inside the front doors, next to the windy stairs with the art prints. *Boy With Tear In Eye. Malaysian Woman. Dusky Maiden In Swamp With Arms Folded Across Chest.* Personally, I'm willing to give John Lewis the benefit of the doubt and assume the reason the store hasn't been touched for thirty years is because the little iron balconies and the lino-tiled atrium are Grade-VII listed, along with the rest of its brilliantly boxy, mud-pie moulded concrete.

Walking on down Oxford Street, the Littlewood's flagship store is more like something you'd find on a condemned council estate, all glass and blue panels to try and fool less observant shoppers into believing they're looking up at a big patch of friendly sky. The Pantheon, the stark black box of '30s M&S Central, is far more stylish – and what dependable undies! I asked my friend Maria what was her favourite place in London, hoping she'd say 'the street where they shot *Absolute Beginners*' or 'Bob Hoskins' house' (nah, she's a bit of a film buff), so I could extrapolate from her statistical sample and make some patronising generalisation about worldwide images of London. To my inexpressible delight, she thought for a second and replied, 'Marks and Spencer's.' The girl ain't got no *culchah* . . .

'Whenever I go back to Madreed,' she says, 'I feel a leest for all my girlfriends and my mother and my seester of the Marks and Spencer's lingerie (pronounced 'lingerie') – eet ees sexy and lasts longer and ees beaudifool.' And to hell with history and art and Bob Hoskins.

At Oxford Circus, the regal sweep of Regent Street unwinds invitingly to the right, but I turn left and walk as far as Langhalm Place, and BBC Broadcasting House. This is one little corner of London whose ideas and ideals shall be forever beamed out across the rest of Britain and the uncivilised world. Constructed in the '30s to leave no doubt about its function, BH takes the form of a battleship's jutting prow; or, come to think of it, maybe it's supposed to look like one of those early Teasmade machines – just as appropriate. Either way, it's topped off with a wonderfully futuristic radio mast, broadcasting zigzag sparks of newfangled electricity direct to the wireless on your sideboard. What a comforting thought, that in the future *every* building will look like Broadcasting House.

'Nation shall speak peace unto Nation', reads the inscription in the foyer, which translates more realistically as 'We Talk, You Listen'. I know from past experience the futility of attempting to bluff my way past the uniformed guards on Lion Bar duty in front of the lifts. Not that I couldn't make up some outlandish excuse, and drop in for a coffee in the sixth-floor restaurant – it might just take

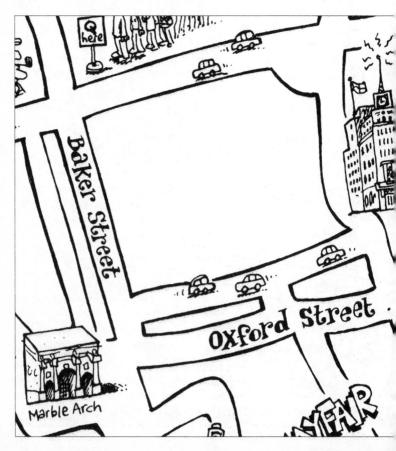

me the rest of the week to get away. Broadcasting House is a
fathomless maze, run roughly along the same lines as Britain
preparing for Nazi invasion. There are no signposts; room numbers
run haphazardly out of sequence; nobody can tell you the way to
Studio B34, because they're lost, too – and they've been working here
for forty years. There's only one way to track down your destination
in BH, and that's with the aid of a 3-D map constructed to order on
the reception desk. Once, to get to an office in the 'new' extension, I
had to go up five floors, along a right-angled corridor, back down
three floors and up an escalator. Another time, in search of office
K754, I was simply told, 'You can't get there from here.' I was late.

For all anyone at the BBC knows or cares, I could still be hacking

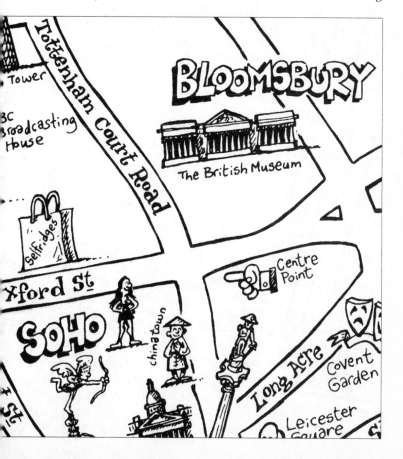

my way through cobwebs or jammed between steam pipes, looking in vain for a way out of the basement, following my delivery of a lively opinion piece entitled 'Ingredients are Useless', later broadcast on Radio 4's *Food* programme. For some reason, my radio career never really took off as I'd hoped. I sat by the phone for months waiting for a call from Radio 5's *Environment News* show — whose producers must surely, one day, commission a follow-up to the lively opinion piece, 'Pandas Deserve to be Extinct' . . .

As you walk east down the final stretch of Oxford Street, bordering on Soho, the shops become gradually more cramped and cluttered and youth-orientated. As the towering op-art honeycomb of Centre Point blocks out ever more sky, the stuffy old department stores are left behind for throwaway fashion, dodgy electrical goods, and various Universities of the English Language tucked away in third-floor box-rooms. APPRENEZ L'ANGLAISE. TOUCH TYPE IN ONE HOUR. The Aberdeen Steak House stands out like a beacon of wholesome values in an area which, no matter how commercialised and cleaned up, still carries faint echoes of an agreeably sleazy past. Centre Point itself stood mysteriously empty for thirty years after it was thrown up in the mid-'60s, and rumours persist about an unofficial police unit (if not the police then MI6; Lesley Wallace says she's heard it's extra-terrestrials) using the top floors as a clandestine surveillance point for central London. God knows, the kind and gentle London bobby needs as much help as he can get on the Oxford Street beat.

Because the door is propped open, I decide to sample the atmosphere of the 100 Club, a survivor from the days when it was possible to get excited about jazz. There was a time when dropping down these two flights of stairs into the cool black coffin of the 100 Club would have been considered a wild and dangerous option — especially by mums and dads, and admirers of Gracie Fields. Here, young people would stay up late, drinking and smoking *with the lights out*, and often in the company of black people. I feel my way onto a murkily lit landing, and press on toward the source of an odd sound — a squeak interrupted by a clatter . . . and voices . . . and old people. I'm astonished to find a lunchtime session is already under way — a free trad-jazz gig for finger-poppin' pensioners. In a curious way, it's vaguely shocking to happen across all these cheerful oldster couples tugging on pints and Pimms, and tucking into big plates of ham sarnies under the huge perspex '100' icon, and original club posters for some of the baddest bluesbreakers who ever woke up this morning. Some of them are even up having a bop to Ronnie Timpson and his Double-Footed Slippers. Don't they care what *time* it is? What would their *parents* say if they could see them now?

In the mid-'60s, the 100 Club was the coolest club in London, and therefore the coolest club in the world. Not only did they book all the greatest soul acts – Otis Redding, Marvin Gaye, Aretha Franklin – when they came over to tour, but also the new school of spotty-bottomed British R&B bands. The Stones, The Yardbirds, The Kinks: none of them were much more than ham-fisted copyists when they started out, but given the chance to do their American homework at the same time as partying *and* giving it the large one, they soon blossomed and, like, found their own trip, maan.

In the '70s, the 100 Club caught another wave and became *the* legendary Punk venue: if half the music journalists who claim to have been at the 1976 British Punk Rock Festival had really been here, proceedings would have to have been transferred to Wembley Stadium. The Sex Pistols, The Clash and The Damned all swore and pouted in a shower of glutinous spittle, and Siouxsie and the Banshees made their début appearance in conditions even less favourable. The Banshees' idea was to play so badly, they'd be bottled off stage in no time, and no one would find out they didn't know any songs. Adding to the teenage Siouxsie's problems (being attacked by *The Sun* and apparently sane women in the street for her spiky black hair and unladylike attitude, her witch's make-up and inflammatory lack of clothes-sense . . . or maybe it was simply her lack of *clothes*) members of The Clash then went and objected to her art-school swastika armband . . .

Such was the lot of the revolutionary female rocker: damned if she did, damned if she didn't.

Bringing the story up to date, the 100 Club missed out on the house music explosion of the '80s, misreading their attendance figures as an indication that people were staying in and watching *Stones in the Park* videos. But now, in the '90s, the 100 Club once again finds itself pushing the envelope – this time at the white-hot vanguard of the over-sixties' foot-tapping scene. And I was there. I saw Ron Timpson. You can't buy memories like that, not at any price.

Long before he invented the Sex Pistols and Londonised punk rock, Malcolm McLaren was working on an arthouse scam – sorry, a *filmic happening* – based on the history of Oxford Street, which he gave the working title *Oxford Street*. (He got a lot better with catchy names.) The film took in Tyburn hangings; the opening, in 1760, of the Pantheon fun palace; the free-for-all anarchy of the Gordon Riots, a few years later, and hundreds of alienation shots of shoppers and office blocks and dolphins jumping through hoops at the (sadly missed) Oxford Street Dolphinarium.

Digging ever deeper to find the truth behind the stories of a dark and dangerous, dolphin-unfriendly Oxford Street, I turn to *Hazell*. In the '70s, James Hazell was just one of hundreds of TV detectives getting into unlikely underworld scrapes on a weekly basis. Like all the others, Hazell inhabited the moral ground between the big-time villains and the flat-footed bogeys. Like all the others, he had a gimmick: here was a slang-shooting, streetwise bit of rough wiv an 'eart of tarnished gold. Unlike all the others, Hazell's sharp line of patter was provided by one of the most successful cockney do-wot? duckers and divers of recent years – sometime nightclub singer, 'businessman' and England football coach, Terry Venables.

While he was still a player at Queen's Park Rangers, El Tel embarked on a part-time career as a writer, collaborating with his friend, the novelist Gordon Williams: as well as exercising his well-tuned ear for dialogue, Tel pitched in with some low-life dirty realism. What you might call a case of fingers in pies, strings to bows, horses for courses, me old china.

'First off I spotted the dog-eye,' relates Tel/Jim in the novel *Hazell and the Three-Card Trick*, 'standing on the corner of Wardour Street with his hands in his sky-rockets.'

Hazell eyeballs his target firm of confidence-tricksters going about their business on an overturned milk-crate on the corner of Dean Street. The dealer-comedian slaps down three cards and, time after time, a lucky gambler picks out the queen and pockets a fiver. He's just a stooge, in on the act. Meanwhile, a 'crowd' forms, making excited noises about someone giving away free money. The unlucky sucker, the *mark*, stops to watch, and clocks the dealer switch cards while his 'victim' is digging in his pockets for money. He's wise to the con. Next deal, someone else in the 'crowd' spots the cheat, and piles his money on the switched card. There are witnesses, egging the sucker on: 'Now's yer chance – screw this rotten berk.'

Out comes the bundle of tenners, previously destined for the handbag of a Soho tart. For once in his life, the sucker can't lose. Triumphantly, he flips the card: the three of spades.

'Coh – you was fakkin' unlucky there,' the rotten berk commiserates, hastily shutting up shop.

'I could ov sworn it,' moans the planted 'loser', betraying his cockney roots with those oh-so-typical spelling difficulties.

Of course, you'd rarely find such a primitive con worked on Oxford Street these days. Hazell mentions the young hustlers sidestepping the law by covering over their pavement displays of T-shirts, beads and umbrellas at the first sight of a beat bobby. T-shirt sellers moved into permanent premises ages ago, and the street traders have moved up-market. Just today there was a gang selling 'Ralph Lauren' shirts from a box by the Oxford Circus Tube; back outside the classier stores, three different teams were flogging pint bottles of 'Kalvin Clein' tap-water for a tenner apiece.

In *The London Scene* of the '20s, Virginia Woolf found Oxford Street 'a breeding ground, a forcing house of sensation. The pavement seems to sprout horrid tragedies; the divorces of actresses, the suicides of millionaires . . .' Worst of all, there were 'seedy magicians' on the street-corner . . . *selling tortoises*. Outside the Bond Street Tube today, I did see one chancer doing his level best to drum up custom for his dancing toy mice on invisible thread; but it didn't look like he'd tapped into a tortoise market.

A couple of months ago I saw a great story in the *Evening Standard*, reported shock!-horror!-style by a self-confessed 'thriller-writer', who'd had a tenner gently prised from his grasp by the well-drilled operatives at one of Oxford Street's bargain auction-houses. If you've ever taken more than a dozen steps on Oxford Street, you'll have been handed a flyer promising giveaway prices at one of these establishments: £100 for a £700 lap-top, £5 for a Walkman, £1.50 for your pick of the Crown Jewels, and so on.

The thriller-writer told the story in suitably thriller-ish detail: how he'd been tempted into one of the open-fronted shops by a man with a microphone giving away free money and goods to members of the public. Large brand-name boxes were handed over the counter to the early bidders, who secured themselves £2 TVs and £5 hi-fis. The thriller-writer admitted he might have missed the clue of the battered-looking boxes, which do get pretty shop-soiled from being handed backwards and forwards over the counter twenty times a day.

Then the ultimate lucky-dip offer came up for grabs. The thriller-writer couldn't lose. Other members of the crowd were urging him on to snap it up, flashing their own car-stereos and desk-top calculators, as the heavies closed in on either side in case of any bovver. Ring any bells?

Some 'thriller-writer'. Coh – you wouldn't catch Terry Venables getting caught by that old racket. Not on your nelly. And you wouldn't catch yours truly falling for a sucker-punch like that. No way, Ho-zay. Not since the first week I moved to London, and unwittingly snapped up a disposable ladies' digital watch with a broken strap and a battery on the blink – a once-in-a-lifetime lucky-dip bargain at a mere five pounds.

Oxford Street may have cleaned up its act since Hazell last expended shoe leather in the name of law and order; but it's unrecognisably squeaky-clean in comparison with the Tyburn era, when public holiday hangings on the present-day site of Marble Arch constituted the capital's most popular spectator sport. Up until the middle of the eighteenth century, unlucky miscreants were paraded through the streets on a three-hour cart-ride from the City's Newgate Prison to the gallows at Tyburn, stopping off for a traditional beer and a haircut and a nice clean pair of M&S Y-fronts along the way. Well, wouldn't you want to look your best if you were going to be flogged, tortured and/or hanged in front of a crowd of 100,000? Hazell/Venables passes on the Tyburn story, throwing in as an aside his dad's two penn'orth of folklore: the old name for Oxford Street, the final crowded mile of the condemned prisoner's journey, was 'The Stony-hearted Stepmother'. And it's still stony-hearted. You might no longer meet your maker at Marble Arch, but it's still all too easy for your hard-earned cash to 'go west' along the greatest shopping street in the world.

Two hundred years ago, I might now have popped in to catch a freak show at The Pantheon (just imagine: before M&S), or visited prizefighter James Figg's infamous 'School of Arms' opposite Poland Street. Here, I could have baited bears or tigers, or watched women tear one another to shreds over a quiet lunchtime sherbet. Today, hot on the trail of some suitably Oxford Street-ish atmosphere, I dodge into the shady five-foot-wide roadway of Hanway Street, which leads into a network of Dickensian crevasses, where the sun never shines.

Danger. Darkness. The Underworld.

Relatively speaking.

The decor at Bradley's Bar is very Costa del Crime – all Spanish sherry barrels, plush alcoves and wrought-iron trim. This pint-size basement bar has been cashing in on cockney bullfighter chic ever since the release of *Tommy the Toreador*, starring lapsed London Elvis, Tommy Steele. The cast-aluminium stools and tables are forgotten design classics – not comfy but curvy, and heavy enough to do spectacular damage in any choreographed brawl. *Ole!* I'm certain this must have been the bar used as a model for the snazzy cellar spy-meet which occurred in roughly alternate episodes of quality London dramas such as *Department S* (gimmick: facial furniture) and *The Avengers* (bloke in bowler hat, bird in leather catsuit: *prrrrr*). This afternoon there are half a dozen shifty, style-drunk extras luxuriating beneath the travel-brochure beachscapes, making Bradley's appear at least three-quarters full.

I buy a beer at the barrel-shaped bulge of the bar, and put a pound coin in the old, 45-flipping jukebox. Engelbert Humperdinck's 'Release Me' is just about the swingingest, nowest sound on offer. It's a textbook London sound . . . direct from the heart of Soul City Leicester. A couple of years back, the golden-tonsilled heart-throb billionaire gave my dad a lesson in the value of spending your youth hanging around mock-Mediterranean working-men's clubs, waiting for rumpled three-piece backing-bands to finish their sound-check. Enge is a top-class darter – cabaret's 'King of the Double-1s'. He thrashed my old man to lift the annual golf-club trophy. So I give Doris Day and Dean Martin a spin, instead.

Back at the bar, it turns out the proprietors of Bradley's Bar aren't Spanish at all, but Thai. We still find plenty of common ground in M&S Y-fronts.

If the function of Broadcasting House was to beam a little bit of London to the outside world, the British Museum enjoys exactly the opposite role, setting out the best of the rest of the world behind glass, thereby enabling Brits to enjoy an intercontinental grand tour without the inconvenience of leaving their own capital. I flop in the warm sun with the foreign students, here to visit their heritage. Soon, I'll be ready to go and scoop up my two voluteered quids' worth of purest knowledge; but first I have to tackle this frazzled bacon-and-avocado-goo roll without dripping any more avocado goo on my step beneath the strict Ionic face of the museum.

On the subject of attaining knowledge, London guides and museum guides are unanimous: 'Don't try and "do" the BM in a couple of hours . . . the collections in the British Museum cannot be studied in a single visit . . . two and a half miles of corridors . . . thirteen acres of galleries . . . allow at least three weeks if you want to see *everything* in the British Museum . . .' But that's reckoning without my patent formula for separating the wheat from the chaff, for *cutting to the chase* around these parts. Namely:

British Museum =
Elgin Marbles + Egyptian Mummies + Piltdown Bloke

The BM Souvenir Guide sets out three whistle-stop tours that allow tourists to hoover up the bare essentials on videofilm. 'They can all be fitted into a morning,' I'm pleased to see the guide admits, 'but you may prefer to linger over one and return another day.'

Pah. All you need to get around this place is a cast-iron plan and some sterling resolve. Ignoring the idiot's tour, I get my head down and cut straight through the corner of Egypt, doubling back from a dead-end in Assyria before finally running aground, stuck in Ancient Greece. Given that I've done the museum a couple of times before, it's strange that I don't recall spending any time in the company of this Nereid Monument – 'the complete Ionic façade of the pedimented tomb of one of the rulers of Xanthos' . . .

So where *is* Xanthos, exactly? And what's a Nereid? Just who are these 'ravishing figures', and have they got any much younger sisters? Above all, how did *this* come to be *here*?

Three-quarters of an hour later, I limp up to the Elgin Marbles. Recently rehoused in the Duveen Gallery, itself a wonder of complementary architecture, these statues and friezes, which once decorated the Parthenon on Athens' acropolis, are at once the museum's most visited and its most controversial exhibits. Apparently, there's a small group of Greek troublemakers who can think of an even more complementary setting for our relics: decorating the Parthenon on Athens' acropolis. It's this dangerous brand of logic that lands British museum-goers with awkward questions like, 'How would *you* feel if the pickled remains of Princess Margaret were put on public display in Athens in the year 4000?' and 'What if one of these mummies was *your* mummy?' Luckily, the authorities can easily justify our continued safekeeping of other nations' property. After all, in the Marbles' case, by the time Lord Elgin happened upon the scene in 1902, the Greeks had already mislaid the colossal gold-and-ivory statue of Athena that once stood inside the Parthenon. And not only had they allowed Athens' Turkish garrison to use the temple as an arms dump, they'd also neglected to put up adequate NO SMOKING signs: *ker-boom*! went 90 per cent of the treasures when some bright spark lit up a ciggie and threw away his match on a ten-ton mountain of gunpowder. So thank the Lord the noble Elgin arrived in time to liberate the remainder in the name of disinterested conservation.

Also, it should be remembered that Elgin did first *ask nicely* before touching so much as a measly metope, and indeed made payment for his haul – if only to the commander of the occupying Turkish Army. Best, perhaps, draw a veil over the hasty chipping, winching and carting that preceded Elgin's sailing with his first consignment, all of which occurred in one night, under cover of darkness.

The Parthenon was built as a fantastically opulent tribute to Athena, patron goddess to the city below. The carved pediments from either end of the temple, originally richly painted and high-lighted in gold, are still beautiful even in their dilapidated, vandalised state, and their very presence seems to bridge the chasm of years and culture between Athens, 500BC and London, AD1997. Admittedly, the average day-tripper of today will find little religious significance in a scene showing Athena's birth, emerging fully grown and armed to the teeth from an axe-wound in Zeus's head. But eerily close to home, sociologically speaking, is the string of reliefs from beneath the pediment, which relate the story of King Perithoös' wedding feast, where half-man half-horse centaurs had too much to drink and tried to carry off all the female guests . . .

While I'm busily scribbling notes, a Japanese-American tourist sidles up and asks if I'll take her picture. Immediately, I stop tutting and sniffing at all the Japanese and American trippers walking about the museum with video-recorders plugged into their faces, and become all friendly and helpful.

'Just press the button,' I'm told. 'It's toadally audomatic.'

She goes and stands in front of a 'languid pose of a naked youth'. I spend a few seconds in artistic consideration of composition – 'Shove over a bit, you can't see his willy' – and click. Only the camera doesn't click. 'It didn't click,' I tell her. 'Did it flash?'

'It can be kinda tempramennal,' says my subject, generously. 'It's taking a light-reading. Hold the button down longer.'

After waiting a couple of minutes for a party of Italian children to clear out of the way, we try again. She says cheese. I press and hold. For ages. But no click or flash. 'Is there anything else you need to do?' I fret. 'Is it wound on? It must be jammed.'

She looks just a teensy bit exasperated, looking for knobs to fiddle with on her toadally audomatic camera, but she's still as nice as pie.

'It's not working,' I assure her. 'Go on, you have a go.'

And that's how an American tourist ended up with a photograph of me looking puzzled in front of a naked, headless youth.

Tempted by the promise of 'the largest marble foot you have ever seen', I skip past the junior sphinxes and the Rosetta Stone and the gates from the village in *King Kong*, and head into the basement. The foot belongs to Zeus, and it is undoubtedly large. The big toe alone is a foot and a half long. The whole foot (so *that's* why we went metric) must have measured something like three yards. Yessirree, that surely was one gigantic statue that stood over Alexandria in the second century. But I don't care. I'm statued out.

This is one of the unavoidable effects of the BM: tap me on the shoulder in the pub and unwrap from your hanky a Roman coin or an ancient vase or a fragment of colossal statue, and you'll have my undivided attention. Show me seventeen rooms full of ancient vases and, almost instantly, I'll be vased out. I sense it's time to change tack and visit seventeen rooms full of old books.

On the way back through the entrance hall, I go for a peep into the famous domed reading-room, shared between the Museum and the British Library in its East Wing. The Copyright Act dictates that one copy of every book, newspaper and periodical published in Britain must come to the library, currently overspilling from the doors of the new, inadequate St Pancras site at a rate of two shelf miles per year. Today, the reading-room is closed to the general public, because there simply isn't room for anyone else to join the stew of worthy academics in their solemn research . . . taking turns to pose at desk G7, where Karl Marx wrote *Das Kapital* . . . in between visits to the economics stack, to check the finer points of Adam Smith and *Big Ones Fortnightly*.

At least the British Library's manuscript saloon is accessible from the Museum, and here, within balconied walls book-clad to the ceiling, I lose myself among the collection of original handwritten texts and historical documents. The dying Nelson's half-finished letter to Lady Hamilton! A deed signed by Willm Shakspe! Original Beatles manuscripts, with the lyrics all wrong!

The giants of British and Irish literature are represented: James Joyce and his red crayon scrawl; Lewis Carroll: very strange doodlings, for a twelve-year-old. And how on earth did Virginia Woolf, George Eliot and Emily Brontë manage to write in such *microscopically* tidy hands? My own amateur beginnings of a graphological theory of literature suggest it might have been a good idea for all three to *get out more*. And then there's the little matter of Eliot's ugly block crossing-out: what on earth did he have to *hide*?

Finally manuscripted out, I make a move for the mummies – and find out that the Museum shuts at five o'clock. It's seven minutes to. I tell the guard on the stairs that it'll only take an old hand five or six minutes to do the Piltdown Bloke and the mummies, but she's not having it.

'There are postcards in the museum shop,' she attempts to lessen the blow; but I don't find anything in stock featuring my pet favourite off-the-beaten-track exhibit, the one collection I was looking forward to seeing again more than anything: the religious nuts. They're amazing. A whole 3-D world of soldiers, animals, Virgin births and crucifixions on crosses no thicker than a strand of cotton, all carved by a miraculously steady hand, inside half a walnut. I've no idea who could have carved them (Emily Brontë springs to mind as a suspect), how or when or where. I'll shift them to the top of my itinerary next time I visit, which should increase my chances of finding out to around 50 per cent.

I may have missed Tutankhamun and the mummified cats, the crocodile-skin armour, the Middle Ages, Lenin's application for a reading-room ticket, the Magna Carta, the Oriental World, the leather-bound Swamp Man, the religious nuts and all the vases; but I still say it's possible to gather the *gist* of the history of civilisation in one expertly structured dash.

Just remember to kick off your quest for knowledge some time before four o'clock.

7 In the City

In order to stave off the uncouth advances of Boadicea and the East Midland Brits – wahey! – the Romans built a fortified wall around their outpost of Londonium, which to this day marks the boundaries of the City. The names of the seven gates in the battlements survive in street names: Aldgate, Moorgate, Newgate and so on. The Barbican Centre's Museum of London stands on London Wall, quite literally astride one of the remaining fragments. Maybe it would have been a good idea for me to start my day-tripping here – at the beginning.

The sheer weight and volume of London's history is daunting. Standing at the beginning of the green neon time-line with Raquel Welch and her fur bikini from *One Million Years BC*, any summary or attempted overview of this, the most important city in the world, seems impossible, even in a hundred fat volumes of closely printed type.

A couple of hours later, I've thrown off my mood of pessimism and whittled it down to a hundred words:

1,000,000BC: Ungowah!

0–AD500: Romans.

500–1066: Dark Ages and Saxon London. Port. Trade. Vikings. People stay in a lot.

1070–1400: Medieval. William the Conqueror builds Tower of London. William II builds gift shop.

1400–1600: Tudor London. Will Sharpspeer and the Globe Theatre.

1600–1666: Early Stuart. Cromwell axes the monarchy . . . and decides to take over as king himself for a few years.

1666–1714: Late Stuart. *London's Burning*. Wren rebuilds in stone instead of balsa wood.

1714–1830: Georgian. Four kings called George. Dr Johnson writes dictionary, omitting 'sausage'.

1837–1901: Victorian. Docks and railways. Big Ben. Britain bosses the world.

You know the rest: Suffragettes and railings, World War x 2, Carnaby Street, *Only Fools and Horses* – all of which brings us neatly up to . . . (insert today's date here).

Just as I thought: Madame Tussaud's two-minute London ride didn't miss out anything of *real* importance, except for Dr Johnson and 'sausage'.

The most eye-opening exhibits in the Museum of London are the models of the city as it looked at various points in the past. Based on excavations, paintings and bird's-eye-view maps, historians have been able to recreate a version of Roman London; an amazingly detailed miniature of the city just before the Great Fire, its covered bridge bulging with shops and houses; and then London after Wren's rebuilding, the dome of St Paul's floating on a sea of church spires. Most disappointing is the much-vaunted Fire of London Experience: a darkened model with an orange torch shining up from underneath the old, wooden St Paul's. An illuminating voiceover, from the diaries of Samuel Pepys, makes up in part for the lack of fireworks. There's nothing here that couldn't easily be fixed with a keg or two of Guy Fawkes's gunpowder.

As usual, it isn't the set-piece, star attractions of the museum that

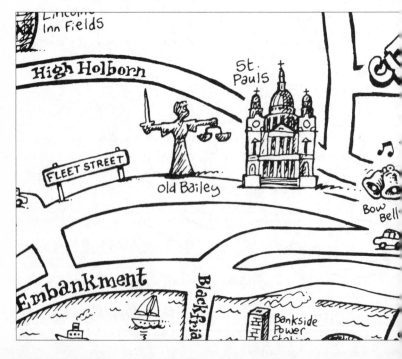

stick in the memory – the Lord Mayor's state coach, the Georgian prison cell – but instead some of the odd, unexpected handles on history, thrown up by the marvellous randomness of the collection. It's difficult to imagine how anyone really lived in Stuart London, but something undefinable crystallises once you've seen their underwear, and yearned for a bounce on their child-sized four-poster bed, which they slept in sitting up. I loved the tiny, wooden sedan chair from the same era, which gave a smooth ride through twisting, congested streets, but gave rise to a storm of protest about Englishmen being treated as beasts of burden. Like the proverbial child who throws away the toy and plays with the wrapping-paper, I gave the original Selfridge's lifts a cursory glance – yes, they're beautiful, overblown, priceless Art Deco – and spent fifteen minutes poring over the sweeties and knitting patterns on a pre-war counter from Woolworth's – NOTHING IN THESE STORES OVER 6d. I should coco.

Costumes, posters, photographs and ambient sounds draw visitors into a succession of lost London milieux, each to his or her

own. Here are *artefacts* which, just ten, thirty, three hundred years ago, were merely such-and-such's pocket-watch, such-and-such's barber shop, or Ford Cortina. I love the democracy of a museum where the Sunday-best armour of the rich and powerful is displayed alongside a green-white-and-purple Suffragette's flag and an uppity old hippy's badge collection. I'M NOT A TOURIST I LIVE HERE. JOBS NOT POMP. MURDOCH IS BAD NEWS.

In the final few yards of its Time Tunnel, the museum focuses on the ultimate outcome of all those unconnected gobbets of history, with exhibits on London's economy, health and traffic, made palatable to tired trudgers via displays of see-through fashion, sophisticated '60s ciggie wrappers and Dinky toys. Questions like 'Who Decides What London Looks Like?' are tossed casually into the air, alongside a genuine planner's dream of Piccadilly Circus buried alive under multiple hexagonal layers of pre-stressed concrete. In a few years' time, the buildings we ignore, the cars we drive and the clothes we wear will all be history – some sooner than others, admittedly. As a London resident or a visitor, the museum's trick is to fit both you and your lifestyle into its complex game of consequences. A Recent Acquisitions cabinet includes a packet of Nicorette patches, a tape of agony aunt Clare Rayner, and a 1951 boy's suit from Harrod's, donated because its owner 'disliked the suit's formality and seldom wore it', oblivious to the fact that it was nineteen sizes too small and forty-six years out of date.

One day, that could be *your* I FOUND THE BARBICAN CENTRE badge on display. Possibly even your MAKE LOVE NOT WAR.

In the gift shop I can't make my mind up between a Tube map mousemat, a Tube map pencil-case, a set of Tube map coasters or a pair of Tube map boxer shorts. Then I find my Tube map hidden at the bottom of my bag, and opt instead for an historical slice of cherry flapjack.

When work on the Barbican Centre was started in the early 1960s, the idea was to bring back some humanity to the City by boosting its tiny resident population, and also to give the average Londoner a reason to visit the City, to see an exhibition or a film, or catch the Royal Shakespeare Company or London Symphony Orchestra playing at home. The Barbican's teething troubles show little sign of abating, though it is still considered by many to be 'difficult to find', off the beaten track, vaguely grim and unwelcoming. Its trees, lawns and creeper-covered piazzas must help make the pricey flats bearable to live in, but beyond the 'model community' image, it's really no more than three lanky concrete Stickle-Brick blocks, and several more laid on their sides. The Barbican Arts Centre was originally touted as 'The City's gift to the nation'. If I'd been around at the time, I must say I'd have preferred a nice box of Quality Street. At least something positive arose from the experiment: this fully realised dream of a City in the Sky led to the developers being reined in on concrete-crazy schemes for Covent Garden and Whitehall as well as Piccadilly Circus. That said, the plan to slab over the Thames would have saved a fortune on bridge maintenance.

Having found my way down from the Barbican walkways to the romantically named 'Gate 8', I walk south down Aldersgate Street, cut through to Newgate and sight Justice balanced precariously on the pinnacle of her Old Bailey dome. This was the site of the infamous Newgate Prison, as poor an advert for eighteenth-century London as it's possible to find. Typhoid was rife in the stinking, cramped cells, with no ventilation or provision of running water. Sitting judges at the Old Bailey still wear a posy in their buttonhole, once vital to combat the stench of the prison next door. In 1780, fifty thousand disaffected Georgians rampaged through the streets of London for five days: so hated was Newgate, the Gordon Rioters tore it down by hand, releasing thousands of inmates. But it didn't take long to build it back up again – with Lord George Gordon on the inside, and rioters swinging twenty at a time on the gallows.

Newgate was traditionally the start of the journey for condemned prisoners on their way to Tyburn, but crowds later paid to watch hangings inside the prison – the road outside the Old Bailey still widens to accommodate the cheerfully sadistic throng. Split into three blocks designated for debtors, male and female felons, the bad boys' yard welcomed a number of celebrity guests: the Quaker William Penn, later of Pennsylvania; Ben Jonson, Christopher Marlowe and Daniel Defoe; the famed escape-artist Jack Sheppard (immortalised by cockney rocker Tommy Steele in *Where's Jack?*), and the highwayman's super-rascal colleague Jonathan Wild (tough luck, he only made it into a Henry Fielding novel). Wild is said to have drawn a record crowd to Tyburn, with more than two hundred thousand Londoners claiming to have been on the front row when he pickpocketed a corkscrew from his chaplain, and was hanged with it held aloft in his hand. Predictably, conditions plummeted to their most appalling in the women's quarters, which make *Cell-Block H* look like tea at the Ritz. Jailed along with their children, kept half-naked and drunk on porter, the women's straw-strewn cells acted as little more than personal brothels for the turnkeys. Inmates begged for pennies through the bars, pushing sticks down into the street for 'garnish money' to bribe fellow prisoners for a sight of the fire. Conditions remained abysmal until the intervention of the brave reformer Elizabeth Fry in 1810, who instituted schools for the prison children, and eventually brought about the abolition of flogging of women – a very generous concession.

The proud tradition of British law is upheld at the Central Criminal Court, the forbidding Imperial stage for so many classic courtroom dramas (The Crown versus Ruth Ellis, the Great Train Robbers, *Lady Chatterley's Lover*), all the most gruesome murder cases (J.R. Christie, Dennis Nilsen, Rosemary West), and popular show-trials (Oscar Wilde, Second World War propagandist 'Lord Haw-Haw', the Ali-Bye-Bye Four/Five/Six). In recent years, the Old Bailey has figured in the news less for headline prosecutions, and more often upon the release of innocent victims of the system. Today there is no chanting crowd filling the street, baying for the blood of an 'overenthusiastic' police forensics expert; no hunched figure being bundled into the back of a police car under a hail of stones. Just a group of bored paparazzi standing behind a yellow line on the pavement, zoom-lenses at half-cock, waiting to take their pictures of a man with his hand in front of his face.

Like the lawyers and judges, the snappers get paid no matter what the result – guilty or not guilty, fine or prison, right or wrong. It's watertight. A beautiful system. Open to all. Like the Ritz.

As an innocent at trial, the more you pay, the more inadmissible evidence, fabricated evidence and withheld evidence will come to light; then a dozen sleepy quiz-show contestants have to vote which side is better at lying. Great British Justice has come a long way since the days when you could pay a lawyer threepence to watch someone horribly murdered.

After the short walk down Ludgate Hill, I cross the fetid Fleet River, flowing thick with sewage, dyeworks' chemicals and blood and guts from the local slaughterhouses. At least, that's what I would have seen (and smelled) here up to the middle of the eighteenth century, when the Fleet was buried in a sewer pipe and its course transformed into Farringdon Road. Now only traffic flows under the Holborn Viaduct, and there's little call for the iron mooring rings still set in its brickwork. It's a romantic notion that this car- and cab-clogged artery was once a babbling brown stream but, I must say, I don't miss the stench one little bit.

I turn off the busy Fleet Street pavement into the subterranean half-light of St Bride's Alley, overhung by the dangerous-looking church wall. The Punch Tavern is boarded up, but carpenters are hard at work on its interior. Unlike the satirical magazine that was founded here and borrowed its name, the pub should be up and running again for summer. In fact, Sweeney Todd's demon barber-shop stands more chance of a successful relaunch than poor old *Punch*.

England's first movable-type press was set up next to St Bride's as early as 1500, and the name of Fleet Street has been synonymous with print ever since. The first daily newspaper, the *Daily Courant*, was published here in 1702; for years, bookbinders and sellers, mapmakers and dictionary-compilers (Dr Johnson, to give just one example) lived and worked in the surrounding alleyways and courts. At the turn of this century, the era of press barons and mass media began in earnest, with daily circulations first topping one million. At Lord Copper's *Daily Beast*, 'the bells of St Bride's chimed unheard in the customary afternoon din of the Megalopolitan Building . . . in grotto-blue light, leagues of paper ran noisily through machines . . . on a hundred lines reporters talked at cross purposes . . . sub-editors busied themselves with their humdrum task of reducing to blank nonsense the sheaves of misinformation which whistling urchins piled before them' – at least according to the atmospheric evidence of Evelyn Waugh's *Scoop*.

Just fifteen years ago, the dailies were still being printed on lumbering Victorian hot presses, and Fleet Street typesetters' jobs were still passed from father to son, along with the family eye-shade. Thanks to a royal decree of 1523, woolly mammoths were still guaranteed employment as ink-sloppers, with hula-hoop breaks set at twenty minutes in the hour. Meanwhile, in the real world, desktop systems were already in existence enabling a child of ten to produce an issue of the *Currant Bun* alone in his bedroom. Nevertheless, it still rankles that Rupert Murdoch, the 'Dirty Digger', had to be the one to show us the error of our comfortable, Luddite ways.

Now Fleet Street is a graveyard, littered with buildings which used to be the home of a paper, a printer or publisher standing empty or inhabited by drear money men. How I'd love to see just one cigar-chomping, stripy-shirted news editor waddling out of a showdown (with someone wearing a PRESS tag in their hat) at the Cheshire Cheese or the Stab In The Back, doing that thing they're supposed to do with those twangy gold armbands.

Across the face of one office building, iron letters still trumpet the existence of the Edwardian London Press Agency; another is scarred for life with inlaid adverts for its former inhabitants from the *Sunday Post*, the *People's Friend* and the *Dundee Evening Telegraph*, who must have taken a tragically wrong turning on the A1 somewhere south of Newcastle. The Press Complaints Commission and Reuter's news agency do their best to keep up the neighbourhood, but Lord Beaverbrook's arrogantly blind, black curtain-wall *Express* building (1931; doesn't look a day older than 1961) is steadily falling into disrepair. The stepped Deco cliff of the *Telegraph* building is still in use, but its symbol of British torchbearers tearing around the world seems thrown away on the insurance executives who lurk behind its pencillated columns and comically colourful clock.

On the way back past St Bride's, I make a happy discovery. No, not the printing museum housed in the crypt, nor the Roman mosaic pavement which was only uncovered when the 'journalists' church' was bombed in the war; St Bride's four-tiered spire was one local Ludgate pastry-cook's inspiration for the *wedding-cake. That's* a cool church.

St Paul's Cathedral is more than a cool church; more, even, than a big cool church. First sighted as a disembodied dome, then through the crack in the buildings at the top of Ludgate Hill, St Paul's keeps expanding until it fills the sky. Everyone walking towards the cathedral is looking up, craning for a better perspective, even as they trace a way through the picnickers encamped on its broad steps, and disappear inside.

Ian Nairn, for argument's sake the most passionate and vital of all Londonographers, writes not of St Paul's grandeur or drama, but of the 'overwhelming compassion' of the place: 'no wonder that cockneys love it, and see it as a badge as well as a symbol'. St Paul's does lack the usual chilliness of a church, partly because of the blurring of its religious role with social and political gospels, and partly because it's full of tourists on the Princess Diana Fairytale Trail. Nairn paid a heartfelt compliment to the universal, anti-authoritarian atmosphere of St Paul's when he wrote that the great arched, octagonal space beneath the dome could just as easily house a mosque or a Hindu temple as an Anglican cathedral. I hope the Church appreciates what he was driving at: that's why the tourists keep coming.

I'd never heard of Ian Nairn before the BBC made up an anniversary excuse to repeat one black-and-white, late-'60s episode of *Nairn's Travels* – simple, effective TV of a classical cut – which featured the architectural critic poling about Norfolk, oozing warmth and spitting Scots venom into a single, understandably shaky, camera. *Nairn's London* is 'an intensely subjective search for the really good things in London', and I treasure my second-hand copy.

Quite what Nairn would have made of the sightseers who come to relive the wedding of Prince Charles and Lady Di, I'd love to know. Royalists must be celebrating the day our future king secured the continuation of the Windsor line, but any less detached perspective is bound to bleed into some degree of cynicism.

'Are you in love?' called one cocky snapper at a press shoot, months before the Happy Event. Lady Di blushed and averted her eyes, and dared to peep up at Charles to gauge his response.

'Whatever that means,' he called back, coolly.

That's royal rhyming slang for 'no'.

The wartime image of St Paul's dome against a flaming sky, of the cathedral miraculously still standing amid a smouldering wasteland of ruins and overturned buses, gave a late fillip to its 250-year-old status as the living heart of London. For another three hundred years before the Great Fire, the gothic wooden structure of Old St Paul's was just as popular, housing an extraordinary collection of alleged holy relics (a lock of Mary Magdalene's hair! Jesus's pocket-knife!), with the nave even doubling up as a marketplace. Some say it's never been the same since the street-women and cut-throats were cleared out of the aisles, and laws passed to forbid swords being drawn and mules being led through the Cathedral.

Apart from the tombs and monuments of the Great and Good, St Paul's also remembers thousands of ordinary people by name, reminding us of who we are, whoever we are, without presuming to tell us what we should do about it. As we clamber to the summit of the dome, St Paul's even provides us itinerary-ticking tourists with a thoroughly modern version of a spiritual uplift.

Well, it is a stunning view – and you do have to struggle up hundreds of stairs, braving vertigo in the dizzying spiral section between the inner and outer domes, then squeezing through a gap all of eighteen inches wide before popping out, gasping, halfway to the greater grey dome of the London sky.

The air up here is unusual: it's fresh. People smile at recent arrivals – '*Woo!* Serious *height!*' – and take each other's windblown photographs against successive segments of white stone city spread below. The brown river, with its pleasure-boats and teeming bridges. The multicoloured stalagmites of the City. The light on the Crystal Palace TV mast flashing over the sprawling estates of South London. The West End and the pencil-thin Post Office Tower. Primrose Hill. The Old Bailey. White-shirted office-workers in windows. Workmen shirking on a flat roof below. People like ants . . . a distant siren floating up from the street . . . toy London buses: ah, there's nothing like a good, cathartic climb to set the cliché juices flowing.

I wonder when the trip to the top of St Paul's first became a regular activity for Londoners and tourists, and when it started to take over as the prime experience. Did Christopher Wren foresee the draw of his perch in the sky, unequalled as a lookout for nearly three centuries? Were the funfair pleasures of the Whispering Gallery provided merely by accident, or for those in need of a breather halfway to the heavens? And what about the Big Drop? As you make your final ascent to a landing just short of the Golden Gallery, there's a tiny window in the floor, next to which is sellotaped a hand-scrawled sign on a scrap of paper: LOOK. This is the quick way down to the middle of the nave, 340 feet below, and straight on to Nelson's tomb in the crypt, ten feet below that – no need to bother with the steps. The inner dome is made of brick, eighteen inches thick. It weighs *64,000 tons*, and at the point directly beneath your feet, the brickwork is *horizontal*.

Glory be.

Back safely on the ground floor, Ian Nairn isn't quite so keen on the cathedral monuments, which he brackets together as 'a prodigious display of incapacity . . . what a mess of marble'. Just as he warns, the spectacle of endless worthy gentlemen (generals, politicians, dictionary-compilers), either heroically posed or idealised in togas, does eventually bring on fits of 'nausea, boredom or the giggles' – a novel mixture of all three, in my case. Nairn doesn't hide his contempt for the groups of 'pudding faces', going so far as to blame them for burdening us with modern, abstract art. But since Ian's day the Church has played a trump card to counter his criticism: Henry Moore's *Mother and Baby* is a twisted blob of marble *with a soul*, completely in keeping with Nairn's idea of a universal spiritual space.

In another healthy reverse of orthodoxy, a guide tells an American couple that people are encouraged to touch the inviting marble. When they've cleared off, I have a feel. *Mother and Baby* is cool and smooth.

Walking east along Cheapside, I linger for a few minutes outside the church of St Mary-le-Bow, and wait for the bells to ring two o'clock. A true cockney is said to be born within earshot of Bow Bells, and although I'm a little matter of thirty-four years late, bonus points are surely given for *proximity* to the famous dull clanging. I think it's fair to say that I now fall well within the broadest definition of cockneydom, as applied by cockneys themselves. I may not be an official cockney, but I'm a cockney once or twice removed; a cockney cousin; a *mockney* . . .

Gor strewf strike a light guv – at the centre of the City of London, seven roads collide at the furious traffic intersection known simply as Bank. Sitting here on a bench on the tongue of land extending from the Royal Exchange into the maelstrom of noise and fumes, it would be all too easy for an outsider – even a cockney outsider – to feel intimidated by the hustle of the traffic and the suits; by the encircling white stone of colonnated heavyweights. The Bank of England. Mansion House, the Lord Mayor's residence. The head branches of the high street banks. You clearly have no business in this neck of the City unless you're wearing the uniform – that's an *optional* pinstripe on a *charcoal-grey* business suit; a *plain* shirt and a *Dennis the Menace* tie – and you're quite prepared for summary dismissal if you're caught wearing *scuffed Hush Puppies* (that's *paisley tights and strappy platforms*, if you're a woman). The famous five o'clock 'sea of bowler hats' may no longer flood out of the banks and over London Bridge, but the brollies, briefcases and amusing neckwear still offer the snapper of essential London sights a telling tribal photo-opportunity. Ancient trade signs hang in Lombard Street – the gilt grasshopper, the cat and fiddle, the king's head – and no one who belongs here has ever had to ask what they stand for.

For eighteen years the moral values of the Square Mile – sameness, selfishness, sell, sell, sell – were imposed across the country, across the board, to stocks, schools and souls alike. Finally the country reverted to type and voted for a change. At the weekend I read a newspaper article by the novelist Hanif Kureishi, in which he likened the past era of deregulation and privatisation to colonisation by a foreign power, and looked forward to the resumption of normal British service. Welcome back responsibility and respect, momentarily forgotten in the headlong rush to the bruising anarchy of the open market.

I don't know how the majority of these City workers voted, but they seem to have adjusted quite happily to the financial sector's former role of servant and guardian – even if it was good, sick fun playing Masters of the Universe. I, for one, am applying a new, moral attitude to my part-time, temporary share of a job in the City, where, on the odd weekend, I secrete my scuffed Hush Puppies under the expanse of someone else's desk and reduce sheaves of misinformation into ambiguous American jargon. No more gazing down on the clouds from someone else's bombproof window. No more shuffling decimal points to see if anybody ever notices the difference between a thousand million and a hundred billion. The bull is back on its leash.

In the '80s free-for-all, City businesses trumpeted their attitude by tearing down whole blocks of beautiful, gentle, listed buildings and replacing them with their own towering totems. Planning permission presented no problem: the potent combination of hard cash and deregulation saw to that. For years, low-rise London was preserved by a law disallowing development above the height reached by a fire engine's fully extended ladder. When the laws first started to come crashing down, the City suffered for the lack of an overall plan. Speculators chipped in to pay for the crumbling roadways and, in return, converted the sky into ugly and inessential office space.

The new Stock Exchange building is a block of slitted concrete, its unmistakable message to the passer-by, 'Keep Away – Keep

Walking'. Sadly, the old Exchange of the 1850s incorporated elements of reserve and decoration in its design which could be construed as *soft* and *weak*. On the positive side, the new building is computer-friendly, and should last at least a couple of years into the new millennium, when an instantaneous banking and trading network will render it officially disposable.

The NatWest Tower was London's tallest building when it was thrown up, but no one was ever interested in scaling its height to sample the view: it's just a bank, after all, and it looks like a gigantic fag-packet. Now they've changed its name to the 'International Finance Centre', and as part of its image makeover it has become not a bank, but a *prestigious new corporate address*. I'm still finding it easy to contain my enthusiasm.

Lloyd's of London attracted fleeting interest when they commissioned a new concrete and stainless steel HQ, with lifts and snaking lengths of aluminium ducting running up and down its exterior. The inside-out building is an easy party-trick played once too often. I don't care if each individual office is wallpapered on the outside and filing cabinets are suspended in mid-air outside each window, Lloyd's of London is still an *insurance company*, and insurance companies are *boring*. Still, every dog has its day. For a short time, the institutionalised money-shufflers came to believe they were sexy, but now they're settling back to their harmless business, no more than a necessary evil.

A trip to the dentist is more packed with mythological potential than a visit to any bank or civil court, to any livery company hall or the legal Inns of Temple perched between Fleet Street and the river. Suffice to say they've all had their moments – but only in the history of stationery. Even my own personal lawyer (read: college flatmate), Geordie Mick, admits he enjoys nothing like the adventures of the TV young guns of *This Life*; although he assures me there is something to be said for a life at the bar.

The eighty-four livery companies scattered about the City are the old union headquarters of once-powerful trades that don't exist any more: there's the Barber-Surgeons' Hall, the Tallow Chandlers' Hall, the Cordwainers' Hall – which trades still vie in a medieval league table of self-importance. Still, they do a lot of work for charidee, and *someone* has to dress up in ruffles and big-buckled shoes for the Lord Mayor's Show . . .

Someone has to look after the Queen's swans on the Thames on the odd days when she isn't down there tossing them stale bread herself – and it may as well be the knickerbockered and tricorn-hatted members of Ye Anciente Periwig and Syrup-Knitters' Company.

I was going to try and have a peep at Lloyd's to see if it was raining inside the building, or plastered with pigeon crap, but Leadenhall Market brought about an abrupt change in my plans: I'm surprised some of the underwriter's all-powerful 'names' didn't file to have this Victorian iron and glass market-place demolished in the '80s, because its simple functionality and immediate charm make their new pad, unfortunately right next door, look as cheap and flashy as a West End superloo.

Leadenhall's butchers and fishmongers set out their stalls in shallow shop-fronts, beneath a deadly row of meathooks which date back to the opening of the building in the 1880s. The airy arcade was sensitively refurbished, scrubbed and refreshed in cream and maroon in 1990 . . . *and they didn't tear out the old meathooks.* The vaulted glass roof is built in a cruciform, to shelter the cobbled intersection of Leadenhall Place and Whittington Avenue, and its maze of connecting market alleys. Cast-iron griffins, escaped from the City's coat-of-arms, lurk in every corner of the rafters, and the plasterwork is alive with posies and bird-life.

Leadenhall was originally the market-place at the heart of Roman London's forum. Like, *wow.* And, as the street name hints, the land was gifted to the city by Dick Whittington, the fifteenth-century Lord Mayor whose real story diverges from the panto version only in that spooky Bow Bells messages, cats, knotted spotty hankies on sticks and poverty did not feature. But, hey, no one ever said the streets of London weren't paved with gold.

Office workers on a late, late lunch spill out of the cafés and *two* unspoilt pubs, with engraved glasswork and hanging lanterns. Leadenhall Market beats any money-market hands down. It must be a positive pleasure for a merchant banker or futures analyst to walk from the beetle-glassed City streets into this fragrant oasis of flowers and food, for a well-earned pint and a beef and mustard cob at the Lamb Tavern. I know it was for me.

Earlier this year, Simon the English Tutor went out on the City heritage trail with a group of his students; first stop, The Monument: the world's largest free-standing column, started five years after the Great Fire, to symbolise London rising from the ashes. Si's history lesson ground to a halt as soon as they arrived at the bottom of the 202-foot pillar: half the students decided they weren't interested in going to the top when they discovered Wren had foolishly neglected to install a lift.

And 202 feet is the exact distance from the foot of the column to the baker's shop on Pudding Lane where the Fire of London started on 2 September 1666. The story of the fire is told on a series of entertaining murals surrounding two sides of a vacant site on the corner of Fish Street Hill, in the shadow of the Monument. Eight people were killed as the slow-spreading fire took five days to level four-fifths of the City, proving the early complacency of the Lord Mayor, Sir Thomas Bludworth – 'Pish! A woman could piss it out!' – sadly inappropriate. A more effective fire-fighting method was hit upon by the newly restored Charles II, who took to the streets and appealed for assistance – not forgetting his large bag of silver pieces.

After scaling the 311 steps of the Monument's tight spiral staircase – nowhere to rest, nowhere to hide – it comes as some relief to step giddily into the iron-barred viewing cage under the golden fireball, if only to be faced with the politely pointless, ultra-British notice: THIS WAY AROUND→ . Having first checked for potential witnesses, I ignore the sign as a matter of principle. View-wise, the first thing you notice is that 202 feet is *high* – not cathedral-*woo!*-toyland-buses high, but still high enough to clear all the modern buildings for a respectable distance around. Also high on the list of views is the compressed corkscrew down the middle of the staircase which is second to none for an *indoor* view, and offers the interactive opportunity of dropping sweet-wrappers onto the clear perspex sheet wedged in place over the embattled ticket-collector's head. If he cuts up rough and refuses to give me my official Monument-climber's certificate on the way out, I'll just blame these Aussie new arrivals. It'll serve them right for not even getting out of puff on the way up.

It's at times like this that I wish I were dragging my parents around London with me. Mum would have prevented me letting myself down with my Opal Fruit wrappers. Pop would have remembered to bring binoculars.

Looking all around, a church spire seems to appear every second or third street, although many are now obscured by the financial institutions' pink marble and brown-and-blue plastic strongholds to the north. The Great Fire destroyed over 13,000 houses and 93 churches, of which 52 were rebuilt to Wren's specifications, and 24 survive.

Even as the fire still raged, plans were being drawn up to criss-cross London with grand boulevards, and create a new model city. But, as soon as the fire had finally burnt itself out, the people returned to their old corners on the naked medieval street-plan – bakers to Pudding Lane, stonecutters to Stonecutter Street, crutched friars to Crutched Friars – set up tents and shacks, and resumed their lives. The city was rebuilt in stone, to the template dictated by the people in the front-line.

When London was once again set ablaze, at the beginning of September 1940, a similar proportion of the old city was demolished. This time, in the face of no concerted resistance, the planners have had their way, tirelessly standardising, burying old under new, nibbling away at a job left tantalisingly incomplete by the fire-bombs.

By the time I've walked to Tower Hill, the prospect of climbing all over another landmark has lost most of its appeal. I'm knackered. It's crowded. A photographer, working the same tourist scam Michael Caine tried in *Alfie*, sidles up and waggles his Instamatic: 'Hello, sir. Take a picture for you, sir? A nice souvenir of your visit, sir?'

When I first moved to London, the Tower was one of the first day-trips I enjoyed on a celebratory Grand Tour of London Things with Lesley Wallace. At the time, we thought the Tower was good value; a bit short on Beatle-osity, but undeniably a dead old building.

Only when I'd read *Nairn's London* did I realise that the whole experience had, in fact, been rubbish. Ian Nairn rates the Tower as the 'one big hostage to the unreality of organised sight-seeing' in London. 'Still,' he adds, 'if it is a joke, it is at least full-blown farce, and enough historical events have happened to make invention unneccessary.'

Meanwhile, *Europe on $10 a Day* goes all trembly and tearful, describing the Tower as 'the most profound experience of your London stay', unreservedly recommending a plunge into little old England's gory history show. Doubtless speaking with humility born of personal experience, Arthur Frommer warns his fellow American culture vultures not to get too familiar with the Beefeaters, who have 'heard the gag about the gin hundreds of times'.

Admittedly, the long-suffering Beefeaters' walking-tours succeed in bringing to life only an iceberg-tip of historical melodrama; but who expects an objective, year-by-year lesson in social history from a cartoon character dressed in a red-and-black kung-fu dressing-gown? So far as the story goes, the nephews of the evil hunchback Richard III were smothered *on this spot* in the Bloody Tower. The imprisoned Princess Elizabeth (later crowned here) walked *these very walls* by the Beauchamp Tower, looking down on Tower Green where her mother had been executed on the command of her father eighteen years before. Walter Raleigh was dangled from *these very chains* as punishment for bringing back the potato from South America, and losing the recipe for chips to the French. Unbelievably, real people with real problems were rowed through this Pinewood stage-set Traitor's Gate, the weight on their shoulders dependent on whether they were destined for the royal palace, the fortress, or the chopping block. Elizabeth I. Anne Boleyn. Henry VIII. You know the names, you know the numbers – why not drop in for a chin-wag, and hear all the gossip?

From outside the Tower, the oddly scruffy collection of buildings visible over the wall doesn't look as if it dates back nine hundred years – irregular brick walls built on top of stone; a small greenhouse abandoned at the top of the Bell Tower – and indeed most of it doesn't. One of Nairn's principal objections to the Tower is the mock-medieval curtain wall built in the 1840s, at the same time as they filled in the moat. Clues to the date of the outer wall appear every few yards in the form of post-medieval drainpipes, unfortunately marked 'VR' – although the view plaques overlooking the moat coyly avoid the issue by admitting only that the walls were 'started thirteenth century'. The latest plan is to reflood the moat, but I think realism would be better served by simply removing the signs on the surrounding fence, which shout WARNING: TREATED WITH ANTI-CLIMB PAINT when *everyone* knows there's *no such thing* as anti-climb paint. Nairn has another minor grouse about the White Tower being re-clad in yellow stone, and bemoans the various fairy-castle alterations which have helped make the Tower irresistible to families wearing matching Bermuda shorts.

There can be little doubt that Ian Nairn was right about the

Tower, and I was wrong. Come to think of it, I do remember feeling vaguely insulted by the moving pavement that whisks you past the Queen's collection of sparkly hats, but no one seemed to complain – hard-core hat enthusiasts just doubled back and trundled past time after time. According to legend, when the ravens leave Tower Green, the White Tower will crumble and fall along with the Commonwealth. They're not leaving anything to chance, mind: it's easy to feel cheated when you find the birds' wings have been lopped off. Since we visited a couple of years ago, the White Tower armoury has been shifted to Leeds, so no more comedy codpieces. Good news for fans of grisly torture implements, however: *Carry On Henry* is out on video.

Hundreds of tourists are milling about outside the Tower, waiting to lay gentle siege in crocodile formation. Straw-boatered schoolgirls sprawl on the lawns, absent-mindedly sketching a wall, Tower Bridge, an ice-cream van, each other. One tourist consults his copy of *Streetwise London* to find the entrance to the Tower, but ends up asking a Beefeater with a walkie-talkie. The same wiry old snapper comes over and double-checks that I haven't changed my mind about that valuable souvenir portrait: 'How about a smile, sir? It'll be a picture.'

On the sparkling brown river, the only working barge is in the driftwood business. The *Viscountess* pleasure-boat ploughs upstream, engines easing off to allow a PA précis to impart the *real* highlights, the most *expertly pared* condensation of the Tower of London story in twelve seconds flat.

Maybe I'll go and buy myself a 'Tower Bridge Experience'. There are Victorian engine-rooms, musical Tower Bridge decanter-and-soda-syphon sets, and spectacular views if you climb to the top.

8 Walking Down the King's Road

Walking down the King's Road on a summer Saturday afternoon, a history of modern British fashion flashes before your eyes. It's in the very bricks and mortar of the shops; it's draped around the narrow shoulders of the startled shop-window mannequins; but most astonishingly it shines back, like an image in a shattered mirror, from the unconscious mix-and-match sampling of styles on display in the street. The infamous British youth tribes, every one London-born and bred, may have died out as pop music has gradually slipped from central status to just another take-it-or-leave-it supermarket commodity; but glimpses of all the purist styles still crop up as fragments of confused new images: a hippy tie-dye skirt, a mod target T-shirt, punk piercing, a biker jacket . . . and that's just one fourteen-year-old girl.

Dressing up is fun.

Mary Quant opened London's first 'boutique', Bazaar, on the corner of Markham Square in 1965. Within a few years, every clothes shop catering to the happening (under-)60s set had adopted its informal walkabout style. The Mother of the Mini's breezy hemlines, her black-and-white op-art styles and trademark angular bob were all recognised as instant design classics. Apropos of nothing, the master manipulator used to shave her pubic hair, and announced the fact to the world.

'Once only the rich, the Establishment, set the fashion,' she said. 'Now it is the inexpensive little dress seen on the girls in the High Street. They may be dukes' daughters, doctors' daughters, dockers' daughters. They are not interested in status symbols. They don't worry about accents or class. They are the mods.'

That's just the sort of thing I'd come out with if I were married to a backer called Lord Alexander Plunket-Green.

The new 'classless' teenagers were undeniably big business, and the rest of the King's Road was quick to cash in. In the '60s, all you needed to open up a fully stocked boutique was half a yard of psychedelic-print cotton and a dodgy monicker: I Was Lord Kitchener's Valet; Connecticut Yankees In King Arthur's Court;

Granny Takes A Trip. Tommy Roberts, self-styled 'Father of the Hot-Pants', opened up as Mr Freedom, and the King's Road claimed another wildfire trend. This mile-long ribbon through the hairy headland of Chelsea has provided the trimmings for a dizzying succession of lifestyle cults ever since, regaining the dynamic impetus it had lost by the late '60s (to Kensington, and Barbara Hulanicki's floppy, floaty Biba) with the emergence of punk and Vivienne Westwood. Foppish fads such as futurism, new romanticism and goth came and went. Sterile label-ism came and hung around: it made money. Throughout the '80s and '90s, cult revivals and trouser circumference cycles were peddled at an ever-quickening rate. Until now, the ultimate fashion: no fashion. Self-expression. Individualism. Any style and every style. And no such thing as old stock.

Far too many high-street chain-stores have muscled into the northern end of the King's Road. Don't they understand that people don't travel from all over Britain and the world to buy a khaki trouser-suit? They come here to show off and watch the other show-offs; to ignore all context and dress for fun in styles they like, but don't know *why* . . . like a guileless fourteen-year-old schoolgirl. Whom I watched extricate herself from a wheeling group of older teenage boys. And she crossed the road. And I looked again. And it was only *Kylie Minogue* – model mistress of postmodern irony . . .

Steinberg and Tolkien's grannywise grotto is lovingly arrayed with costume brooches, beaded purses, flappers' feather boas, an Erte sequined bodice and some suspiciously interesting Dior and Pucci eveningwear. Steinberg and Tolkien, admittedly, deal in vintage clothing – the cufflinks in the men's department give the game away. Boy (*Rocky Horror* red stockings, fluffy red suspender belt, quarter-length leather jacket), Red Apple (purple velvet flares, yellow slim-fit shirt) and Phlip (lace-up hipsters) are strictly cutting edge.

Far too many shops stock identical suede and leather jackets. When it comes to the delights of dressing up, cowboy fringes are a surprisingly widely acquired taste; stitched-yoke shirts and bootlace ties, too. And black-and-white snakeskin boots. With cuban heels and lizard logos scampering up the ankle. This is one purist scene left well alone by the mix-and-matchers, for obvious reasons. In cult terms, they are the distant descendants of '50s teds and '60s rockers – in the flesh, they are portly forty-somethings sipping coffee with their boots up on the café table, discussing shades of purple sage and their revving role models in *The Mild One*. Park up your Harley and pull up a piece of pavement with the last of the *Leather Boys*: 'the motorcycle cowboys who live for fast machines and faster girls . . . who ton-up along the motorways, terrorising drivers and defying the law . . . who marry unthinkingly and live only for the next kick'. Well, possibly in their younger days.

In the past, Chelsea earned a reputation as an artsy haven of individualism, now manifested mainly in locals' stubborn belief that their borough is a village. If Chelsea is a village, then London must be a vast daisy meadow, thoughtfully circumnavigated by the M25 for conservation reasons. The relatively late development of the area (until 1830, the King's Road was quite literally a private country lane leading to Hampton Court) gave rise to a streetplan with less inherited scribble than the rest of London. Parks and squares and leafy sidestreets sprout along the length of the road, and in its western half, especially, the hustle does give way to a relaxing laziness, a willingness to sit and watch the beautiful freaks and belly-buttons go slouching by. Not a village, then; but, in the straight bordered by the red-brick Vale Terrace, not unlike the high street of some unfeasibly trendy market town in rural Leicestershire. It's the balanced mixture of the King's Road which makes it so perfect for a Saturday afternoon stroll: people apart, there are bookshops and noodles and tarot readers and antiques. The bright white of Terence Conran's stucco and enamel '30s Bluebird Garage now nurtures a fruit market and café in its forecourt, only yards from his original Habitat furniture and lifestyle store; the '60s cubeforms of the Chelsea Fire Station and King's College's halls of residence are just enough but not too much. The dark-red brick of the Terrace absorbs the bright sunlight, making a Kodacolor picture of the lime-green leaves and ultramarine sky.

Chelsea *used* to be a village: that must be the source of its residents' misunderstanding. When Sir Thomas More built his home here in the 1520s, Chelsea was a humble fishermen's hamlet, normally reached only by river. Tipped off by his Lord Chancellor's real-estate deal, Henry VIII built a palace in this most desirable Thames-side hideaway; other courtiers and statesmen followed, and Chelsea soon became known as 'the village of palaces' (even then, everybody with cash wanted to live in a village). Henry thanked More by sending him to the Tyburn tree, and took his chances with the tone of the neighbourhood. It seems More had objected to the King's divorce and remarriage to Anne Boleyn, and refused to acknowledge him as head of the new Church of England. It's also just possible that a Humanist and future saint might have had certain reservations about the King's serial-killer personality profile – a point alluded to more delicately in most history books, and rarely in polite conversation with the Queen.

We'll never know, until *A Man for All Seasons* comes around again on TV.

The furthest western reach of the King's Road is known as World's End, an apt destination for the tatty trail of pilgrims who have turned too late down one of fashion's evolutionary blind alleys. Spiky hair, torn jeans and studded leather jackets have all entered the pick 'n' mix fashion mainstream from the once-shocking wardrobe of punk. Today there's really No Excuse for a tartan bumflap, even it is a family heirloom. There's No Point pretending to have No Fun, acting ugly for the benefit of (No) potential mates and (No) tourist snappers outside number 430 King's Road.

Only the clock in the window of Vivienne Westwood's World's End boutique – numbered 1 to 13 and spinning wildly backwards – gives a mocking clue to its place in London legend.

No Future.

A nihilistic battle-cry hilariously mistaken as a cue for Mr Bumflap to spend £120 on a pair of nostalgic steel-shinpad booties.

In 1974, Malcolm McLaren stole the idea of dressing (other people) in rubber and leather fetishwear from a postal catalogue advertising 'scandalous lingerie and glamourwear', and his partner Westwood went into production on her sewing-machine. A stock of teddy-boy drapes and crepe soles was ditched and, in 1976, the name of their shop was changed from Let It Rock to SEX – in pink plastic letters ten feet high. 'Out of the bedroom and into the streets': the aim was to shock and offend middle-class middle-aged middle England. And, oh yes, to grab media attention. Instead, SEX became a focus for the fledgling punk scene at this, the 'wrong' end of the King's Road. McLaren wasn't finished yet. Playing streetwise Svengali, the art-school sloganeer set out to create the ultimate antedote to the plodding rock and disco industry, to work and boredom and hippy love and peace: the Sex Pistols. When agitprop lyrics and a pub-rock back-line were thrown into the pot with Johnny

Rotten's snarl and Sid Vicious' skinny legs (all leather, zips, chains and rips courtesy of SEX), 'Anarchy in the UK' exploded . . .

For those of us without the benefit of first-hand exposure to London's violence, drugs and unemployment, there were at least some fast records with snotty words. Although never addressed directly in the anti-everything lyrics of *Never Mind the Bollocks*, homework deadlines and lawn-mowing chores seemed valid sources of disaffection on the streets of downtown Oadby. With all the inky music papers and tabloids screaming youth rebellion, stripes were picked out of school ties and worn with the skinny end to the fore. It felt *cool* to defy Miss Horsepool and chat in the Language Labs; to take a black felt-tip and write 'The Undertones The Jam Motorhead' on your woodwork apron. Confusing times for us Dave Dee fans; but, then, I've always been a disappointing spitter.

From her stronghold next door to Chelsea Conservative Club, Westwood went on to produce bondage trousers and rubber zipper T-shirts for the Sex Pistols, incorporating liberal-baiting swastikas and commie-baiting Karl Marx patches and badger-baiting dog-collars. That's dog-collars, as in the studded leather worn by Spike out of *Tom and Jerry* – although the church fête look could have been just as shocking in its own way. Viv's modern-day catwalk garments tend to take the more distant past – anything from Tudor times to the 1800s – as inspiration; but today her window-display features a maroon-and-chocolate crimplene tie, almost identical to one owned by my dad in 1977.

In this far-flung corner of the old borough, flags and banners are still hanging from windows long after Chelsea Football Club's victory in the 1997 FA Cup final – their first since 1970. Chelsea's current team, managed by the dreadlocked Dutchman Ruud Gullit, starring Player of the Year Gianfranco Zola and a host of international talent, have put Chelsea *back on the map*. Chelsea buns are selling like hot-cakes. Chelsea boots are cool. Chelsea Clinton is . . . Bill and Hillary's daughter. 'Chelsea Girls'; Chelsea Pensioners; 'Chelsea Morning'; 'Midnight in Chelsea'; Chelsea Flower Show; '(I Don't Want To) Go To Chelsea (Er, Only Kidding)'. Thanks to football, Chelsea is back in the big-time with a bang. Strange, then, that Chelsea FC's Stamford Bridge stadium is not in Chelsea at all, but in Fulham . . .

As a stripy-scarved twelve-year-old, the highlight of the football season was an M1 away-trip to watch Fulham take on the mighty Leicester City. Mum spotted the floodlights, not far off the Fulham Road. Dad found a parking space, just around the corner from the ground. We didn't *think* there were many people walking to the ground or milling around outside, at five to three . . .

For years, Chelsea have struggled to live up to their reputation as London's 'glamour' club, originally earned in the '60s (when the team included Jimmy Greaves, the greatest goalscorer ever; 'Gorgeous' George Graham; a teenage Terry Venables), but finally cemented into popular mythology by that Cup-winning side of 1970. Osgood, with his woolly triangular sideboards. Hudson, subsequently pinched for allegedly running a brothel. Hutchinson, with his spectacular 'windmill' throw-in. The ever-popular Ron 'Chopper' Harris . . . In order to lift the silverware, the swaggering playboys of Chelsea had to overcome Don Revie's Leeds United, a team run along lines of 'family values', strict discipline and homicidal tackling. Jackie Charlton. Billy Bremner. Norman 'Bites Yer Legs' Hunter. Ugh. Revie's idea of building team spirit was to organise a game of carpet bowls, a couple of hands of gin rummy for matchsticks, and early to bed. Meanwhile, Dave Sexton ordered his Chelsea team to test out the old succubus theory of sex before the big match. They even sang their Cup-final song, 'Blue is the Colour', on *Top of the Pops*. There hadn't been such a clear-cut case of goodies against baddies since the mod-rocker Bank Holidays, or the Beatles versus the Stones.

The current Chelsea side would doubtless run rings around their 1970 counterparts. They're more highly skilled and tactically adept, and they're all honed to a peak of physical perfection by personal trainers and dieticians who have never even heard of cake. But if Gullit's men stayed up until four on matchday morning, knocking back blue cocktails and frugging with frolicsome fans at the Bag o' Nails, and then on to the Bird's Nest discotheque on the King's Road . . . then it might just be a different story.

Chelsea's modern-day fan-club numbers John Major and Richard Attenborough. David Mellor's reign as Heritage Secretary came to a halt with the appalling tabloid revelations of his fondness for SCORING AWAY FROM HOME wearing his Chelsea shirt.

Back in the glam old days Chelsea's number one fan was *Raquel Welch* . . .

It's only a short walk from this end of the King's Road to Cheyne Walk and the Embankment. As I turn the corner out of Edith Grove, a welcome blast of cool air hits me in the face, and I think *seaside*. The tide is out far enough for the houseboat colony at Whistler's Reach to be resting at a slope on the salty-smelling shoreline short of Battersea Bridge. The flat-bottomed boats are built up with every conceivable design and colour of cabin, from basic garden-shed affairs to New Orleans Imperial and DIY submarine styles. All linked together with communal barge-walkways and freshly-painted gangplanks, this could be the last bastion of true Chelsea individualism. Fluttering flags, porthole windows, a healthy jungle of houseboat-plants; bright red calor-gas cylinders for that long-lost caravan smell. There's only one word for it, and that's *gay*. What a marvellous place to live, just three minutes from the King's Road, and no extortionate rent to pay. And when the Thames starts to get choppy in the winter months, just float your shed out to Monte Carlo and park next hatch to Omar Sharif or George Michael.

When Cheyne Walk first established its reputation as the focal point of Chelsea's enclave of writers, artists and intellectuals, its elegant rows of tall, red-brick houses were open to the waterfront. The deep, gently sloping beach was subsequently reclaimed from the Thames in the 1870s, separating Cheyne Walk and the beautiful Physic Gardens from the serenity of the river, but providing London with the Chelsea Embankment, whose thundering highway now continues as far north as the Houses of Parliament. At the Tate Gallery, just a couple of miles downstream, riverscapes by Cheyne Walk's own James Abbott McNeill Whistler show the Chelsea of old, complete with the original, rickety wooden span of Battersea Bridge. Whistler was a controversial Yankee dandy, with a white lock in his black hair. His most famous work is a portrait of his mother, which he clearly thought about long and hard before arriving at the title *Arrangement in Grey and Black No. 1*. Infuriatingly for Whistler, the rest of humanity preferred plain old *Whistler's Mother*. The Tate is even more famously hung with J.M.W. Turner's abstractions of the watery river light at Chelsea. Turner, England's most famous artist, was a dwarfish, grumpy cockney, who lived in Cheyne Walk under the alias 'Mr Booth', known to locals as 'Admiral Booth' for his habit of surveying brooding storm clouds from his windows.

Rossetti, Augustus John, John Singer Sargent. Carlyle, George

Eliot, Isambard Kingdom Brunel. All past members of Cheyne Walk's chattering Chelsea Set.

A handy clue to judging the reputation of these dusty Chelsean characters is by their total number of names (odd numbers are always promising) or whether they are known solely by their initials. Thus Whistler trumps his local compatriots Mark Twain, Henry James and Judy Garland, despite rarely being referred to as 'J.A.M.' There's no need to stipulate 'Jonathan' when referring to Swift; but 'George' will always need to be prefixed by 'David Lloyd' – the man was greater than the sum of his parts. Carlyle, the mono-monickered 'Sage of Chelsea', is still renowned as a great writer, even though the last time anyone read *Frederick the Great*, Chelsea was synonymous with *fish*. Julie Christie is just a common old two-name, but wasn't she smashing in *Doctor Zhivago*?

Moving onto more pressing concerns, the first shared flat of the Rolling Stones' Jagger, Richards and Jones was on Edith Grove. In the '70s, Jagger moved into number 48 Cheyne Walk, and Richards occupied number 3. Meanwhile, before the Sex Pistols could put their revolutionary ideas into practice, they had to steal some musical equipment: a cabaret band's PA system from a van in Hammersmith; a guitar-tuner from a Roxy Music gig; most of a drum-kit from BBC TV Centre, and so on. Guitarist Steve Jones's foray from World's End to Keith Richards' house provided only a colour TV set and several pairs of wholly unsuitable cowboy boots. John 'Rotten' Lydon is now himself a resident of Cheyne Walk, still waiting hopefully for his invitation to join the Neighbourhood Watch.

It's a good job the Sex Pistols never ventured so far from World's End as the delicate cobweb structure of the Albert Bridge, hung loosely over the river by an ingenious Victorian combination of the cantilever and suspension principles. Which makes it uniquely susceptible to rhythmic movements. Such as mass pogoing. The potentially disastrous warning sign – ALL TROOPS MUST BREAK STEP WHEN MARCHING OVER THIS BRIDGE – still hangs on the redundant toll-booth like a red rag to any Art Terrorist bull.

Since property prices rocketed in the '80s, Chelsea no longer resonates with quite the same amplitude of Art Terrorist bull. Studios and loft apartments, which should rightfully be packed with bearded students and bohemiennes, are now merely inhabited by people who can afford them. As I stand in the middle of the Albert

Bridge, doing my best to get things bouncing without drawing too much attention, a young woman walks by carrying a large speckly-purple perspex sheet, in which a pyramid-shape and a cluster of bumps have been artfully moulded. The School of Art still brings in a smattering of embattled dreamers. We look into the skittering reflections of the sun in the river below, an inspiration to so many artists before her. But she's not so good at sky, boats or straight lines.

To the north, a string of riverworthy craft – no sheds here – are moored midstream, off the flimsy frame steps of Cadogan Pier. Seagulls scavenge on the decks of these slick launches, where the riverboat colony attracted only landlubber sparrows. Battersea Power Station is reportedly in the midst of an unlikely transformation into an arts centre and gallery, a theme-park or a funfair – possibly all four – but for me the impact of its four fat smokestacks will always be ruined by association with everybody else's dozy big brother's Pink Floyd album cover. The Peace Pagoda, fully deserving of a double- or triple-take amid the green curtain wall of Battersea Park, is a jarring folly in the rich London tradition of the Albert Memorial, the Monument or Nelson's Column.

A fascinating version of history can be pieced together using the size and expense of London landmarks as a guide, together with dedicated buildings, street names, and so on. The resulting picture does seem to be rather dominated by minor royal figures, Victorian dogooders and favourites of government. Just as well most things already had a name by the time Margaret Thatcher and Lady Di enjoyed their brief period of Londomination. St Denis's Cathedral just doesn't have the ring of St Paul's. And how would it feel to walk the streets of the East End overshadowed by Phil Collins Wharf?

On my way up Royal Hospital Road, I drop off at number 34 Tite Street to gaze through the ground-floor study window where Oscar Wilde, the embodiment of Victorian Chelsea's wit and style, wrote *The Importance of Being Earnest* and *The Picture of Dorian Gray*. Wilde lived for eleven years in this red-brick terrace in the ivy-grown heart of Chelsea. During this time he made a living editing *Lady's World*, a society bible of good taste, and was happily married to Constance Lloyd: neither position was tenable for long after Oscar set eyes on 'Bosie', Lord Alfred Douglas. Tite Street was the scene of the famous showdown with the Marquis of Queensberry – Bosie's dad, 'the most infamous brute in London' – which made Wilde enemies, and eventually led to his arrest and conviction for sodomy. The interior and contents of the 'House Beautiful' were broken up and auctioned off for loose change. On his release from Reading Gaol, Wilde never returned to Chelsea, but lived out the remaining three years of his life (and the century) travelling abroad under an assumed name, Ron 'Chopper' Harris.

More exciting than Tite Street is my scheduled visit to Royal Avenue, and the bolt-hole *pied-à-terre* bachelor-pad love-ranch of James Bond. My hero. Even if he is a macho pig, an anachronism and a suspected *Telegraph* reader, I'll never shake off my jealous schoolboy crush on Bond and his lifestyle. Today I ate buttery scrambled eggs for breakfast, and drank strong filter coffee and Kwiksave fresh orange juice, all in honour of this moment. For reasons of national security, Ian Fleming – himself another noted resident of Cheyne Walk – could never disclose the exact address where Bond lived with his trusty Scottish housekeeper, May; but I'm willing to take an average and assume it wouldn't have been far from this sober black door in the middle of the terrace. Naturally, Bond would have lived on the western side of the side of the street, not the commie east. Even if you were making it up, there could hardly be a more perfect place for Bond to live: barely a pitching-wedge from the bustle of the King's Road, but then only a wristy mashie from the hyper-English setting of the cricket pitch and bowling greens set before the beautiful brick and bell-tower of Wren's Royal Hospital. Parade-ground sounds from the Duke of York's Regimental HQ float over the rooftops. A sports car speeds around the avenue's one-way U, and its twin-barrel three-inch rebored ejector exhausts sound authentically *throaty*.

Chelsea Royal Hospital was built by Charles II at the insistence of his 'big-hearted' lover, Nell Gwyn. The King was not averse to the idea of an old soldier's home on his recently commandeered private road, and went along with the idea for an easy life. As I'm crossing the central, tree-lined walk which lends Royal Avenue the atmosphere of a Bloomsbury square, a couple of Pensioners amble homeward in their immaculate dark-blue uniforms, their shrunken chests full of ribbons, seemingly inhabitants of another time, another London. War. Guns. Death. Duty. What must they think of me, in my unpressed jeans, and not a single enemy confrontation under my belt? I'd go and ask them some patronising questions, but they must be tired of dissolute children and their trivia. I'd gladly buy them a drink if we were in a pub; but I wouldn't want them to think I was buying their time. I'd like to tell them they have my respect; but I've never done a thing that might earn theirs. And now they've disappeared through the gate into the playing-fields.

Indulging in some playful mental arithmetic, I feel a further, childish sense of loss at the realisation that either one of those war veterans could have been Bond himself.

We might not have got on.

Having walked an unhurried two-and-a-half-mile loop in the stinging Saturday sun, a refreshment break is overdue. For inspiration, I turn again to my all-swinging, gunslinging *London Dossier*. The 'Photography' chapter is written not by Len Deighton, but by one of his flowery-cravated chums, roped in to flesh out an all-round vision of the city. Adrian Flowers is a jobbing photographer – hey, he took the *Dossier* cover pic of Twiggy – with a studio in Tite Street, and a fine line on capturing the light of London. Adrian pays cab-drivers fifteen bob to drive him around Soho, snapping as he goes; he sets up a time-lapse tripod for Sunday supp. shots of Westminster Bridge; flies flashing around the markets, the monuments, the parks and policemen. A Chelsea specialist, he recommends the buildings of the Royal Hospital, the Pensioners' parade on Oak Apple Day, and the bizarre sights of the annual Flower Show held in its grounds. But when it comes to Saturday afternoon, there's only one place you'll find our Adrian: *birdwatching* on the King's Road:

'Flocks of these creatures occur welded to the folded hoods of vintage and modern open cars . . . 3.30 p.m. is peak display time. If you want to see and not be seen, a good tip is to grab a window table in a pub called the Chelsea Potter.'

How can I resist?

I pick up a fab 'n' gear pint of lager and take a vacant seat by the windowsill just along from the open front windows. Just as Adrian promised, the road and pavement are jammed with 'suitably stationary' subjects for the London scrapbook. A pencil-thin Japanese girl, barely stretching her lycra. Another woman, massively pregnant, a cluster of rings piercing her bulging belly-button. Some obscure sub-species of rocker, who has seen fit to tie a scarf around his knee. Three stripy-shirted twits in a jeep. A middle-aged woman in an American convertible, tossing her hair and drumming her fingers on the steering-wheel. Not one of them *needs* to be caught up in this mayhem: the King's Road simply exerts a magnetic draw over people who think they need to be seen here. On the King's Road. Just in case anybody's looking.

The January 1972 issue of *National Geographic* magazine, recently rescued from the black hole under Mum and Dad's stairs, takes up the King's Road Saturday story in that special anthropological tone normally reserved for photo-captions of African tribeswomen adorned in ceremonial beads and warpaint – but who were always otherwise, quite coincidentally, *butt-naked* . . .

'The young pour in to shop the King's Road, but above all to parade, while staider folk come to enjoy the show. It is the sort of show the police would have closed down when I was a boy,' admits Assistant Editor James Cerruti, loosening his fat-knotted crimplene tie as he slowly goes purple in the face. He recovers sufficient professional composure to scientifically catalogue 'a covey of decorative "dolly birds" . . . their elegant long legs . . . fresh English complexions . . . a lovely young lady in hot pants . . .'

At which point Assistant Editor James Cerruti explodes, splattering the steamed-up lens of Adrian Flowers with spittle and shreds of sweaty safari-suit.

My big sister Lynda used to go down the King's Road in the '60s, with her hippy friend Alison. Men took pictures. 'We were fifteen. We used to iron our hair and dress in cheesecloth and walk along pretending we were on drugs. We used to practise our stoned look for hours in the mirror.'

It's the story of the King's Road in thirty words.

I hop on a number 11 bus and crawl up the King's Road as far as Sloane Square, whose rows of plane trees and fountain of Venus could so easily be Parisian, given an added sprinkling of rudeness and Martini umbrellas. SWEET THAMES RUN SOFTLY TILL I END MY SONG, reads Venus's inscription, easily legible because the fountain is broken. Standing out from the square of Victorian stone façades of the pubs and restaurants huddling close to the Royal Court Theatre, the glass frontage of the Peter Jones department store was considered a marvel in the '30s, its curve elegantly rounding the corner into the King's Road with a gurly flourish.

In the second half of the '70s, Sloane Square became known as the spiritual home of the Sloane Rangers, originally a like-minded crowd of officer-class hoorahs, who – almost incredibly, now – spawned a wannabe cult following in the years that saw Margaret Thatcher sweep to power. The Sloanes shopped at Peter Jones and The General Trading Company, and held utterly blissful cocktail parties for their muckers in Laura Ashley quarters. Sloane Man was called Charles or Timmie: he wore tweeds, *knew the form*, and went point-to-pointing for a giggle. Sloane Woman was called Diana or Caroline: she wore an utterly blissful Hermès headscarf, navy tights, skirt and blazer, and *added tone* wherever she Ranged in her Rover. Peter York's *Sloane Ranger's Handbook*, a jokey extension of his articles in *Harpers & Queen*, briefly succeeded in making green wellington boots fashionable among England's non-farming classes. Let's face it, some of them didn't even own a window-box.

As I walk away from the King's Road, up Sloane Street towards Knightsbridge, street fashions gradually cease to be a function of personality, ideas, theft and downright daring, and become noticeably more *off-the-peg*. The classic silky lines are immaculate, beyond any possible criticism; but what's missing here are those precious King's Road elements of *freedom* and *fantasy*. In the windows of Gucci, Cartier, Chanel, Lacroix and Vuitton, handbags and trouser-suits worth millions are laid out by price-tag, so shoppers can snatch up the most expensive items they can possibly afford, without having to concern themselves with questions of taste. These are the same wealthy Americans and Europeans who marvel at the way British women manage to look *great* wearing *rags*. That's why the wildest London style-samplers and -stitchers – Alexander McQueen, John Galliano, Stella McCartney, Jean-Paul Gaultier – are all now on Parisian bankrolls: to supply the very dashes of wit and improvisation that are here to copy for free on the streets of London. It might take them a couple of years to bleed down from the innovators to the designers to the catwalk to the shop-windows, but soon all of Knightsbridge and Kensington will be top-to-tail in £5,000 couture target T-shirts and second-hand bumsters.

In the days before fax-machines and e-mail, Harrods' cable address was 'Everything London'. If that fact alone weren't enough to blow away my reservations about coming along to watch people with orange suntans go shopping, the gabbling excitement of the tourist crowds and the comic, over-the-top opulence of the store have soon won me over. ENTER A DIFFERENT WORLD proclaim the spotless green-and-gold doormats, missing out on a chance to use the far funnier IF IT'S WORTH DOING, IT'S WORTH OVERDOING.

The first sight that makes me laugh out loud is the Egyptian Hall, whose pillars and ceiling are carved with a cool £25 million worth of cod-hieroglyphics: using my handy pocket-size *London Hieroglyphics Guide*, I roughly translate the symbols etched across one ancient tombstone-cum-sales counter as 'Cat beetle fitted kitchen heli-pad spend spend spend'. The window-display is centred around a life-size pharaoh sitting in a giant flower, playing a harp: it's a music box, an ideal drawing-room conversation-starter for a megalomaniac Bond villain. The metal mini-sphinxes standing around the display are tagged at £1,295 each.

'Wooooooo!' a posse of American women shout at each other.

'Ah'm goan have tuh *pud a chain around you* . . .'

'Abso-lootly *waaaaaaow!*'

Back on planet Earth, a grubby cockney infant complains to his mum, ''E ain't even touchin' ver fakkin' strings.'

I start wandering aimlessly from hall to hall, following the smell of ninety-seven types of freshly ground coffee, a crocodile of foreign diplomats' wives, the trail of ludicrous bargains: a piano that plays itself (£8,899); a piano that plays itself, being tinkled upon by a tiny old lady in a polka-dot dress (£8,899). Obviously, I have to ask her whether she comes all-inclusive or costs extra, and so find out exactly how Arthur Frommer felt when he told the Beefeater the one about the gin. Having been amazed by 'the aesthetics of the Nineteenth Dynasty recreated by modern craftsmen' in the Egyptian Hall, I am stopped dead in my tracks by the phenomenal tooling quality and gaudy period detail of the Egyptian Escalator . . .

Harrods just keeps getting better and better. The world-famous Food Halls feature a Sushi Bar, an Oyster Bar and a Bar Fromage. Don't you agree 'Cheese' sounds a bit *cheap*? The Meat Hall is sumptuously decorated with Doulton tiles, its glass counters packed with mouthwatering delicacies, an extremist Temple of Taste. Above the poultry counter, stuffed rabbits, pheasants and pigeons are posed in a vulgar woodland spray around the bodies of more recently expired birds, hanging on spikes for connoisseur consumption. For those of us who are scared of dead animals, guinea-fowl, quail and their little friends are plucked naked and arranged artistically in the fridge. A ceramic shrine to fish stands in the corner, chrysanthemums and gaping snappers dangled over tasty mermaids. Cooling spray wafts over parrot-fish, shark, octopus. This isn't a food hall, this is a *zoo*. The air is full of the aromas of blood and oils and *fromage*. I want to kill and feast and orgy.

When I win the pools, I'm going to come and snap up a four-poster bed with built-in quadrophonic radio, cassette-deck, turntable, radio alarm, pop-up colour TV, coffee percolator, cocktail cabinet and refrigerator (£8,298 in 1975). As a man of wealth and taste, I'll lunch only on Harrods hampers; I'll make sure I'm seen with Roger Moore when he switches on the Christmas lights; I'll order a(nother) Harrods alligator for Noel Coward, and a(nother) Harrods baby elephant for Ronald Reagan. Even going for a piss in Harrods is more satisfying. It must be: it costs a quid.

Everything about Harrods is overstated, exaggerated, extravagant. It manages to be fun without a fortune to spend because it's more than just a shop: this is London's living Museum of Boundless Luxury. Cloud-cuckooland. Plucked and ready to gobble.

Mohamed Al Fayed admits, 'From the first moment I stepped over the threshold, I knew this was the most exciting place in the world': in fact he liked the shop so much, he bought the entire House of Fraser Group for £615 million.

Not so long ago, Al Fayed bought Fulham FC. Let's hope he doesn't think he's bought Chelsea.

9 Notting Hill Gate

Notting Hill comes drenched in more of yer actual pop-cultural history than any other area of London. In Soho you may find more clubs and more On This Spots to loiter near; but in Notting Hill you can actually *live* three flats along, two flats back and six up from a bedsit once shared by the drummer out of Alvin Stardust's backing-band. Notting Hill is crammed with people revelling in such vicarious vibes. If anyone ever printed up a Notting Hill souvenir tea-towel to sell to triple-hip tourists, you'd hardly be able to see the hopelessly out-of-scale street map for the welter of arrows, circles and badly drawn famous faces.

Of course, in reality there would be a severely limited market for the triple-hip tea-towel. Personally, I can't imagine any self-respecting hipster washing up in the first place, let alone *drying*. If a hipster were to compromise their cool in the kitchen, they'd surely be more likely to wash and *leave to drain*, rather than diving in at the square and mumsy deep-end of drying and putting away. But if you *forced* a hipster to use a tea-towel, they'd surely prefer a plain, checked, or understated paisley design – the sort that might double up as a bandanna – over anything featuring the line MY BROTHER / SISTER / MUM / DAD WENT TO NOTTING HILL AND ALL I GOT WAS THIS LOUSY HIPSTER TEA-TOWEL. Tourist souvenir tea-towels printed with hip or otherwise hipster-orientated information would be doomed to commercial failure. Tea-towels are anathema to hipsters. They would sell like cool cakes. That's why I'm asking you to bear with me on this one.

Pride of place in the hipster tea-towel history of Notting Hill would be taken by the famous CARNIVAL, Europe's biggest outdoor festival. GEORGE ORWELL lived at number 10 Portobello Road. MICK JAGGER, JIMI HENDRIX and VAN MORRISON lived the life in Notting Hill and Ladbroke Grove; indeed, one of them lived so hard he died here, although you'd never guess which one from looking at recent photos. COLIN MacINNES'S novel *Absolute Beginners* was an influential, hipsterised version of the 1950s' Notting Hill race riots. I bet DAVID BOWIE and PATSY KENSIT wish they'd never appeared in the dismal song 'n' dance film version. MICHELANGELO ANTONIONI swung open the door of the '60s when he shot *Blow Up!* in northern Notting Hill streets; NIC ROEG slammed the door in the decade's face with his *Performance* in Powis Square. THE CLASH could later be heard refining their nastiness every weekend at the Elgin pub on Ladbroke Grove. Notting Hill even managed to be at the centre of something worth while in the 1980s: the FRANKIE GOES TO HOLLY-WOOD sound was created by Pop Producer of the Decade TREVOR HORNE at his Psalm West Studio on ALL SAINTS Road. The singing group cheekily pinched the name of the street when they were record-ing there unsuccessfully in the early 1990s. HANIF KUREISHI (*My Beautiful Launderette*) and MARTIN AMIS (*London Fields*) are just two modern novelists inspired by the area, although only one of them actually likes it. Blur's DAMON ALBARN, one of Colchester's few true cockneys, lives on the Hill with his lesser-rockin' girlfriend – just a little bit like Mick Jagger and MARIANNE FAITHFULL brought up to date, they hope. And yesterday I made the timely discovery that the projected sequel to *Four Weddings and a Funeral* is to be called NOTTING HILL GATE, ensuring a new influx of American tourists to rub elbows with the backpackers way into the next millennium.

Notting Hill Gate sounds like a pretty unlikely name for a film, from where I'm standing – or maybe that should be from when I'm standing. Film names and band names, place names and baby names have a habit of settling down over the years, and becoming easier on the ear. As William Shagspere once said, 'What's in a name . . . eh, Nigel?' 'The Beatles': now there's a bloody corny pun-name for a band. History will probably lay the blame for that one at Richard Starkey's door. But what about 'Elephant & Castle'? 'Reginald Dwight'? 'Shoot-Up Hill'? 'Elvis Costello'? Hey, *Notting Hill Gate*'s sounding better already.

If the location researchers do their homework, *Notting Hill Gate* will be set at least partly in the upstairs bar of the Devonshire Arms. I can picture the title sequence now: a long, slow zoom into the pub's curved corner frontage, still promoting Double Diamond beer to a gratefully Double Diamond-free world, and on in to Hugh Grant sitting contentedly at the open window, the sun in his eyes and a lunchtime sherbet in his hand. Scene One: Hugh leafs through the bargain paperbacks he's picked up second-hand from the local Book Exchange, pausing only to gaze out on the busy junction with Pembridge Road, leading north to Portobello Road and all the real action. A sip of lager. Hugh takes in the Dalek turret of the Coronet Cinema along the one stretch of the Gate that escaped the standard '60s streamlining into four-storey office blocks, all glass and grubby panelling. Another sip of lager. Pan across the nineteen storeys of the tower-block Hugh calls home, in the middle-distance. Window-boxes. Washing-lines in mid-air. Small children dangling from balcony railings. Local colour. Enter Andie McDowell. She'll waltz up with her half of cider and asks Hugh if she can join him (meaning here, in front of his quintessentially cinematic backdrop). He'll say maybe later, in the car. And there, sadly, our two stories will diverge . . .

Statistically, as an average denizen of Notting Hill, Hugh is most likely to be cast as a counter assistant at one of the Gate's ever-growing number of Exchange shops. First, there was the Record and Tape Exchange, then came CDs and books, musical equipment and cameras, more recently followed by clothes and esoteric furnishings, electrical equipment and computer paraphernalia. No less than eleven Exchanges now compete for customers on Pembridge Road and both sides of Notting Hill Gate. At some point, every new arrival in West London, every student and backpacker, gets to stand behind an Exchange counter and enjoy their first taste of real power – or at least how it feels to be a deputy bank manager. Remember, only *statistically* does Hugh Grant have this *frisson* of excitement to look forward to: far be it from me to suggest that he might instead be typecast as one of the yuppies who started to infiltrate the area in the '80s, pushing house prices through the roof in oases around select sushiterias and wine-bars with topiarised hedges spelling out their names: 'Beach Blanket Babylon'; 'Let's Talk Salaries' . . .

Notting Hill is nothing if not a mixed community. Generation after generation of bohemians and outsiders – beatniks, hippies, punks – have drawn inspiration from these vibrant, rumbustious streets. Today's New Age of Notting Hillbillies – beatnik hippy punks, approximately – still gather in the market cafés and pubs of Portobello Road to talk noisily about sex and drugs, politics and art, and high scores on the Space Invader. As the session wears on, it is traditional for each participant to stake a claim for true local status over the trendy bond dealers, the antiques dealers, drug dealers and fruit-and-veg dealers; even over next-door neighbours who have lived in the area for considerably longer than twenty-five minutes: Irish, Afro-Caribbean, Portuguese, Asian, English people of every colour and creed. Results of a recent poll conducted around one scientifically selected sample Notting Hill pool table indicate a population comprised of true locals and longtime faces on the scene (100 per cent), Johnny-Come-Latelies (0 per cent) and embarrassed interlopers from unhip neighbouring boroughs (0 per cent). Diversity and individuality are important: 80 per cent of the sample are mock-dreadlocked, dyed green or shaven clean; are trailblazing cybernauts, alternative stallholders or underground musicians, all deservedly reclaiming Friday afternoon to wind down from their busy week at the office.

I spent the last hour or so in the Record and Book Exchanges, where I was chuffed to pick up one much sought-after out-of-date London guide, and help myself to the information that when Hendrix died he was living with his girlfriend Monika Dannemann on Lansdowne Crescent. Most of the other customers seemed to be using the shop as a free library, too, except for the sluggish flow of green-dreadlocked twenty-somethings attempting to use it as a bank. Every so often the door would tinkle, followed by the sound of boots clumping straight to the counter. A carrier-bagful of comics and sci-fi novels (or CDs and LPs) would be emptied out, and a counter-assistant (they take it in turns) would slouch into humiliation mode:

'Let's see.' (30-second pause.) 'I'll give you four quid.'

'*Four quid* for this rare Prodigy bootleg?/collectable *Swamp Thing* mag?/signed first edition of the Bible?'

'No, mate. I'll give you four quid *for the lot.*'

And that's that. Take it or leave it. Another bank manager in the making. Another heirloom collection pawned to the only bidder, repriced and flogged off within the hour. I must admit to a certain prickle of righteousness when I took *The New London Spy* to the counter and handed over my £2.50, even though the book was still clearly marked with an old price from another bookshop: '1st ed. 1966 – £6'. Could it be they haven't realised these superannuated London guides are bound to catch on and be worth big money one day? Oh yes, mate – I'll give you four quid *for the bagful* . . .

In the Devonshire Arms, I learn that the original *London Spy* was published by Ned Ward, landlord of the King's Head, near Gray's Inn, in 1703. This first-ever London guide lingered on the various leisure pursuits of the time – hiring a harlot, baiting lunatics in Bedlam, gaming and dog-tossing. Two and a half centuries later *The*

New London Spy was reworked as *A Discreet Guide to the City's Pleasures* by Hunter Davies, the original Beatle-ologist. There are promising-sounding chapters on 'Night Clubs', 'Underworld' and 'Speciality Services'. Although the book probably hasn't been opened for thirty years, it still falls open on a page which kicks off: 'Nudes on Real Ice, The Girl in the Golden Fish Tank, The Golden Nude and nude films in sin-erama.' Intriguingly, the corner of a page is turned down to also mark 'Lesbian London' – definitely cool for 1966. This is my kind of London book – one which earned its dustjacket disclaimer: 'The intention is neither to condone nor to corrupt, but to record . . .'

The skinny mile-long strip of Portobello Road is split up into distinct thematic zones, which are clearly signposted on schematic roadsigns: it's straight on for SECOND-HAND GOODS, via ANTIQUES and FRUIT AND VEG; but first it'll be necessary to navigate through GLOOM AND DOOM. This top end of the market is dominated by antique shops whose entire stock looks like (once again for the lawyers: *looks like*) it's been knocked off from church property and dilapidated Gothic castles all across Europe. I wonder who flogged these giant stone balls from the top of someone's gateposts? And what about these graveyard urns? A painted wooden triptych? Either some cash-strapped Spanish priest is quite legitimately selling off the contents of his church and graveyard at four quid per bagful, or else . . . or else the artefacts must be worthless fakes! It's the only possible legal explanation. But nonetheless one which begs the question: who wants a dubious altar-piece on their sideboard, anyway? Catch me using an antique angelic urn as a plant-pot holder without a *full* service history, guv'nor. It's enough to give you the willies.

Further down Portobello, the shops begin to specialise in antique furniture, glass and silver, bone china and . . . *ostrich eggs*? A couple of shops are displaying a nest of the eggs in the window, alongside infinitely more sensible nicknacks. I've half a mind to put my head round the door and ask how much they cost, or if you have to buy them by the half-dozen. An ostrich egg: that could be the perfect surprise gift for the woman who thought she had everything. But hold on: *The New London Spy*, already earning its keep, says: 'When a dealer takes a stall in the Caledonian Market, he adds 20 per cent to his prices, *and in the Portobello Road 40 per cent.*' Best shop around, then . . .

At first glance, Alice's (Est. 1887) looks like the perfect London antique shop: its windows are packed high with colourful curios, and inside it's so cluttered there's only one square yard of floorspace available for the owner – whom I shall call Alice – his four browsing customers, intent on fumbling everything in sight, and a small dog. ALICE'S is painted over the door in the kind of lettering you only *ever* find above the doors of antique shops, unless you happen to own a Donovan album called something like *Merry-Go-Round* or *Grannie's Magical Attic*. Alice's is so hyper-authentic, it comes as something of a disappointment to discover not everything here is *real*. *Some* of the antiques are almost certainly real – piles of plates, chests of drawers, ostrich eggs – while others are, on second glance, only *apparently* real. A 'Fry's Chocolate' mirror. A wooden sign for the 'All-England Lawn Tennis Club'. Another one that says 'Est. 1887', but is it true? These deceptive wood and enamel advertisements have cropped up in every pub refit in the '90s, all chipped and aged to exactly the same degree. If you know a pub in London that has clung onto a genuine period interior, you can look forward to it being stripped out, knocked through, and thoughtfully replaced with Alice's amusing 'Cobbler's' sign. There'll be a high shelf strewn with Random Old Things, too. It must be a dealer's delight to be asked for a skipload of colour-coded crap, pre-1987 if possible: empty bottles; broken dolls; books that have escaped the bonfire only to be sold by the yard; framed photographs of anonymous dead people.

As unlikely as it may sound, the hipster tea-towel history of Portobello Road almost pales into insignificance in comparison with its not-very-hip-at-all history. Let's not forget, it was to his Portobello Road antique shop that the kind Mr Brown brought one marmalade-fixated Peruvian bear he had found lost on the platform at Paddington Station. And never mind James Fox in *Performance* (or in *Absolute Beginners*) – this is where Angela Lansbury came looking for a magic spell to help repel the Nazi invasion in Walt Disney's *Bedknobs and Broomsticks*. Without wishing to spoil the ending, the story involves a white witch and three young cockney evacuees who fly to London on a magic bed in preparation for a football match against a team of cartoon animals. The exact circumstances are unimportant – it all makes perfect sense when you're six – what *does* matter is that I'm standing on the very spot where Angela Lansbury all-too-briefly locked horns with Bruce Forsyth's memorable psychopathic spiv, give or take a yard or two for the liberties taken by the Disney set-builders. This is where the great David Tomlinson sang '(You'll Find What You Want) In the Portobello Road', the Disney writers taking fresh liberties with bric-à-brac-related rhyme. Tapping into the theme of diversity, Disney choreographers then pressed servicemen from every corner of the world into performing a version of their national dance, along with corresponding members of the local population. West Indian military calypso, Ghurka banghra, Irish jig-a-jig with golden-hearted good-time girls: could this be lost footage of the first-ever Notting Hill Carnival?

How refreshing to witness history and language being trashed in the name of infant entertainment, with Anglo-American market-speak along the lyrical lines of *Spuds two bob a kilo?/the Venus de Milo!/Old instruments of torture/Cor! wot a scorchah!*

Running at right-angles across Portobello Road is Westbourne Grove, where even the most exclusive antiques shops finally give way to art galleries and interior design studios. This, I fear, is the *Notting Hill Gate* where Hugh Grant will be sent to snap up a statue, a tigerskin rug, a crystal chandelier from Andie the investment consultant. Paddington Bear would be skinned alive if he came sniffing for marmalade sarnies around here.

At Let's Talk Salaries, a single plate-glass window allows punters to sip and swagger inside, while remaining fully visible from the street. Pressing my face against the window, I could almost be watching a scene from *Miami Vice*. Big suits. Big hair. Stiletto heels. Golden ankle and belly chains hung with mobile phones. It's the Beautiful People and their horizontally mobile chums. Across the road, I'm astonished to discover a designer outfitter's that specialises in *handbags*. In 1997. In the window of Frocks To Get Cocks hangs a dress that costs £1,000, and *it's royal blue* . . .

Before heading down the hill to the market proper, I cross back over Portobello Road and follow my *A–Z* to the Hendrix deathplace, off Ladbroke Grove. If only the Book Exchange had a bigger music section, or if my pilgrimage had been anything other than an after-thought, I could have looked up the number of the house where Hendrix died; the precise flat, the actual stain on the carpet. Luckily, given no choice, I prefer to take a more impressionistic, spiritual approach to the place where Jimi returned after the 1970 Isle of Wight Festival, and tragically choked to death on his own vomit – or, more accurately, on a couple of ounces of damp white powder and some carroty bits.

In Paris, the arrows to Jim Morrison's grave in Père Lachaise Cemetery start at the end of the Eurostar platform. At Gracelands, just follow the queue to touch the lavatory where Elvis gagged on his liquidised hamburger. In Britain, we treat our dead heroes with much more respect – which comes as a blow if you're expecting the odd graffitied clue to where you might be looking. All things considered, and, once again, given no choice, Westbourne Crescent seems a nice place to die. An even nicer place to live, but that's rock 'n' roll. A four-storey sweep of stucco terrace curves away out of sight; twisted trees grow around railings and porticos, climbing to upper-storey balconies. The terrace backs onto a quiet, leafy garden shared with the houses from the next street. Uniform creamy stucco relaxes into subtle contrast with all the other wedding-cake colours, as is the style from Holland Park across Notting Hill to the hotel quarter of Bayswater. There's lemon, powder-blue, pink, even the odd brick-red and darker blue in the shade of great green oaks. This is where I shall picture Jimi gently strumming away eternity. Even if he was staying on the other side of the street, and really spent all his time in Ladbroke Grove getting stoned in his pyjamas.

Back on Portobello Road, the cake-icing colours of the squat, flat-roofed terracing lend the market a distinctly southern European look, which is heightened further by the bright fruit-and-veg stalls taking up three-quarters of the road's width. Looking back up the hill from the pandemonium of the market-place, the green dome on the yellow stone of St Peter's stands out against the pale-blue sky, and the scene could easily be mistaken for Lisbon – especially by someone with an at-best patchy memory of Lisbon. The whiff of oranges and incense and fish barbecuing at the roadside hint at somewhere far more exotic than a crumbling suburb in the south of England.

At Saint's tattoo studio, which presumably has no affiliation to the Salvation Army, next-door-but-one, it is possible to buy a florid inky scar in the shape of a woman taking her jeans off. NO TATTOOS ON FACE are allowed, mind, just in case you fancied a semi-clad cowgirl sitting astride your nose. If I were ever press-ganged into the navy or a real punk rock group, and were forced to have a tattoo, I think I'd plump for the classic James Bond/Sean Connery SCOTLAND FOREVER, in honour of Lesley Wallace;

possibly a cunning combination of the text and a picture of her taking her trainers off. SAFE BODY PIERCING is promised, and equally politely declined: the holes I've already got in my body cause enough problems, without adding to the list.

Incidentally, not a lot of people know that, in piercing circles, a metal stud driven clean through the penis is called a 'Prince Albert', named after the device's most famous adherent. Now that's what I call an Albert Memorial.

Hopping about in front of the defunct Electric Cinema is a cheeky dyed-green beggar, attracting record donations with the startling honesty and originality of his plea: '10p for a tab of acid, guv? Spare 10p to help me get off me head?'. He's so upbeat and smiley at the prospect of spending twelve hours trying to count his fingers, just about every passer-by is chipping in 10p. Even I chip in 10p, and I never chip in 10p. 'Cheers, only one-fifty to go now,' he smirks.

Dawdling on through the market street, I suddenly feel my heart drop. It's nothing to do with the fart sweets, the pumpkin perfume hair oil, the packets of plastic flies or the mosque alarm-clock displayed in the eyecatching window of Wong Singh Jones. I've been had! If that cheeky beggar kept up his act for a few hours, it dawns on me, he'd make himself thousands of pounds. But when I double back to see if he's still there, he's already earned his passage and left for Neptune, as good as his word, blissfully unaware that he's just passed up on the finest entrepreneurial opportunity in Rotting Hill since Richard Branson agreed to expand the business interests of his dingy, incense-dripping record-shop by pressing up a thousand copies of his drippy mate's hopeless LP, *Patchouli Smells*. (Some say the first sign of Branson's nascent business acumen was his suggestion to change the name of the electro-monstrosity to *Tubular Bells*.)

The density of CD, clothes and bead shops increases noticeably in the stretch of Portobello Market approaching the Westway motorway flyover. Rough Trade Records for indie and punk. Honest Jon's for funk. Receiver Records for Donovan and my kind of junk. Fashions change quickly in these parts: every twenty yards and every twenty minutes. Fly-posters hardly have time to dry before a fresh one is slapped in place – on the most popular walls the thickness of hundreds of layers of paper overhangs the pavement by five or six inches. In the seething clothes market forty feet beneath the motorway gutter, more suede jackets than you would ever have believed were made in the '70s are now on sale again, along with second-hand jeans, second-hand platform boots and ex-army gear. One bleary-eyed raver hold ups a microscopic stretch-lycra top, puzzling over how four square inches of material will ever cover up her belly-button *and* her Wonderbra (it won't), or whether pink, purple and red love-hearts will clash with other items her in her matchbox-sized wardrobe (yes, they will – she'll take it!). Every third stall has house music blaring and, just to add to the confusion of the mix, a freelance tambourinist is banging and rattling along with his own funky tapes. An elderly couple pop out of the crowd into the roadway, looking stunned by it all.

The market peters out among car-boot stalls as Portobello Road finally comes to an end at the Golborne Road. Foodwise and junkwise, anything you can buy on Portobello Road, you can get cheaper on Golborne Road. The Golborne Road is noticeably poor, even run-down; it's cheap, but none too cheerful. On another day I might have bought half an Oxo cube from one of the old blokes hanging around the street corners, and grabbed the chance to practise Len Deighton's authentic drug slang; but today I feel like a real sad square. My *chick*'s real tuned in to that *kick*, every time I see her she's doing a *flip*, but she's never got enough *bread* to give the *pusher*. She's real *gone*, dad; and she's never coming back . . . On another day I might have tried out one of the Portuguese and Algerian cafés, but this early in the evening they just look empty and uninviting. I console myself by imagining how the proprietor of the most lively and thriving (the only) Portuguese restaurant in London must have felt when another one opened smack-bang opposite. And then a Portuguese deli opened up next door.

My first impression, and the whole mood of the area is adversely affected by the overbearing ugliness of Trellick Tower, a sheer shadowy cliff-face of badly judged sci-fi flats, which blocks out the sky and apparently walls off the road east. The most depressing building in London would have made a fitting home for the area's most famous resident, Keith Talent, Martin Amis's vision of the Working-Class British Male.

Keith Talent is an Oxford Street con-artist, a rapist, a drunkard, an adulterer and a wife- and child-beater. What's worse, he wipes his mouth with the back of his hand. Keith Talent drinks, dirty-deals and darts in the fictional Black Cross pub on the Portobello Road –

in fact not a million miles from the Warwick Castle, long recognised as a centre for anti-social music, anti-social pies and unmentionable personal habits. I follow in Keith's fictional footsteps and drop in for a pint. Martin Amis had TV AND DARTS painted across the door of his own personal hell-hole – to which was tacked a piece of cardboard, adding AND PIMBALL. At half-past five on Friday, the Warwick is already full of smoke, slumming Hillbillies, teenage women shouting at their children, and old black barflies wearing an optimistic assortment of post-Rasta headgear. The paintwork is brown. The noticeboard carries a yellowing advert for 'Cleaning Services', and a police missing persons poster. A regular is bartering with the barmaid for his pint of snakebite: he stumbles away, and she shrugs at me.

Behind the counter is a sign with today's date on it, advertising PHYSCO NITE – 'Come Prepared Come Dressed'. Added as an afterthought, in the same mauve felt-pen, is a note: 'I must be mad, no H'.

Psycho Nite at the Warwick Castle. How will they ever know who's come as themselves, and who's in fancy-dress? Fifty years ago, the notorious necrophile mass-murderer John Christie went about his grisly work on other side of Ladbroke Grove. But Christie worked as a projectionist in the Electric Cinema, just along Portobello Road. And I'm sure I remember a scene in the film *10 Rillington Place* where Richard Attenborough is the life and soul of his local pub pool team . . .

In truth, the dangers of the Black Cross were somewhat exaggerated by Amis, himself one of the regular window 'crowd' up at the arty 'dentist's surgery' gastrodome. By the time my mate Pat turns up, I'm happily lying about my local status to anyone who'll listen, including one young rasta who assures me I've got the wrong end of the stick about Trellick Tower. He says the sci-fi flats are literally out of this world – split-level wonders of optimistic '70s architecture, with built-in tigerskin rugs – 'like *tartal* luxury'. Pat tells me about the time he sat next to Timothy Spall on a flight to Spain. They got on like an illegally sub-divided house on fire, both being true Notting Hill locals. Yes, it's true: now I'm being asked to believe that *film-stars* used to live in DeathStar Tower.

Pat has really earned his spurs as a true local Portobello fellow. Apart from the incidental geographical advantage of living just around the corner, he makes a living as a techno DJ and *recording artiste*. Alas, he won't listen to the arguments for dying his hair green.

As the market closes down, the pub begins to fill up with the whole range of street-traders, and shoppers with bulging bags of knock-out bargains. The origins of a rough-and-ready market first appeared in this area as long ago as 1837, when the ill-fated Hippodrome racecourse was opened. Unfortunately for the gentlemanly racegoers, a public footpath across the land allowed an invasion of hawkers, gypsies and thieves. Locals opposed the fencing-off of such a large area of private land, but resented the influx of the few gypsies even more. By the 1870s, they were trading horses and herbs on the farm track leading from Notting Hill Gate (which served to keep the riff-raff out of Royal Kensington) to the Porto Bello farm, and before the end of the century, regular Saturday-night markets were being held, lit by flaming naphtha lamps.

Disputes over local status. Racial tension. Rich rubbing shoulders with poor. Night life. Just last year Portobello Road hit the headlines when James Christie – no relation to the mass-murderer, but brother of Olympian Linford – was shot dead in the street, allegedly over the trading of herbs. Some things never change.

Before the start of the Physco Disco, we head out into the street to take up one of Notting Hill's famous foodie options. There's no backtracking to the Portuguese and North African cafés on Golborne Road, even if they are haunts of the international jet-set. By now, the Spanish supermarket and Falafel King will be shut. The last time we met up, I suffered a brainstorm and dragged Pat out for a cut-price Chinese buffet – 'All you can eat for £4.50' – which turned out to be approximately fifteen pence worth of onions, curry powder and hollow spring rolls. Chinese is off the menu tonight. Pat votes for the Malaysian-Thai café, wedged under the Westway, but it's closed for a refurb. Walking back up Portobello Road, we call in on a West Indian sidestreet café, but it's also shut. Along the road, a premium selection of new bistros, brasseries and bijou butteries are open for business, but I don't much fancy nouvelle medallions of panda in celery gazpacho. Any fool knows July isn't panda season.

On the subject of food, it's only a couple of months till Notting Hill Carnival time. Now, I know the initial idea behind the Carnival was to fight back against the racist attacks of 1958, when busloads of teddy-boys and common-or-garden white pinheads poured into the area to assert their superiority with crepe soles and brick-ends. In 1959, a few church-hall events and a Trinidadian-style parade were designed to build a sense of community and pride in the local black neighbourhood. In 1965, Carnival took to the streets, and began to take off on giant glittery butterfly wings. Over a million people every year now cram into the streets around the three-mile carnival route. It's still dominated by London's Afro-Caribbeans, but it has been allowed to grow into a brilliantly non-exclusive event. Carnival weekend is all about elaborately costumed, face-painted kids waving from flatbed trucks, while their parents dance through the streets for ten hours solid; it's about the sound of a thousand whistles being blasted in your ear; giddying waves of techno and reggae and calypso hammering from floats. It's about flung-open windows and overflowing balconies. And I don't just mean the annual tabloid front-page shot of a gulping bobby peering from between the voluminous breasts of a Carnival Queen.

But what about the *food*?

At Carnival weekend, there's nothing quite as satisfying as commandeering enough room for one buttock on somebody's garden wall, and digging into a big plateful of bony curried goat with peas and rice. Ooh, the smell of sweetcorn and banana, fresh from the barbecue. Home-made patties and saltfish fritters. Jerked chicken. Ackee and dumplings. All washed down with Sea Moss: that's non-alcoholic Guinness made out of seaweed, which, not surprisingly, tastes better than it sounds . . .

I can't possibly come to the cosmopolitan cooking-pot of Notting Hill and end up eating some time-honoured English staple like *curry* or *pizza* or *pasta* or a *burger*.

I've got to sample something foreign, something exotic and *strange*.

Flicking in desperation through my *Let's Go: London* guide, we hit upon the perfect solution:

'It's disturbing to watch your meal dumped in a vat of boiling oil,' warns a queasily disbelieving American gourmet, 'but the final product is ample consolation . . .'

An authentically exotic Greek treat will fit the bill perfectly.

It's got to be fish 'n' chips at my old favourite, Mr Costa's on the Gate.

10 Bull and Bush

When I'm doorstep day-tripping, I like to throw myself into the deep end of London: why make do with climbing some isolated chunk of history when you can combine a West End elevator trip with a fountain dip, a casino cruise and a picnic with a soldier with a bear's bum on his head? There's so much textbook London to track down and tick off, I always tend to head where the pandas and the palaces come thick and fast – which does mean the singular charms and curiosities of the outlying boroughs can be overlooked. Orton's Islington. Royal Crouch End. Harry Enfield.

Then there's the Sunday afternoon sensations along the river at Richmond. Dreamy Kew Gardens. The Windsor Castle Experience. I've heard Weston-super-Mare is worth a visit . . .

So today, in the interests of balance, I'm taking a trip to Shepherd's Bush.

A couple of months ago, I read a short *Evening Standard* lowdown on the Bush, which wrote it off as an area 'with characteristics, but no character'. That was *harsh*. The brimming strip of market, the noisy Aussie and Irish pubs and the overshadowing presence of the BBC were all mentioned in dispatches; but the terrific pop-art sheep grazing over the subway entrances must have somehow escaped the reporter's attention, and nowhere near enough was made of Shepherd's Bush's place not a million miles from somewhere fairly close to the heart of entertainment history.

Shepherd's Bush is an *unspectacular* swathe of west London, neither as groovy as Notting Hill nor as desirable as Holland Park and Kensington to the east. Bushians who live in the west of the district claim to live in chi-chi Chiswick – *Jayne Mansfield* opened their single-lane Meccano flyover – or Ravenscourt Park, at the very least. Meanwhile, near-neighbours living in the east of Acton have been known to talk up their address as 'virtually Shepherd's Bush'. For the past three years I've lived with Lesley Wallace in sunny Acton Vale, *right on the border* – and only two minutes' walk from a corner of Acton that locals almost justifiably think of as Chiswick. To the south, Hammersmith basks in the glamour of backing up to the river, while the Bush huddles, unassuming, around its threadbare triangle of green.

The Bush has towerblocks, but it isn't inner-city. It has endless streets of Edwardian villas, but it isn't exactly sitcom suburbia. Proximity to the Beeb keeps property prices high, while White City is one of the biggest pre-war council estates in Britain.

Shepherd's Bush is average. But, in London, even average can have its moments.

Fast-food outlets crowd the northern side of the triangular green, leading down to the Central Line Tube station in the neck of the funnel, and the Shepherd's Bush roundabout, the stopper. A few yards on from the station stands a huge stucco concrete arch: the old façade of a disused cinema, yes; but also the original front entrance for the 1908 Franco-British Exhibition and Olympic Games! The *Olympic Games* were held in Shepherd's Bush! Up until recently, White City Stadium was still (partly) in use as a 50,000-capacity dog track; now it's the site of a new BBC annexe. If you walk from the Green toward BBC TV Centre, you can still see the 'ghost' Tube station of Wood Lane, where less-than-Olympian Exhibition-goers were ferried on a special loop of track built out from the Central Line station. Grown men with jotters can often be seen taking rubbings of its painted-over sign, and shedding a specialist tear.

The western end of Shepherd's Bush Green provides a potted history of mass entertainment in Greater London. The Empire was built in 1903, one of the Stoll-Moss chain of theatres strung across the capital to quench the public's insatiable thirst for music hall. In its early years, audiences enjoyed the antics of Fred Karno's Fun Factory troupe, whose number included Charlie Chaplin and Stan Laurel. In wartime, rafters were regularly raised and home fires kept burning by local London legends Flanagan and Allen, Vera Lynn and Max 'the Cheeky Chappie' Miller. Bear in mind, by this time the music hall didn't offer any unofficial extras in the orchestra stalls: people just used to come *for the jokes.* Plaster angels still strum, peep and percuss on the balcony beneath the Empire's château cupola, but the innocent charm of the great pre-war variety acts is wasted on modern ears. All together now: 'My Hat's a Brown 'Un.' See?

As early as 1906, the threat of cinema sprang up right next door to the Empire. Along the length of the alleyway at the side of the tile-faced Walkabout Bar, an original price-list is still set in stone:

'CINEMATOGRAPH THEATRE – CONTINUOUS PERFOR-MANCE – SEATS 1/- 6d & 3d.' In the era of mass cinema, the tiny Cinematograph was put out of business, dwarfed by the hulking hangar of the Pavilion, which in turn grew up next door. When the popularity of TV dictated that oversize picture-houses should convert *en masse* into Top Rank Big Bingo parlours – MEMBERS ONLY, MEMBERSHIP FREE – the Empire took over as the new cinema on the block. Then its lease passed to the BBC, and it became the TV Theatre, where the *Wogan* chat-show was filmed three nights per week in its '80s heyday. How did *that* ever happen? And now the Empire has turned full circle, and reverted to a thriving music venue. Forthcoming attractions include Cockney Rebel, New Model Army and a Queen tribute band . . . all the ingredients, in fact, for Civil War II.

Around the corner in Goldhawk Road, the atmosphere of Shepherd's Bush Market spills into the street. African and Arabian textile shops abound; shopfronts are split in two to save space and spondoolicks, and interspersed among the typically exotic bills of fare is some classic London cuisine. Mid-afternoon, and it's buzzing at Harris's CaféRest. According to a menu untouched for years by foodie fashion, a choice of boiled bacon or braised liver with boiled potatoes and cabbage is just £3.10. Spam fritters, chips and peas come in at £2.70. Home-made jam roll and custard is 70p. I'm sorely tempted, only I've promised myself to another. With more old-fashioned greasy spoons per yard than any other shopping street in London, the Goldhawk Road is paradise for the more sedentary shopper. I haven't even glanced in a shop window before I'm queueing up at the counter of Cooke's caff, over the road.

Cooke's is the only traditional pie 'n' mash shop I've come across in all of west London, surely vindicating the modest boast on Mrs Cooke's badge: PROBABLY THE BEST. As if that weren't sufficient to get the Londonometer rumbling in anticipation, Cooke's was also Phil Daniels' nosherie of choice in *Quadrophenia*. The choice is simple, unchanged since 1899: pies, mash and eels are available in quantities divisible by one, and something called 'liquor' will be slopped all over unless the slopper is expressly told to hold her fire. That's what the sign says. The couple in front of me order double pie, double mash (him) and pie, mash and eels (her).

Mrs Cooke nods at the sidelined queue of diners, and explains,

'We're waitin' fer ve eels to come up.'

To come up to the boil? To come slithering up the stairs? To come up on the football pools? These are exciting moments for a stewed eel virgin.

When the bucket of boiling eels have been brought up from the basement kitchen, and have been ceremonially tipped into their stainless-steel sink behind the counter, the liquor-slopper gets on with her eel and pie backlog. I sit at Phil's free table amid pushchairs and pensioners, casually open up my newspaper, and risk a peek at my meal. One big dollop of mash. One smallish pie. A good half-dozen sections of stewed eel . . . And liquor is *parsley sauce*! Why didn't they say so? At last the gloomy brown tiling and pale green paintwork make sense: the whole shop is cannily designed to make any passer-by think *pie 'n' liquor* . . . I'll 'ave a bit of that.

Stewed eels are, if anything, even more of an *acquired taste* than their jellied cousins. As a loyal cockney, I'd describe the taste as *subtle* – not unlike slightly fishy parsley sauce.

The Who's *Quadrophenia* LP was all about a spotty herbert with a motor-scooter, so the film version was always going to be my favourite of 1979. Quite coincidentally, it's brilliant: a London classic; a rights-of-passage classic, and a stylish put-down of youth-cult herd mentality (I missed that message on my first five viewings). What's more, the pre-Brighton Bank Holiday scenes are all set around Shepherd's Bush, the Who's early-'60s stamping ground. The Goldhawk Club. Cooke's pie shop. Saturday-shopping cuppas, swapping party rumours. There's even a mod-rocker rumble with Ray 'Scum' Winstone in the dingy confines of the alleyway that's better known in these parts as the market-place.

The Who add up to a major portion of sunny Acton's local mythology, of which I am inexplicably proud: Pete Townshend, Roger Daltrey and John Entwistle went to school at Acton Grammar. Lionel Bart, *Oliver!*'s composer and lyricist, lives over on the other side of Acton Park. The George and Dragon in the High Street is one of several hundred London pubs with alleged Dick Turpin connections. It gets better: just along the Vale from our house is a thrilling blue plaque which marks the one-time residence of a Royal Navy Paymaster General! And right on our street lives the actor who once played MacGregor, the black Scottish head-case out of *Porridge*. Beat that, Brentford.

Having read *Reed All About Me* – Oliver Reed's autobiography, needless to say – at a dangerously impressionable age, any mention of the Who's drummer Keith Moon still plagues me with disturbing images of the first meeting between London's top two hellraisers. Note: I have since learned that 'hellraising' isn't big and it certainly isn't clever. Any man who feels it necessary to perform a handstand on the bar after drinking his own weight in lager needs psychiatric help – not my secret, pathetic respect.

'Hi! I'm Ollie Reed!' shouted Ollie, pissed as usual, as he burst in through Moonie's hotel door.

'Hi! I'm Keith Moon!' replied Keith, slightly muffled, from the bottom of a pyramid of jiggling groupies. 'Let's have a drink!'

The shanty-town shops and stalls of Shepherd's Bush market cling to the curve of the overhead Hammersmith and City Line between Goldhawk Road and Shepherd's Bush's second tube station. The grander shops hunker down in the railway arches themselves, obscured by a long row of semi-permanent lean-tos, all leaning hopefully on each other. On the other side of the narrow tarmac track, every clapboard garden shed manages to stock about five normal shopfuls of pots and pans, Irish country and calypso cassettes, nylon fashions and fruit and veg.

You know you're in a proper London market at Shepherd's Bush, because there's a kitchen table set up for a lippy chancer to demonstrate his ingenious patent vegetable-peeler-cum-tomato-zigzagger-cum-masher-grater-dishwasher. As seen on TV. And people are readily handing over their money. Not seven-pahnd-fifty or four-pahnd-fifty. Not one-pahnd-fifty. Not any-pahnd-fifty. And so on.

At the Goldhawk Road end of the market is a flattened demolition site called 'Steptoe's Yard' – ANY ENQUIRIES ASK ALBERT OR HAROLD . . . and then a phone number, obscured with black paint. The BBC's sitcom rag-and-bone men, *Steptoe and Son*, lived in a Shepherd's Bush junkyard on Oil Drum Lane, mercifully fictitious. This was the screenwriters Galton and Simpson's little in-joke, to set their plague-infested rubbish tip in the Beeb's own backyard. More insidious evidence of the BBC's presence in the Bush used to crop up on *Match of the Day*: all of my schoolmates who used to kick around at playtime were up in arms at how regularly Queen's Park Rangers were shown, especially when other London matches were called off. At the time, the bias was as inexplicable as it was scandalous.

As the mistimed volley flies, QPR's Loftus Road ground is all of two hundred yards from the back of TV Centre: a single zoom-lens stuck out of the DG's office window, and the programme was saved.

An early black-and-white series of *Steptoe and Son* is being rerun at the moment, and it's showing its age: people nowadays don't give their junk away to professional litter-sifters, they come along to Steptoe's Yard themselves and try to sell it out of their own car boot.

Honestly, the things people refuse to throw out. The things people *buy*: half-empty pots of make-up; broken music-centres; souvenirs of other people's holidays in Bracklesham Bay. Napoleon must have imagined he was taking *le pi-pi* when he called the seafaring English a nation of shopkeepers. Now we're a nation of car-booters. At least, those of us with jinxed Lottery numbers are car-booters.

I spend an hour clocking up absurdities, manfully discussing the merits of various defunct power-tools, picking sniffily through LPs retrieved from the bottom of budgie-cages, and feeling guilty at the good-spirited desperation of it all. But how about these *bargains*? – a packet of ten stolen razor-heads, on sale at two quid; a plastic Piccadilly Circus ashtray, only slightly singed; a rare 'Corkette' pump-action bottle-opener, complete with instruction leaflet and all its original packaging. In retrospect, hardly a promising selling point for a twenty-year-old miracle labour-saver. Which, I later discover, doubles up as an explosive needle-bomb.

Still, not bad for ten bob.

I walk out of the northern end of the market into Uxbridge Road. This is the longer way round to where I've dumped the car in Lime Grove, but it's worth it to pay a visit to my favourite shop in Shepherd's Bush: no, not the wonderfully evocative House of Pies chippery, but Meldrum's the Bakers. As usual, I call in for a large bloomer loaf and one of those 'Craftsmen Baked in Fulham', advertised so prominently. Oh, you should see the look on those jolly cockernee faces.

In Lime Grove, the only sign of one of London's best-known film studios is now in the name of a cul-de-sac of new flats: Gaumont Terrace. Open for business as early as 1913, Gaumont Studios was five storeys tall, with a glass front and roof to provide plenty of daylight for illumination. When British film production was scaled

up in the Golden Age of the '30s, the industry gradually left behind
its glasshouses, its converted roller-skating rinks and dancehalls and
moved to new studios in the countryside west of London. Ealing,
Pinewood, Shepperton, Elstree: not only did the new studios offer
space; they were also clear of the smog which normally blanketed
central and east London. Twentieth Century-Fox eventually sold on
Lime Grove to the BBC as a ready-made production unit. By the time
Doctor Who was shot here in the '60s, electric light had been
invented, but they were still using scenery and props made out of
egg-boxes and old cereal packets.

It's time to pick up Lesley Wallace from her own particular branch
of the BBC's London Dream Factory, the North Acton Costume
Store.

Actors call this regulation '70s office block 'the Acton Hilton',
but then most of them are wicked ironists. Facilities are basic across
the costume warehouse floors and upstairs in the rehearsal rooms, as
befitting a workshop where programmes are hammered together
from raw materials; where dramas are first enacted and punchlines
tested out to the echo of bare walls; where characters are created,
drilled and dressed before they're sent out to be shot for your
viewing pleasure.

Having picked up my 'Visitor' badge from reception, I take the lift
up to the third floor. Captain Peacock grunts and I nod as we cross on
the threshold.

'Uuh-uh,' he grunted – *Captain Peacock*, the real, live pompous
floorwalker out of *Are You Being Served?* He grunted at *me* – the same
grunt and raised eyebrow that hailed each and every addition to
Lloyd and Croft's 'Mrs Slocum's Pussy' canon back in the '70s. The
man is a legend, of a sort.

When LA hooker Divine Brown was interviewed after her
remunerative kerbside ordeal with Hugh Grant, she went on record as
saying, 'I knew he was English 'cos he sounded like Captain Peacock.
We have *Are You Being Served?* on *Classics Theater* . . .'

This is the kind of run-of-the-mill thrill they're conditioned to
taking for granted at the Acton Hilton. These costumiers, set-
hammerers and prop-pickers are too close to the job. When they're
busy mythmaking, they imagine they're just dressing up an actor as
a Jane Austen hero, as a seven-foot-tall slice of cake or a grumpy, ex-
army shop assistant. From inside the Dream Factory, the autograph-

hunters and gentle stalkers on the pavement outside seem almost *extreme*.

Lesley Wallace is the costume department's Queen of Light Entertainment. On TV, you can always tell one of her LE costumes apart from the standard period gear: LE goes a step or six beyond stodgy old *realism*. Realism is *easy*. Example: when one of the BBC's acknowledged comic geniuses – let's say Russ Abbot – appears in a football sketch, he can't possibly wear a regular shirt and shorts: not *funny* enough. Not *football* enough. And so, Russ will be suitably attired in LE football kit. Cavernous, baggy shorts. Odd-sized boots. A big stripy shirt, spattered with LE stage-mud and handprints. He turns round, and his number's on upside-down. Now that's *funny*.

In true LE style, Lesley Wallace's left hand is tattooed today with a mysterious blue biro message: NIPPLES. Go on then, Sherlock, pick the bones out of that one. Logically enough, it transpires that one of the nipples has fallen off her LE gorilla-suit, and NIPPLES is a reminder to bring her glue-gun from home, so she can stick on the patent drag-artiste's nipple she's painted specially to match.

All in a day's work.

The LE costume store reminds me of nothing so much as a walking tour through a quick succession of old *Carry On* films. Outside Pantoland, these shelves full of paste-jewelled turbans could only ever have been worn by Kenneth Williams' Khasi of Kalibar in *Carry On Up the Khyber*: Englishness personified. One big box is labelled HAREM BRA TOPS. All that's missing is the cackle of Sid James's laugh. Moving easily from east to west – just two corridors over – I find a hairy monster's foot from *Carry On Screaming*, a Carnaby Street punk, and a whole set of LE Pearly King suits, awaiting the next emergency comic callout for *Carry On London*. Lesley Wallace pulls out Ronnie Barker's LE Beefeater's coat. A whole rail of red and black, for a child-sized LE changing of the guard. A drag-artiste's Queen Mother costume. Gawd bless 'er.

I can't resist slipping on the jacket of the electric pink LE Sergeant Pepper uniform, topping off the effect with an oversize, over-fluffy LE bearskin busby: Mr LE London, 'imself. I love the idea of all these visual short-cuts; these stock characters ready at hand to prop up a harmless stereotype or provide the butt of some prehistoric joke. After all, how are you supposed to recognise a TV cockney unless he's sewn 50,000 buttons onto his trousers? Unless, of course, he's wearing an LE used-car dealer's sheepskin jacket, or singing 'Dahn at ve Old Bull and Bush' . . .

Strangely, the period costume departments are hardly less confusing than LE. Blackadder's frock-coat hangs comfortably alongside serious costume dramas' serious costume knickerbockers. Fun Queen Bess's dresses dangle amid a sadistically sensible array of stays and bustles, paniers and fontages. Whatever one of them is.

In 1910-to-date, Lesley Wallace pulls out a blowsy barmaid's barmaid-blouse, as once worn by Angie Watts in *EastEnders*.

It looks real enough to me.

Instead of walking into BBC TV Centre through the entrance under its familiar bulbous façade, staff and visitors are now ushered through a new reception hall grafted onto the side of the building. After a five-minute walk following an empty connecting corridor through a maze of doors and right-angles, you're back where you would have started, at the hub of this whirling, ever-expanding complex.

Not a lot of people know that the bulging belly of TV Centre's façade is, in fact, the only outwardly visible section of a complete, cylindrical office block. Like the Post Office Tower, TVC is a triumph of positive self-assurance: when it was started in 1955, television was just about to take off and take over, with the BBC in the role of the nation's educator, entertainer and moral guardian. No matter whether the futuristic hula-hoop design was practical; whether the seven outlying studios actually needed to be clustered so tightly around the Inner Circle of management and production offices: the building is a beautiful symbol of its age. The possibility of any future need to change, to expand or specialise, were confidently ignored. Mosaics and tiles shimmer in shades between the faded parsley and pale soupy green of Mrs Cooke's famous liquor. In the centre of the circle, thrust up toward the heavens from the fat barrel of the Beeb, is Helios – the Greek god of getting stuck naked up a pole with a tambourine.

Under the controllership of John Birt, controversial strides are being made to wipe out the BBC's various historical legacies, and to prepare Auntie for the impending age of digital TV. Critics complain that the Beeb should simply concentrate on what it's good at: making quality TV programmes. But what do *they* know? So far, Birt has sold off healthy departments, increased management salaries, and spent a comical amount of other people's money on a new corporate logo, which is the same as the old one. A broad new band of middle-management strategists, co-ordinators and consultants has been whisked in to replace those terribly old-fashioned producers, directors, writers, designers and technicians, who, quite frankly, were trouble.

Birt's response to the outdated innocence of TV Centre has been to build a new entrance hall – and to excavate a suite of offices in the Helios fountain. I kid you not. It's anybody's guess how long the Corporation will survive under the knife of this medieval cosmetic surgeon.

On the internal noticeboard, almost buried among the latest Birtian invitations to reskill, rethink and/or resign, is a plea to all staff to spend next Tuesday lunchtime on the seventh-floor balcony overlooking Helios's roost, cheering and waving as Alexei Sayle chases the Director of BBC1 around the Inner Circle with a big stick.

We trail up the open-plan mosaic stairs, and complete a circuit-and-a-half of the second-floor viewing galleries – in itself a potent argument against office blocks with circular corridors. There's nothing cooking under the banks of spotlights hanging in the gloom of the warehouse studios. The rib-tickling interior of a sitcom semi is hidden away behind plywood walls on one studio floor (*hahahahahahahahahaha*). In another, a red chat-show sofa peeps through a suspended scaffold canopy of lights, monitors, booms and fat, creeping cables. CLAP. WHOOP. CHEER. PLEASE?

I can't resist continuing upstairs to the rooftop, just so I'll be able to hang TVC's scalp on my tourist belt alongside those of The Monument, St Paul's and the Tower. The *Post Office* Tower, that is.

The last time I dropped by the BBC bar, the fourth-floor reception area was hung with a rogues' gallery of publicity mugshots featuring all the giants of the BBC's Light Entertainment programming: Noel Edmonds; the Two Ronnies; Les Dennis and Dustin Gee – the latter of whom, even then, had been dead for two years. Slick new superstar portraits – Dale Winton, from *Supermarket Sweep*; the woman off *The Lottery Show*; purple Teletubby – now line the walls as you follow the endlessly unfolding curve of the corridor in search of some corporate hospitality.

The BBC bar used to figure high in my Top 100 favourite London places – 72 of which, I must confess, are licensed. Something of the air of a gentleman's club used to pervade the original two-tier bar, with its teak fittings and deep leather settees set out on the lower level. Everyone from technicians and newsreaders to off-site employees, Top of the Poppers and scruffy, high-powered BBC lifers used to use the bar as an extension of their own offices, to wind down after a show, or just before one. But ever since a recent wave of reforms, it has been made illegal to refer to the bar simply as 'the bar'. The bar is now to be known as 'Visions'. It reminds me of the sort of bar routinely installed in municipal leisure centres: a bright, shiny, angular bar, where you're invited to down a well-earned Britvic orange, and *go home*.

This is a bar built to suit a new class of trim, mono-motivated, mentally healthy employee. It's an image thing. Only Brendan the Doorman remains from the era of Dustin Gee, and he's set to retire next year. Placed under intense pressure ('Hello, Brendan'), he is apt to snap and start spilling fond reminiscences from the days when he used to call time and the punters would be queueing five-deep at the bar; when staff would dive in for an afternoon snifter, hiding from their bosses in the Members' Bar (now a nasty little gymnasium). The marvellous old school-dinner cafeteria has been swept away, too, and replaced with a food-bar with *salad* on the menu.

Ah, I remember the happy evenings when we would call by for a scoop or two of lukewarm stodge; when it seemed as if the BBC would limp on unchanged forever. Still, forcing the grand old Corporation to eat salad seems an unnecessarily hard policy decision, not exactly akin to forcing the Royal Family out of their palaces and onto council estates, but not far short of suggesting they might one day like to start paying taxes. Start shifting the ground-rules of our few remaining national institutions, and anything could happen. Anarchy could be ushered in. Compelling the BBC to eat salad is like forcing Sarah Ferguson into a too-tight mini-skirt and asking her to host an American TV chat-show. It's undignified. It's untraditional. It's modern. It's the beginning of the end.

We sit at a stripped pine table in the middle of the stripped pine floor, and pine for the old comforts. A magnificent view across west London is blocked only by the sloping roof of the adjacent annexe, ergonomically designed for the pleasure and convenience of all staff members standing over six foot four inches tall. While all the bar talk is of low morale, low pay and immovable misfits at all levels, there's still an embattled feeling of familial worth and togetherness to be sniffed in the BBC bar. Even if you're just visiting.

For all its faults, the BBC still makes programmes that no commercial company could ever hope to make. Even if the BBC is now being run like a just-pretend commercial company. That's why subsidising a national TV corporation works in everyone's favour. Even if they do get by without one in America, and in every other country in Europe.

Unlike any other TV news, BBC news is *neutral*. And the BBC makes prestigious, quality drama like *Pride and Prejudice*, and – well, *Pride and Prejudice*. *That's* what makes it worth paying the licence fee.

Quite apart from maintaining the attractively subsidised bar prices here at 'Visions'.

Lesley Wallace refuses to be budged as I pester her for a BBC anecdote to end all BBC anecdotes. I want to hear an anecdote with star quality; an anecdote dripping with multi-purpose nostalgia; a story about the nature of fame, about dressing up . . . a *London* story.

But Lesley Wallace's long proximity to celebrities in underwear has made her virtually impervious to everyone else's fascination with the stars fully clothed. Obviously, she could drop names and trade secrets into any conversation, but her lofty professional standards ensure she upholds the corporate principle of neutrality, and respects the privacy of her clients.

So, anyway – one lunchtime, Lesley Wallace was sitting eating her jam roly-poly and congealed custard at the Acton Hilton, along with all the other costumiers and wardrobe assistants, when an excited yet professionally detached whisper went about the canteen: 'Look out – it's Del-boy and Rodney . . .'

The stars of *Only Fools and Horses* collect their school dinners, sit down and get on with the business of their rehearsal break. No big deal.

Until an excited yet professionally detached whisper emanates from Del-boy and Rodney's table . . .

'Look out! It's *Joan Collins* . . .'

11 Hotel on Mayfair: £10,000!?!

Spotted . . . The clerk on the front desk has noticed me lurking suspiciously between reception's potted palms and the cool marble hall where afternoon-tea is being served. She's giving me a helpful smile, encouraging me to surrender with good grace. I might be a billionaire, after all. It's so hard to tell, these days.

'Just having a look around, okay?' The excuses I've prepared earlier vie for preference, only now they all sound decidedly limp: I'm meeting a friend; I'm Lord Somebody-or-other's butler; I'm on a top-secret government mission, so *please* keep your voice down when you call over the porter to kick me out in the street . . . But the Dorchester receptionist has already said yes, of course, that'll be fine.

'Thank you. Sorry.' I perform an awkward curtsy as I step away, and kick over a briefcase and a tubular package cleverly balanced two inches behind my heels by a bona fide hotel guest. 'Sorry. Thank you . . .' I crouch away and melt into an armchair in the sepia lantern-light of the tea-lounge, and sit with my knees together, grinning in intense appreciation of the piano floorshow.

The pianist seems to be having a contest with the tea-sippers to see who can tinkle the quieter: him crouched over his joanna playing a stilted ragtime 'Death March'; or them cutting edible niblets from their crustless cucumber sandwiches. Hushed whispers float out of the pink-and-gilt gloom. I pretend to study the menu, but quickly put it down when a waiter in full tails shows signs of getting attentive. When he isn't looking, I hook over to my side of the table the small green box of souvenir Dorchester matches, then transfer it to my right palm and – cough – into my shirt pocket. Unfortunately, my diversionary throat-clearing is sufficient to attract the attention of the lizard-reflexed waiter, who is hovering in my direction by the time the matches have hit the bottom of my pocket. I tell myself he couldn't *possibly* have seen . . . and begin working out a way to put the matches back.

When the waiter swoops on an unsuspecting oldster leafing through the *Daily Mail*, I escape and pretend to run an eye over the hotel tariff. Relaxing just a fraction, I take in a few of the numbers I'm reading. One night's kip in the rooftop Terrace Garden Suite costs a cool £1,968.13. That price *does* cover VAT, but I can't find any mention of celebrity massage facilities, six months' free family shopping vouchers, or takeaway mini-bar access for everyone you've ever known. For two grand, I expect they throw in tea and cornflakes, and don't make you unpack your luggage to check for stolen soap.

A green-toppered doorman gives the revolving door a shove a fraction of a second before my hand alights on it, and I'm jettisoned into the noise and daylight of Park Lane. We exchange our mutual thanks and apologies, and I keep walking. The heat of the sun tickles as it dries the sweat on my back, and eventually I find I'm able to unclench my buttocks.

I turn left down Curzon Street, cutting through the sedate streets of money-laden Mayfair, the W1 address which became fashionable with the migration of Soho aristos in the eighteenth century. This is *Upstairs, Downstairs* and *Forsyte Saga* territory, beloved of every fan of Galsworthy, not to mention Thackeray and that other hidebound Victorian Trollope. Cutting through to Piccadilly, I pass down Half Moon Street, whose smart terraces' most celebrated inhabitant is Bertie Wooster, closely followed, as ever, by his butler and master, Jeeves. When the Roaring '20s ticked over into the Flirty '30s, Wooster would doubtless have heartily approved of taking tea at the brand new Dorchester, flanked by the last of the spiffing flappers. I don't know whether the ritual itself has changed very much over the years – the mothballed surroundings and clientèle certainly haven't – but I can't help thinking Bertie would have been stuck for jolly japes today, what-ho! More larks to be had at Crockford's on Curzon Street, provided Aunt Agatha can be persuaded to foot the bill. At this most élite of London's gambling clubs, gentlemen have been cashing in cheques for chips and chips for fresh air since Regency times. William Crockford founded the club in 1827, when gambling was first a craze in Mayfair and St James's; but he never succeeded in upsetting the odds so spectacularly as on the day he died – of a broken heart, after his horse had been beaten by a ringer in the Derby.

Walking up the incline of Piccadilly, with all the space and shimmering plane trees of Green Park to your right, the crushing weight of old money and crumbling stone lie dead ahead: the Edwardian *faux*-château of the Ritz Hotel on the corner of the park, then the great defensive pillars of Barclays Bank, the Royal Academy, and 'top people's stores' like Simpson's, and Fortnum and Mason's. Not content with tiptoeing between hotels on the plush purple squares of Park Lane and Mayfair, I'm now going to drop in on a knot of institutions a hundred times more exclusive: London's gentlemen's clubs. *The New London Spy* provides a guide to these last outposts of privilege, all-male games and gossip, but isn't so common as to print their full addresses. Black-ball offence, and all that. On the top stretch of St James's Street, I soon identify the clubs – they're the buildings with doormen and no nameplates – but can't decide which is which. Terribly bad show, getting your Brooks's confused with your Boodle's. Hanging offence in certain circles.

As is the case with 99 per cent of impossibly obscure London facts, Louise Nicholson comes up with the goods in the microscopic print of her 400-page *Definitive Guide to London*. Want to know who lived in any house in the metropolis in 1876? Want to find out the symbolic importance of the stuffed hippopotamus held aloft by the Thames watermen in the Lord Mayor's parade? Need a good stiletto cobbler in the vicinity of Goodge Street? Best consult Louise. Her guide is 'the essential manual for everyone visiting or living in London' – provided they don't mind wading through whole pages of unedited, comprehensive, *definitive* facts before finding the one they're looking for. Like the addresses of Boodle's and White's. Or the fact that the gambling room of the latter was once known as Hell. And they still keep books full of the crazy bets accepted here. Like the £3,000 Lord Arlington once wagered on two raindrops racing down a window-pane. And the fact that Louise doesn't know whether he won or not – otherwise she'd have said.

The various clubs on St James's and Pall Mall attract different types of member. Some were originally services- or politically-based, and carry through the tradition; others are favoured by actors or horse-owners or academics. Generally, it seems rich old men join gentlemen's clubs in order to ignore a better class of person, or else to drink too much and reminisce about public-school floggings, jam roly-poly and Edwardian adventures up the Nile Delta. The first club I approach is Boodle's, a dark brick Georgian block with a sunny arched window on the first floor. A ground-floor bow window is open, and from the pavement red leather armchairs are visible in a dingy drawing-room. I'm up on the railings, craning to locate the source of a clatter of cutlery, when a doorman appears and issues an unambiguous piece of advice. First impressions count in clubland, and even a servant's word still counts for something, so I abandon my plans to join Boodle's seventy-year waiting-list for membership and pass on up the hill to White's at numbers 37–38, the most aristocratic and prestigious of all the clubs. From over the road, I can see the chandeliers above the gaming tables in Hell (Hell, on the first floor?) and the portrait of the ultimate clubman dandy, Beau Brummell, who once reduced the Prince Regent to tears when he criticised the unfashionable flounciness of his cravat.

Ian Fleming usually lunched at Boodle's because he 'liked dull clubs', and was put off White's because the members 'gassed too much'. In fiction, he made M, the head of the Secret Service, a member of Blade's, an approximate amalgamation of the two clubs. James Bond appreciated the clubbish touches of an ironed newspaper and freshly minted change, and approved of the discreet arrangement which could occasionally magic a fresh young waitress to a member's room. This provision was far too civilised (and the fictional members far too well *connected*) to be considered as prostitution, which has, of course, never been a service on offer at any real London club. Clubbers are good fellows, with firm, dry handshakes. Decent sorts. In *Moonraker*, M alerts Bond to the possibility of impending national catastrophe. Never mind that Hugo Drax is a psychotic, disfigured ex-Nazi hell-bent on dropping an A-bomb on Betty Windsor's back garden – the man is a member of Blade's, and he's suspected of *cheating at cards* . . .

Fuelled by champagne, whisky and an envelope of Home Office benzedrine, Bond is given further special dispensation in Hell to cheat back in the name of a greater justice, and teach the un-English cad a lesson he jolly well won't forget in a hurry.

If I'm going to make it through the door into White's, I'm going to have to rethink my playground attitude. The one time I did actually make it into one of these inner sanctums of costly Conservatism, the occasion was a Christmas book club launch at the RAC Club on Pall Mall, and I was buried in a large suit borrowed from Lesley Wallace's costume store. I felt like a million dollars, and looked like a sweaty bloke fiddling with his collar and tie. In conversation with a woman stealing the nametags of semi-celebrity no-shows, she accidentally stepped back onto a dainty size eight belonging to that top political historian, Norma Major. We couldn't help sniggering, once the coast was clear. Hellish bad show. Black-ball offence, and all that.

Once I was accepted as a member of a club, I'm sure I could drink enough champagne, make enough idle boasts and ignore enough statutes to fit in. Bondish drugs and upstairs-downstairs arrangements aside, I like the idea of joining in the London Golf Match, teeing off from the steps of the United Service Club on Pall Mall, negotiating a tricky faded mashie around the dog-leg into St James's, and holing out through the door of the Berkeley. I could join the Reform Club, and jet *Around the World in 80 Days* on a fine point

of principle. I could join in the food fights at Bertie Wooster's Drones club, and put the whole lot down to *high jinks* . . .

Realistically, I don't think I'd get far, knocking on the door of White's and asking if Mr Fleming fancies a sherbet. It's as much to do with style as attitude. Not a single member batted an eye when Ronnie Kray dropped in for drinkies with his alleged lover, Lord Boothby: you could call Ron a racketeer, a thug or a plain old psychopath, but he was always *well groomed*. I knew I should have called into Trumper's, the Court barbers, back on Curzon Street. I bet they could do wonders for a hopelessly threadbare number-two cut, teasing any remaining stubble into a more clubbable short-back-and-sides, topping me off in lavender unguents, exotic oils and lotions, and generally buffing up my skull a treat. On Jermyn Street, Floris (est. 1730), perfumers to Bond and royalty alike, display the badger-arse brushes, cut-throat razors and bespoke aftershaves that could have finished the makeover. Easy on the toilet-water, mind.

Elsewhere on Jermyn Street, I earmark a bowler, a boater and a jaunty old-school cricket cap from Bates' the hatters, and a cigar-cutter in the window of Astley's the tobacconists. A fat cigar is a certain indicator of breeding and money to burn: unfortunately, they taste like smouldering rope, so the shorter the better. Across Piccadilly, under the fluttering flags of Old Bond Street's society jewellers and glovers and handbaggers, Swaine Adeney Brigg's royal warrants confirm their provision of leather goods to Prince Charles, whips to the Queen, and umbrellas to the Queen Mum. Asking no unchivalrous questions, I set my heart on a sturdy custom-built swordstick – this *must* have been where Professor Moriarty had them made – and a spiky crocodile-back briefcase from Grimaldi in the Royal Arcade, to help cement a predatory new persona. Finally, I pop along to Savile Row to bagsy my whistle and flute. Surely, no club could turn away a chappie turned out in such an eminently sensible pin-stripe from Prince Albert's own tailors . . .

And then I see it in the window at Norton and Sons (est. 1821). It's the ultimate key to universal acceptability: an authentic Roger Moore/*Sanders of the River* safari suit, complete with big shorts and a shoulder patch to prevent the old rifle doing any damage when I'm out shooting tigers in the Hindu Kush.

Clubland, here I come.

But first I have some more pressing business to attend to on Savile

Row – namely, going along to number 3, and staring up at the roof for ten minutes. I know this roof well, at least the view of it from the pavement. This is where the Beatles made their last ever public performance, occasionally dangling their hair over the dormer windows as they chugged through half-a-dozen tired numbers before having their plugs pulled by the Old Bill. In 1969, number 3 Savile Row was the headquarters of Apple Corps., an organisation fiercely devoted to squandering, giving away and misplacing those vast sums of money which were considered a source of some embarrassment to any serious love-and-peacenik. But times change. Now number 3 houses the Council of Mortgage Lenders and the Building Society Association: major breadheads, as Paul McCartney might have said at the time.

Behind the blazeries and broocheries opposite Fortnum and Mason's on Piccadilly lies one of London's least impressive squares. Instead of being centred around a shady green oasis of calm, the drab frontages of Mason's Yard look out onto a two-storey electrical substation. Originally a goods depot for the Queen's grocery store, this century has seen the yard move steadily upmarket as the art galleries clustered in the backstreets around Christie's auctioneers have overflowed into every blind alley in search of precious wall space. Mason's Yard may not be much to look at, but it was the setting for two of the '60s most influential happenings: the Scotch of St James's and Where John Met Yoko.

Given our modern mass culture of all-week, all-night dancing and drugging, it seems amazing that the germinal discotheque scene in mid-'60s London involved so very few faces, and even fewer places. Plenty of fifteen-year-old girls walked down the King's Road pretending to be on drugs, and everyone *read* about the new disco crowd, too cool for the beat clubs; but when it came around to a midweek night in the West End, most chicks were at home washing their hair and, hey, even hep-cats had to go to work tomorrow. At the time, severe doubts were raised whether there were enough regular disco-goers to support more than a couple of profitable young nitespots. The groundbreaking Ad Lib had already closed its doors by 1967, when Dolly's, on Jermyn Street, and the Scotch of St James's briefly became the In Places – if you happened to be one of London's five hundred rich, pretty or sitar-strumming In People.

According to the *Spy*, the Scotch looked 'like a Scottish roadhouse decorated by a Sassenach set designer'. The bar was see-through, built out of hundreds of empty whisky bottles. The ceiling was decorated with fake oak beams. The upholstery, wallpaper and carpets were tartan. It must have been a sight when the oil-bubble lights were playing across the walls. Especially if you'd eaten one strange Smartie over the eight.

The avant-garde Indica Gallery was next door to the Scotch of St James's. Visible from William Burroughs' window on Duke Street, it was blessed in its early days with many a visit from *Junky* Bill and his various outrageous boyfriends. Paul McCartney was involved in the gallery through his girlfriend, Jane Asher, sister of co-owner Peter Asher. Who used to be *one half of Peter and Gordon!?!* On the sly, McCartney was always the most arty and bookish of the Beatles, though it isn't exactly fashionable to listen to his protestations. He helped put up shelves before the Indica opened, and even designed and printed the wrapping-paper; but the gallery is remembered primarily not for Macca's involvement with the art world, but for John Lennon's.

Dragged along to a private viewing of the usual giant styrofoam hands and giant purple building-blocks, Lennon was naturally suspicious when a crowd of people wearing mauve cravats invited him up a step-ladder to read Yoko's microscopic message stuck to the gallery ceiling. All eyes were on him. He expected something smart and cynical, something to make him look stupid.

Instead, the message read simply, YES.

It was so much better than NOSEY PARKER or GET YOUR BLOODY HAIR CUT. Lennon was hooked.

I was thrilled to read, in a *Big Issue* clubbing column, about a multiply-abused moose-head (cigarette dangling from lips, nether-wear from antlers) which still hangs on the wall at the 'Director's Lodge Club': I'm planning a visit to unearth and lean on that invisible bar. Nowadays, there's no sign of Dolly's in the swanky basement restaurant at 57 Jermyn Street; but there's still plenty of good old-fashioned modern art bluffing its way into the gallery windows in Mason's Yard. Jane Asher is a mumsy TV cake cook.

Since Eros was shunted from centre-stage to side-show, the defining element of Circus has been strangely missing from Piccadilly. Where the traffic used to flow in a whirling vortex around the hub of the tin kid and his toy bow and arrow, there is now a shapeless log-jam within a triangle of white stone and neon bluffs. Cars flash and rev and hoot as they're sucked helplessly through the stop-start system; people squeeze out of the choked Tube exits to take a seat on the fountain steps, and just watch: it's like Piccadilly Circus around here. At least the removal of Eros onto a promontory of pavement means you're less likely, as you dive across the road, to be killed by a bus travelling at three miles-per-hour. It's one of London's unquantifiable pleasures, to sit at the heart of this organised chaos and just let it happen. The noise. The fumes. The crush. At the first grainy hint of dusk, the neon glows brighter red and green and blue. The Friday-night pulse quickens.

One of London's typical postcard punks – a German student – gestures at his girlfriend's purple spikes and net jumper, and asks if I want a photograph. For precious seconds, I toy with the idea of giving them 20p to go and stand by the railings, just so I can pinch their prime perch on the shallow pyramid – top step; clear of spray; gratifyingly warmed up – but no need. An American granny wants to be photographed sandwiched between the lovely couple. I was right about that warm spot.

Buses and taxis may no longer turn in tight circles around Eros's roundabout, but the rest of the West End still revolves around Piccadilly Circus. Looking north, the deep trench of Regent Street curves off to my left, shielding Mayfair addresses from Soho. Cab after cab stops at the Café Royal to drop off precious cargoes of poodles and hatboxes and the kind of ladies who protest at being called a woman.

The colonnaded section of Nash's Quadrant, a few yards east, was demolished in the 1850s due to the nocturnal activities of the kind of woman no one ever mistook for a lady. Under the replacement arches at the end of Regent Street, the pavement is blocked by people buying their *Standard*, flicking through *Club International* for Saucy Spice spreads, and pilfering plastic trinkets. The Piccadilly Circus newsstands are big business: one trader recently made the *News of the World* with the amazing offer, MY KIOSK IS STALL YOURS FOR £½ MILLION! Which sounded suspiciously like a twelve by three-foot pitch in Fantasyland . . . until you found out he's already turned down a bid of £200,000 for his little goldmine. High above the prime-site Angus Steak House, the amusement arcades and brilliantly lit snack-bars, a six-storey curtain of multicoloured neon veils the sins of Soho; but sleaze still seeps out of the backstreets. I can't tell the runaways and rent-boys from the regular school-trippers, or the plain-clothes cops from the perverts, but the story of their ongoing wars is a real downside to the attraction of the bright lights and the big city. COKE. McDONALD'S. SANYO. FOSTER'S. Do this. Drink that. Louder, bigger, cheaper, faster. After all, as the digital counter on the neon wall reminds us, we're all running out of time: there's only 932 DAYS LEFT to Jubilee 2000.

Up Shaftesbury Avenue, London's own mini-Broadway, Ben Elton's *Popcorn* is on at the Apollo, and Jack Dee is playing the Gielgud: I mentioned the Comedy Store regulars going on to bigger and better things, but never said anything about anyone quitting the neighbourhood. In Victorian times, Piccadilly Circus itself boasted two huge music halls. Behind the remaining corner frontage of the Pavilion lies Rock Circus, Madame Tussaud's musical offshoot. Faded, windblown effigies of David Bowie and Annie Lennox look down from the balcony. But which is which? Elvis Costello has dropped his guitar, and his tight black suit shows up the streaks of pigeon-crap. Strangely, the splashy white epaulettes quite suit Gary Glitter. Further on towards Leicester Square, the hollowed-out shell of the Trocadero Palace variety theatre, later the most luxurious of all the Lyons' Corner House tea-rooms, now houses a multi-screen cinema, Planet Hollywood, and a package of six different computerised virtualised laser-driven thrills for ten quid. This is where Lesley Wallace and her Amazonian sister, Kerry, on holiday from Hawick, took on the might of the acid-spitting insect dinosaur in Alien Wars, *and won*: it was only a wee fella in a suit. At Naomi Campbell's new Fashion Café it's possible to lunch on designer-priced lettuce, celery and spring water, and hardly feel guilty at all.

On the corner of Windmill Street, now gathered in by the spreading tentacles of the Trocadero Centre, is the former Scott's Restaurant, the favourite London restaurant of Ian Fleming. Not coincidentally, his right-hand, first-floor corner table was also frequented by Agent 007: the two shared exquisite taste, but little else. Fleming's real-life role in British espionage operations has been greatly overstated – in fact, Roy Berkeley, author of *A Spy's London*, describes him as 'an an intelligence "wannabe": he carried a commando knife and a teargas pen during WWII while working safely behind a desk in London, and subsequently encouraged people to think he'd been involved in wartime matters of great danger and drama'. The anti-Nazi gambling plot of *Casino Royale* was supposedly based on Fleming's own experiences; in fact, the stakes were low, his 'Nazis' were Portuguese, and he played on in an empty casino until he was cleaned out.

Scott's Restaurant was the scene of Fleming's – the humble Admiralty gofer's – most deadly undercover operation: he pestered M (Sir John Godfrey, head of naval intilligence) to let him out on the town with a couple of captured U-boat officers, with the idea of getting them tiddly enough to let slip their minefield strategies. It was a daring plan, very nearly worthy of James Bond himself: the corner-table party succeeded in getting extremely drunk, and began conversing noisily in German.

So the waiters called Special Branch, and they were all promptly arrested.

Eros's original position in the middle of the Circus gave a better impression of the angelic archer shooting the breeze in the very centre of London. Shifting from my seat – it may have been warm, but it's *hard* – I join the punks at their railings, and open up the vista down Lower Regent Street. Here, two more essential London elements are added to the collage: the Victoria Tower of the Houses of Parliament stands stately in the middle-distance, behind the grand old Duke of York's Column at the bottom of the hill. This royal reminder stands on the site of the Prince Regent's Carlton House residence, from which point Nash cut the sickle-shape of Regent Street, with Piccadilly Circus at its fulcrum.

I run after a bus turning left into Piccadilly, catch hold of the post on the open platform, and heroically haul myself aboard. The bus then stops and stands shuddering in stationary traffic for five minutes.

Only marginally later than if I'd walked, I jump off just short of Hyde Park Corner, right opposite the Hard Rock Café. I then backtrack two hundred yards around the underpass, get oily soot all over my hands as I climb the central barrier, and join the lengthy queue which doesn't look as if it's moved since beer, burgers 'n' shameless pop nostalgia were first thrown together on this site in 1971. There's nothing to do except scoff at the hippy slogans painted on the windows (LOVE ALL, SERVE ALL; NO DRUGS OR NUCLEAR WEAPONS ALLOWED INSIDE; SAVE THE PLANET) and try to explain in French, Dutch and German why the tetchy notice DO NOT SIT ON FLOWER BOXES is funny. Funnier, at least, than sooty stripes all down the rear of someone's trousers. After twenty minutes, one of them tells me there isn't any queue at all for the bar, only for tables – and so we all enjoy an example of true pan-European humour. The bastards.

Worldwide, the Hard Rock Café chain is now the leading buyer of music memorabilia, which it uses for wallpaper in its branches from LA to Ouagadougou. I've been to branches abroad, but have never before felt the urge to come to my local branch, any more than a legitimate Londoner would bolt his tea and rush out to watch the adverts in Piccadilly Circus. From my corner of the raised, three square-yard bar, it doesn't seem as though many of this evening's customers have even noticed the eat-through museum they've wandered into, which is a shame. The diner is laid out thoughtfully, so that rubberneckers don't stand drooling over other people's Beatleburgers, and the bobby-soxer waitresses are trained to mask their rage when they find their tight gangways blocked. Nevertheless, I'm the only one who embarks on a tour of inspection of all the display cases; the only one who isn't blithely oblivious to the presence of the Beatles' original blue nehru jackets, and the very bass guitar once strummed on stage by Stu Sutcliffe, the Fifth Beatle. Maybe I missed a sign in a flower-box which warned PAY NO ATTENTION TO EXHIBITS or PLEASE FEIGN DISINTEREST, MAN. Maybe mum's and dad's nachos are done to an irresistibly cheesy turn. But I'd still have thought a half-hour wait outside might warrant a cursory sniff at the London lore soaked like sweat into Sid Vicious's 'My Way' tuxedo; Gary Glitter's pink sequin tunic and girdle; Pete Townshend's pound-note jumpsuit from *Tommy*, and his Flying V guitar. Yardbirds posters. Clash levvahs. Donovan. In person. Stuffed. Here are great chunks of Britpop history that most native fans will only ever see if the London Hard Rock's precious paraphernalia is swapped for a season with the brown café branch in Amsterdam. Phil Collins' autograph is here, too.

'Shut up and look,' I feel like saying to one noisy American family with extra onion-rings. 'Mick Jagger's *baggy jogging pants*.' Okay, not a great example.

The downstairs bar and eaterie are only just opening up, but a bobby-soxer invites me in for a look around. There's a Hendrix axe and a Hendrix jacket and a Hendrix photo taken with his girlfriend, Kay Etchingham, at their flat at 25 Brook Street. It's just around the corner in Mayfair. And Handel used to live at the same address . . .

But my warmest glow is reserved for a framed *Melody Maker* cover from July 1967, which takes pride of place on the staircase down to the loos. No, not BEE-GEES BANNED FROM BRITAIN – I mean the Hard Rock Hall of Fame's Leicester connection . . . 'Only the Beatles stand between Scott McKenzie, the gentle singer with flower appeal, and the top of this week's Pop 30,' reads the blurb. 'But, despite the success of "San Francisco" there are still no firm plans for the Quiet American to visit Britain . . .'

Many years ago now, Scott did the smart thing and turned his back on San Francisco for the positive vibrations of *surf city Hinckley*. Next time you speed up the M69 into East Leicestershire, make like the locals, and be sure to wear some flowers behind your ear . . .

I think I must have been seven when I decided the London Hilton was the kind of hotel I wanted to stay in when I finally made it to adulthood. As our family car sped past on Park Lane, momentarily travelling roughly in the direction of Bexhill-on-Sea, I remember looking up at the tricorn mass of glass and concrete and the curtains drawn across the long window of the first-storey ballroom, and dreaming of the unspecific yet *definably swanky* goings-on I would be party to . . . *when I was a jetsetter*. There would be a tippy-tappy bossa nova band playing, and trays full of green-and-yellow cocktails, and I would be wearing a tight white suit. A barefoot Sandie Shaw would, most likely, be present. But I would play it cool.

Another important factor in my greedy yearning for Hilton Hotel guesthood was the Playboy Club next door: the lop-eared bunny logo was positioned high up on the wall, the very sight of which made me swallow uncontrollably and go sweaty behind the knees. Thanks to the investigative prowess of the *Sunday Mirror*, I knew there were cocktail waitresses at the Playboy Club who wore nothing but a swimming costume with a ball of cotton-wool glued to their bottom. I never noticed the bunny ears until years later.

And now, at last, I'm breezing into the Hilton for a polite sherbet on my own terms. Louise Nicholson's *Definitive Guide* promises it'll be all right: 'Roof Restaurant, 27th floor . . . Mon-Sat 7.30–11.30 . . . required to buy a meal or a drink'. That's okay. I've brought my cheque-book.

Now, act casual.

I make it through the revolving doors without being placed under house arrest, and walk under the billion-carat diamond chandelier let into the foyer's ceiling. I ask a uniformed receptionist which way to the 27th floor.

'Up,' he says, pointing helpfully at the lifts.

'Ah yes,' I reply, rising to the occasion. 'The Roof Restaurant will be open now.'

'Ah yes. You're looking for Windows. That's the 28th floor. It's been open since five.'

Oh, *Louise*. After all those definitive facts I've stolen on trust.

When my ears have unpopped from the four-second ride in the gold-plated turbo-lift, I wobble out in search of the bar. A receptionette stops me in my tracks, casts an eye over my trousers, decides I might just be a millionaire – it's so hard to tell these days – and shows me to a corner table for one.

The Hilton's top-floor bar, Windows on the World, is adequately named. It's a dead ringer for Cloudbase in *Captain Scarlet*. Every wall that isn't a window is a mirror, hung with textbook modern art. The place is full of men stripped casually to their waistcoats, and potential millionaires dressed down in old-style fag-advert chunky-knits. I can see at least four women who may prove to be either Joan or Jackie Collins. The carpet is a kaleidoscope. No wonder Hugh Hefner moved in next door when the Hilton burst onto the London skyline in 1963. The *Playboy* bachelor-pad art and the Collins quads already have my Londonometer needle trembling between 94 and 95 on the dial. Then a waiter glides over with my bottle of Beck's on a Hilton drip-mat, a Hilton bill for £3.50, a packet of Hilton matches, and not one but three large bowls of jet-set quality nibbles: fat kettle crisps, peanuts and almonds, and an assortment of hollow and pimento-stuffed olives sitting in spicy oil. The Londonometer hits 96. The pianist sits back on his stool after a short yellow-and-green cocktail break. He sets a beatbox to bossa nova and tinkles into . . . 'From Russia With Love'. Now a tricky key-change, and it's 'Thunderball'. A Bond score medley!

And, oh Lordie. He *sings* . . .

The Londonometer blows a valve as it peaks on 97, and collapses back in my bag for a well-deserved cigarette.

According to *London Unexpurgated*, the Hilton bar once even went under the name 'Room 007'. How foolish of me to ignore my most imaginative out-of-date guidebook, and assume the Hilton's definition of London urbanity might have altered over the past thirty years. As the great 'Petronius' himself wrote: 'I venture to hope that the swing and the zing, the taste and the smell, the sound and the beat of London are within these pages; the details might change, but the essence remains the same.'

Having learned my lesson, I shouldn't be surprised to find that the basic London ground-rules established by our (wisely) pseudonymous guide still apply, too:

• Open-minded London girls are dying to meet middle-aged American businessmen.
• And invite them to 'kinky' 'orgies'.
• Er, that's it for your basic London ground-rules.

No need, then, for Petronius's readership to delve further into the book — to the sections devoted to identifying and staring at prostitutes, spying on lovers in the park, plucking up courage to buy a 'way-out' nudey-mag, and hanging round the toilets at a selected list of likely bistrotheques . . .

And certainly no need to invest in any of the sad sub-Bondish gadgets that come recommended in a chapter entitled 'The London Peeper': an Owl's Eye image-amplifier ('so darkness cannot hide the faithless lover'); a transistorised stethoscope ('you hear every word and move, next door'), or a Morgan Geo-Phase microphone ('you hear the sweet nothings, but not the trumpet-player').

From the open balcony door at the side of the bar, the view rivals London from a low-flying plane — and that's without the aid of a Butt-Vu Secret Telescope ('it fits into a man's hand'). The green squares of Mayfair sprout from the criss-cross of white stone streets, luminescent in the long midsummer dusk. A great golden eagle scans for the return of pinko protesters to Grosvenor Square, ever-prepared to swoop from its roost atop the boxy American Embassy. When they've finished talking heli-pads and jacuzzis, most of my debonair companions will themselves be swooping down on Berkeley Square, to gamble at the Clermont casino, or boogie downstairs at Annabel's.

Temporarily taking over the reins from 'Petronius' in his excellent *Virgin Insider's Guide*, London gadabout Richard Jobson writes: 'Annabel's is supposed to be the best nightclub in the world – by those few pampered men and women who have never been in a real nightclub.' Sounds superb, eh? According to Richard, the champers will flow; very, very rich people will act like decadent schoolchildren, and no one will take a blind bit of notice. Just imagine the vicarious thrill of watching business moguls and off-duty Arabs, newspaper editors and Tory ex-ministers performing the techno-Hokey-Cokey with girls called Posy and Rosy . . . And then on to the Embassy Club – bolt-hole of the Prince of Wales – where Jobbo breathlessly describes 'naked men and women dancing on the bar' and a 'dancefloor full of young and old men kissing and gyrating . . .'

Naturally, I'm not suggesting *the Prince of Wales* ever got his Owl-Eyes steamed up in Mayfair. Things were probably different in the inter-war years, when he used to go out clubbing with his chums, the Mountbattens.

The brightest lights in Mayfair shine up from Shepherd Market – no longer a market, but a surprising square of eighteenth-century alleys and pubs and restaurants, tucked away off Piccadilly. This is the site of the original May Fair, finally suppressed in the 1730s because of the rowdiness and bawdy behaviour it sparked off. But old neighbourhoods die hard: Shepherd Market is still known as the haunt of the high-class prostitutes favoured by Mayfair's clubmen, politicians and Embassyland diplomats. Strangely, the authorities seem to turn a blind eye to the discreet one-bedroom flats hidden away behind the rows of intercom buzzers. Prostitution's really too strong a word for it. The clientèle are decent sorts, one and all. No riff-raff. The exorbitant price-lists see to that. Two hundred smackers for a soapy tub service. Or so I've heard.

Personally, I'm more of a mind to tag along with the Joans and Jackies to Tramp on Jermyn Street, the archetypal *Bitch* and *Stud*-style London disco, still magnificently denying the arrival of the 1980s. Here, it should still prove possible to rub shoulders with a decent proportion of the faded Rock Circus crowd, plus George Best, Lord Brett Sinclair out of *The Persuaders*, and any number of fairly supermodels.

When you're supping on the rooftop of the Hilton Hotel, the sky's the limit.

12 Waterloo Sunset

This morning I've made a rare journey south of the river, on the trail of *The London Nobody Knows*. A cursory glance at any tourist map shows that there's little point visiting south London looking for The London *Everybody* Knows: spiky skyline London; the London where your big sister went day-tripping, and only bought you that lousy Union Jack truncheon radio.

Plenty of books and bands and BBC sitcoms have been based in the south, but they simply refuse to add up to a cohesive mythology. *Up the Elephant and Around the Castle*; *The Wombles* of Wimbledon Common; *The Lavender Hill Mob*; *The Ballad of Peckham Rye*, set on the same council estate where *Only Fools and Horses* scratch a living. *Citizen Smith* plotted sitcom revolution with the Tooting Popular Front. Carter the Unstoppable Sex Machine shouted about 'The Oldest Living Boy in New Cross'. Richard E. Grant and Paul McGann smoked a Camberwell Carrot in *Withnail and I* – in Camberwell. *Up the Junction* was set in Clapham. Or was that supposed to be *Watford* Junction? *Hancock's Half-Hour* came live from East Cheam, a fictional suburb nevertheless identifiable as an area to the east of Cheam, known only as a place where nothing ever happened. Only one road in south London makes it onto the Monopoly board and, at £60, the Old Kent Road is the least alluring property in the city.

Presumably, something approaching half of London's famous names have hailed from the south. Growing up in Elephant and Castle, Maurice Micklewhite longed to break away and follow south London's three Charlies – the comedians Chaplin and Drake and the gangster Richardson – into the limelight: like the majority of southerners you've ever heard of, Michael Caine has never looked back.

That said, there's no denying south London is a great place to live: it's handy for north London. Even the Tube map seems loaded against the south: why should any newcomer be tempted to explore all that blank white space when even the London Underground can't be bothered?

Tourist-wise, the jewel in the Alice band of south London is the

Imperial War Museum, fittingly housed in the Victorian lunatic asylum, the Royal Bethlehem Hospital – or 'Bedlam'. Here, the First World War 'Trench Experience' will likely leave you shell-shocked, with the consolation of a pocketful of souvenirs half-inched from dead German soldiers. At the London Dungeon, you can look forward to Jack the Ripper tapping you on the shoulder, with equally unpleasant results.

Brixton, on the other hand, is much more fun. Only around 30 per cent of the local population is Afro-Caribbean; but that's the 30 per cent which rises to the fore, making the Electric Avenue market so vibrant and musical and full of excitement – a real, *traditional* London market. Brixton is one of the top day-tripping destinations outside central London – unless you happen to bear mental scars from playing your fourth-ever gig to a paying crowd of seven in 1984.

When I said I'd made the journey south of the river, I didn't mean I'd gone for broke and bussed it down to Penge. I meant I'd ventured *yards* south of the river, just by the end of Tower Bridge.

In *The London Nobody Knows*, Geoffrey Fletcher says 'the appearance of Shad Thames has changed little during the last century'.

Sounds promising . . .

'These Thames-side streets, built up on each side with cliff-like, well-used warehouses, smell strongly of spice, and language heard here can best be described as Anglo-Saxon . . .'

Admittedly, my paperback copy of the book does date from 1965, but things can't have changed that much. David Lynch lit the whole area with gaslight and steam when he filmed the story of Leicester's own *Elephant Man* on Shad Thames, with wonderfully atmospheric results. I'm quite prepared for Geoff's slice of *The London Nobody Knows* to be a shared secret. Even an open secret.

I wasn't expecting to find Jacob's Island here, with its slum extensions and sinking walkways built over a ditch tripling up as sewer, a pets' graveyard and a source of drinking water – as Geoff makes clear, London's grimmest rookery sank into the mud soon after the time of *Oliver Twist* – but neither was I expecting my dark, satanic Butler's Wharf to have been turned into *this*: 'office space' and 'luxury riverside apartments from £129,000'.

Ground-floor shops include estate agents, interior designers and bijou sauerkraut delis. Warehouses have been demolished to make way for something with blue metalwork called Tower Bridge Piazza. Shad Thames has been pedestrianised, post-industrialised, emasculated. Even the Tea and Coffee Museum is decaffeinated. The seven-storey slabs still loom, but their dangerous height has been diminished by polishing and painting up the vertiginous walkways passing between their faces. Butler's Wharf reminds me of a scarred, working terrier tamed and pampered like a poodle. I step back onto the narrow street after a brief foray through an alleyway into river's-edge café society, and an orange-clad urchin sprays my shoes with water: Shad Thames has become the kind of street which can't just be swept clean with a broom or brushed with an electric buggie; it has to be blasted *squeaky*-clean with a high-pressure water-jet.

After wasting my time trawling through the uniformly developed, touched-up backstreets of the old dock, I give up my search for the Unknown and head west down the riverside Queen's Walk. It's grey and hot and muggy, and I'm not in the best of moods. Just my luck: the Queen is nowhere to be seen today.

Just maybe, I finally force myself to admit, I was a *shade* naïve to expect to find Shad Thames still looking like Geoff's agreeably grubby sketch from the mid-'60s. Especially as the byword of his whole book is 'catch these sights now', before they are swept away.

On the opposite bank, fishy weathervanes glint not over Billingsgate Market, but over Billingsgate Temporary Computer Centre. Hay's Wharf is another old docks building to have found a *nouveau* use. Hewn from solid rock by the bare hands of virtuous river labourers and malnourished children, once vital to the Great British tea supply, Hay's *Galleria* is now an executive-class wine-bar and aromatherapy mall, its dock filled in. In the middle of the handsome, freshly sand-blasted arcade is an elephant-sized litter tray, which, on further investigation, proves to be a public petanque terrain. And it's free! The Galleria is also home to the funniest piece of public art that I've come across anywhere in London. David Kemp's *The Navigators* is a twenty-foot-tall junkyard galleon straight out of a Monty Python animation. Like anything, I'm sure it becomes a commonplace sight in time – 'yeah, the tuba's turning up the watering-can power to the paddles' – but I can only stop and stare, and get splashed all over again. The sparrows and starlings love it, too – first taking what must be a blissful shower on the boat's upper lip (*sic*), then diving straight into the deserted petanque pit for a nice deep dust-bath.

Outside, at its permanent resting-place in the Pool of London, the D-Day battleship HMS *Belfast* is camouflaged turquoise and grey against the slick alien backdrop of the City and the heavy sky. On the quarterdeck, its gun-turrets swivel, and twin six-inch cannon lower their sights, drawing a bead on *The Navigators* through the open archway. Only playing . . .

Up ahead, under London Bridge, a family of cormorants is diving optimistically for anything organic among the crap swept into the city on the high tide. I feel like jumping in and joining them in the cool sludge, if only to cough up puddles of authentic London cholera germs on someone's sanitised riverside step. After a further stretch of nondescript glasshouses, London Bridge Road comes as a welcome breath of foul air, the one concession to spurious good taste being an age-old advert on the stonework of the rail bridge running across the street into the bowels of the station, which still sings the praises of

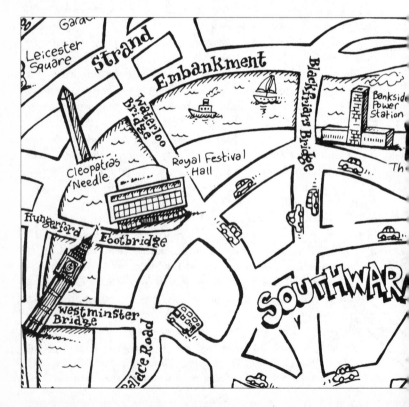

Dry Fly Sherry. The weather lets go at last, and big spots of rain set people running. It'll mean more work for the street-cleaner back on Butler's Wharf, who'll now have this sweet-smelling downpour to blast away with his tanker of slightly sparkling Evian.

It's no use trying to shelter under the bridge because the pigeons have made it to the rafters first. I hurry on down Borough High Street in my thin Hawaiian-print shirt, across the greasy road and into Pringle's Snack Bar. All kinds of people are hunkered down at the clean formica tables – office workers on their lunch-break, rail travellers with their luggage blocking the aisles, even the odd City Gent. It's good to see not everyone with an expense account or Luncheon Vouchers is tucking into kangaroo mousse and starfruit chutney. Here, all-day breakfasts, bubble 'n' squeak and frazzled bacon are the order of the day. People are drinking tea. It's almost like London. Slices, buttered slices and fried slices find their way onto the

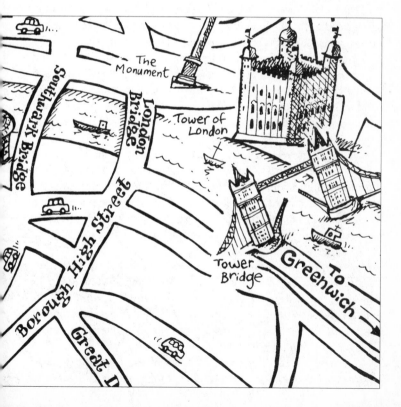

bottom of the me 'n' u, recalling the sole diet of George Orwell when he was *Down and Out* in The Smoke. I get a window seat and take my time over my vinegar-fuming Bernhard, egg and chips – two pahnd ten, all ver best, mate – but the rain has set in and I'm forced to seek refuge over the road at the George Inn.

By the way: that's 'Bernhard', as in Bernhard Langer = banger = sausage = generic pink meat in tubes of sheep-gut prophylactic: *mmm*.

The alleyways running off Borough High Street still bear the names of the coaching-inns that used to line the main road into London, via the city's only bridge, from the south of England and the Continent. White Hart Yard. Talbot Yard, which time has mangled from the name of the Tabard Inn, as patronised by Chaucer's Canterbury pilgrims. The George Inn still stands along one side of its courtyard, London's sole remaining galleried inn. Rebuilt after the Southwark Fire in 1677, the hotel rooms in its north wing were demolished in the 1880s, and its courtyard theatre sadly died a death. Five shallow, bare-timbered bars are strung along the George's ground-floor frontage, blissfully unadorned with carpet and wallpaper and fake brewery mirrors. The upper galleries are closed this lunchtime. I buy a half of Lumpy Old Vernacular, take the very window stool where Shakespeter and Dickens once parked their bottoms, and immerse myself again – this time less credulously – in *The London Nobody Knows*.

Geoffrey Fletcher recommends all of the London markets to the hungry London-hunter: Covent Garden in the confusion of early morning; Billingsgate, 'where the fishy smell has sunk into the very pavements'; Leadenhall – at last, a survivor. There's a tantalising, single-line mention of 'the fruit and vegetable market in the grimy Georgian streets near the Southwark Cathedral', but I'm not going to fall for another sucker punch.

Another half-pint later, the sky begins to clear. For the first time, I realise the black glass and white plastic building blocking the light on the opposite side of the courtyard (along with the George's toilet) may actually have been designed to *blend in*, even to *mirror* the inn. It is a historic example of a late-twentieth- century galleried wine-bar. I'd love to stay and explore, but Bankside calls.

As I descend the steps in the alleyway south of the sunken, yellow-stone Southwark Cathedral, I'm plunged immediately into an atmosphere altogether different from the first leg of the Queen's Walk. I've finally found my way into *The London Nobody Knows* – and this time it's still here. I feel like Charlton Heston in the final frames of *The Planet of the Apes*, when he happens across the half-buried ruins of the Statue of Liberty. Borough Market nestles under the twin railway tracks which diverge as they leave London Bridge Station, bound north for Cannon Street and west for Waterloo. In early afternoon, the iron arches of the black brick market are deserted, except for a trio of wholesalers tidying up and stacking crates in the half-light. The vaulted glass roof is so caked with filth, the watery sunshine only shines in where panes are missing. Outside, iron-fronted stalls bend to fit the curve of the narrow road. I'll have to come back here in the morning, to see this forgotten underworld in motion. And call in for a breakfast-time pint at the market pub on the corner, The Globe. And get myself a proper job, buying and selling and shouting and stacking all the perfect plums at the front, and filling bags from the back. And I bet this place is terrifying at night . . .

Beyond the market is Stoney Street, which more than makes up for the disappointment of Shad Thames. These warehouses look as if they were abandoned in the middle of a day's work forty years ago, and never returned to since. Weighted pulleys hang on heavy-duty chains in front of five-storey columns of warehouse doors, with hinged and chained sills. Windows haven't just been bricked-up – they've been bricked-up, barred, wired and concreted over from the inside, and they're still all smashed. It's just possible to make out a danger sign high on the wall by the winch at Wm. Skinner and Son's: LOAD 20 CWT. And then, at ground-level, a less faded update as a result of who knows what tragic accident: SAFE LOAD 15 CWT. Fair-sized shrubs sprout out of the crumbling mortar along the street. The last door stands wide open: impenetrable darkness starts a couple of yards from my feet, with just one distant stone archway, somewhere under the railway lines, illuminated by electric lantern as a mason chip-chip-chips away at the fabric of the cavernous crypt.

I'm sure dilapidated warehouses and a tatty old market don't add up to everybody's idea of a worthwhile London excursion, but for me there's a real *romance* to these tumbledown back streets. I'm not just talking about the *Sweeney*ish potential of stacked orange boxes and chains dangling outside fifth-storey warehouse doors ('You go rahnd ver back, George. I'll flush 'em aht'), forgotten corners like Bankside serve as a reminder of the basis of so much of London's charm: its gloriously jumbled unpredictability. Turn the corner out of a marketplace and find a theatre, a church, a square, a wharf. A living, working city came about when trading involved meeting and arguing and handling shipfuls of *stuff* instead of a screenful of zeros. When the last factory, the last spice dock and market hall have been knocked down, zoned out of town, converted into flats, banks and arts centres, let's hope there's still a real London left to live in. Just as Geoffrey Fletcher warned thirty-odd years ago, best savour the atmosphere of these streets sooner rather than later.

Just when it seemed my tactic of following the guidebook greats would only give rise to tales of disappointment and disintegration, it throws up another wonderful surprise. When Ian Nairn passed on the tantalising story of a 'gorgeous rose window' buried behind the brickwork of the Bankside docks, I naturally assumed the worst: it was odds-on anything of interest had been subject to casual destruction, and pretty short odds that Nairn had been day-dreaming in the first place. On Clink Street – site of the original Clink prison – some selective demolition has uncovered the fourteenth-century ruins of Winchester Palace, including that intricately carved, weatherbeaten window, an incongruous find amid the railway arches and warehouses.

Soon after the palace was built, the City of London authorities, over the river, entered the history books as Britain's very first NIMBYs. As Puritans and powerful, respectable merchants, they had their own reasons for allowing 'chapels of Satan' (playhouses), bear-baiting pits and brothels to trade . . . but Not In My Back Yard. The Bankside quickly grew up as a suburb dedicated wholeheartedly to roving and ruin. The Bishop of Winchester ruled over the Clink district, whose streets around the Palace were so packed with brothels that the whores became known as 'Winchester Geese'.

Out of sight, out of mind; but just a twopenny boat-trip away, all the same.

This part of Southwark is thick with history. At St Mary Overie's Dock, a notice informs the people of St Saviour's parish of their entitlement to land any goods free of toll: a speedboat full of contraband cocaine might give rise to a tricky test case, especially as the whole dock is flooded with luminous pea soup and devoted to the rebuilt coastal schooner, the *Kathleen and May*. On, past Southwark Bridge, the street names – Bear Gardens, Rose Alley – betray the former sites of Bankside's bear- (and bull-) baiting rings, and Theatreland Mk. 1. Will Sheikspier was a one-tenth shareholder at the Globe Theatre, where he trod the boards himself, and premiered several of his plays. *Hamlet. Macbeth. King Lear.* He really was quite good, wasn't he?

Actors from The Globe used to use the waterfront Anchor pub as a dressing-room. The pub features a tiny one-foot-square room which was put out to rent to escapees from the Clink. And that's just for starters. The Anchor warrants perhaps the most stirring entry in *The Guide to London Taverns* (1927), by another of my guidebook heroes, the swashbuckling H.E. Popham.

H.E. recommends a riverside approach to the pub, staying 'close to the water, by the wharves, under the cranes, over the ropes, and round the barrels, stumbling over a chain every hundred yards . . .

'We are now down at the heart of things, where connection is established between the Mother City and every other part of the world . . . where the things that you actually touch have been or will be handled by some stevedore at Valparaiso or Sydney or Tokio. Silk hats and patent boots are not for Bankside, nor Bankside for them. Coats off here, for there's heaving to be done.'

H.E. lingers for a tankard or two in the bar favoured by 'the greatest of all Englishmen', and gives short shrift to anyone who might prefer the servile flunkeys and five-bob pints of a West End hotel: 'For goodness sake leave us here and take yourself westwards in the first cab that you can find, or swim up up the river if you prefer it. We don't care. We are for a game of darts with our riverside friends in the taproom.'

Cheers, H.E.

The painstaking recreation of the Globe Theatre is to be found on a waterfront pitch two hundred yards from the Park Street plaque commemorating the bard's 'Wooden O'. There are no seats in the stalls, and the back row of the gods is, controversially, well within acting distance of the stage. No more shouting and gesticulating like clowns. No more 'sitting in the dark facing forward to a bunch of people in the light pretending to talk to each other when they are really talking to the audience'. The front row are *right there*, rapt or recoiling, right under the actors' noses, and the open sky. In her

Evening Standard preview of *Henry V*, Germaine Greer concluded: 'The Globe is the one place where you can see the point of theatre.'

On the other hand, a couple of days ago, the *Standard* was worrying that The Globe was in danger of becoming a tourist theme-park, a Bawdy Boozy Bardland. Theatre publicity ominously threatens to 'bring Bankside to life' with an army of 'clowns, jugglers, minstrels, dancers, acrobats, palm- and tarot-readers, singers and sword-fighters'. Wot, no robotic dancers?

Authentic materials, building methods and tools were used in the reconstruction of the thatched pudding. Only in the rush to be ready for opening did carpenters revert to power-saws, builders hurriedly lay new cobbles in concrete, and signwriters show off their ancient craft of spray-painting over cut-out stencils. For those who can't get tickets to see a play, a five-pound walking tour is laid on around the building, although for five pounds I'd want to see more *Love's Labours* than a stack of glueless joints. I take it on myself to warn a leftover workman: you want to get some creosote on those beams, or it'll end in tears.

A *Blue Peter* camera-crew (well, I bet they're from *Blue Peter*) are set up by the river, filming St Paul's above London from the finest seat in the house along Cardinal's Wharf, where Christopher Wren lived and watched his new London take shape. Reminded of the job in hand, the cameraman tracks lovingly across the stuccoed façade of the Pud – and all this time, all he has to do to capture an architectural event of real significance is turn 45 degrees to his right. Choosing instead to soldier on, he captures all the rustic charms of The Globe, accompanied on the soundtrack by the deafening, screeching death-throes of a mortally wounded dinosaur. Bankside Power Station is drawing its last breath: screaming drills and bursts of painful hammering reverberate around its exposed ribcage. The single, square-section, billion-brick chimney-stack is untouched as yet, but the gigantic wings are being dismantled, brick by brick, all around it. Bankside was only finished in 1962 after thirteen years' work. If they'd somehow thrown it up two hundred years before, people would have prayed before its blank, meaningless mass. Everybody passing by on the river path stops and gapes for a minute or two to pay their last respects, hoping to see an explosion or a wall crack and fall, instead of this lingering, undignified end.

Oxo Tower Wharf is yet another South Bank landmark which has only escaped extinction by entering into a Faustian recycling deal. Bankside was too young and too ugly to tempt the developers but, if anyone had shown the necessary imagination, fifty million quid and some nice bright wallpaper could have secured a single-room bedsit with real talking-point potential. Older and cuter than Bankside – hey, the tower spells out OXO! – the former meat coldstore of the Oxo building is now yet another bank of modern flats, its rarity value residing in the non-profit allocation of its living space to locals at the top of the housing list. This Coin Street Development, together with the neighbouring Gabriel's Wharf complex of bars and restaurants, is one brave attempt to forge a real community on the South Bank, and they deserve all the luck they can get. A glass-fronted restaurant, run by Harvey Nichols, is balanced on the roof of Oxo Wharf – it's progress, after a fashion – and on the ground floor you can stock up on art, enamels, textiles and ceramics. As for a pint of milk or a newspaper for the people sandwiched in between it's a twenty-minute walk over the Hungerford footbridge to the 7-11 in Embankment station. And twenty minutes back.

Ever since Tower Bridge, the river has been steering almost imperceptibly to port. The bridges I've passed have gradually fallen away from sight, viewed through subsequent arches. Then, in its approach to Waterloo Bridge, the inrushing Thames takes a sudden dive to the south. From this viewpoint, it seems a mystery how the *south* never developed faster as the city's natural, geographical centre: the *South Bank* is the central hub of London, with the City, the West End and Westminster ranging around it in a shallow 270-degree amphitheatre. No wonder I've spent so long wandering lost after taking some of the longest, most baffling short-cuts known to man: it's so *handy* to picture the river flowing neatly left to right through the centre of town; and it's so *wrong*. Maybe the Tube map is to blame, conveniently shunting this 90-degree meander way to the west, so that the symmetrical grid of central London can appear to rest on a solid foundation. It's a criminal north London bias.

South London is the true centre of London: I've just looked it up on a Tube map which includes the tangled mess of BR lines south of the river, redressing the balance. *Loads* of London is south of the river. Even Ian Nairn couldn't get over the fact that the mid-point between Tower Bridge and Vauxhall Bridge is at Elephant and Castle, not Charing Cross. I take back everything I said about the south. The

Oval cricket ground is in the south, and it's every bit as green and pleasant as Lord's. Crystal Palace is in the south, home of Crystal Palace Football Club and the great Crystal Palace greenhouse, after they moved it from Hyde Park (and before it burned down). Legends filtering north say there be prehistoric monsters on the island in the boating lake in Penge Park, and a sphinx on wasteground nearby – relics from the post-Exhibition Palace funfair. The Horniman Museum and the Old Vic Theatre are south of the river. So is the New Vic. So is Brighton. Half of everyone I know in London lives in the south. Bob Hope was born in Eltham. *Singalonga* Max Bygraves hails from Rotherhithe. The list is virtually endless. Our landlord, Mr Weeraman, lives in Sydenham.

The graceful span of Waterloo Bridge alights in the south – or does it *start* in the south? – amid the site of Europe's largest arts centre, and Cardboard City (which is nothing at all to do with Monopoly). Two of my finest London celebrity spots have been at the streaky concrete-block National Theatre on the South Bank: TV inquisitor Jeremy Paxman and petite boatwoman-novelist Clare Francis. The south is *king*.

No time now for a celebratory southern sherbet at the National Film Theatre bar, so unpromisingly (but, as it happens, so satisfyingly) jammed under the sweeping, cut-away bridge. I'm faced with the task of bolting through 1,950 years of history at the Museum of the Moving Image, and landing safely in the final fifty-year spell where things begin to hot up, Londonwise. To make my job that much more difficult, the museum has stationed character actors in period dress at every corner, who are intent on explaining the workings of the kinetoscope, or talking about Charlie Chaplin as if he's still alive and, even less credibly, still funny.

Having enjoyed the whole loop of British Movietone newsreels, shot by men in hats from the roof of a speeding Morris Minor, I hold on to once again catch Dagwood, the table-tennis cat. Neville Chamberlain may have in his hand a piece of paper promising six years of Total War, but I find myself cheered up no end by this amusing item at the end of the news: Dagwood could catch on. I'm quite happily studying one of Baird Television's new home reception sets (who can resist the idea of 'seeing by wireless'?) when I'm accosted by a pair of smartly uniformed commissionaires wot talk a bit fahny. Inadvertently, I've wandered into the foyer of the Muswell

Hill Odeon – in 1946.

'Oho, so wot 'ave we 'ere, Cynthia? A gentleman of the local press, mayhap?'

Cynthia Crawley explains how the officious Mr Williams took a narsty bit of shrapnel in the 'ostilities. Terrible business . . . GIs . . . buzz-bombs . . . nylons . . . rationing. Not from vese parts, ven?

It turns out we're in 1946 because this is British cinema's greatest ever year, with an unbeatable number of films being produced, and an all-time record 1,650 million bums on seats. I follow Cynthia's snood and stocking-seams to a gallery of all her current 'eartfrobs. She dishes the dirt on David Niven (allegedly a petty crook, allegedly deported from Hollywood, he allegedly fought on both sides in the Cuban Revolution, allegedly), and tut-tuts about Margaret *The Wicked Lady* Lockwood's controversial cleavage, which is having to be reshot for release (or otherwise) in America. 'John Mills, now – ooh, 'e's a luvverly sort. But he battered poor old Stewart Granger black and blue in *Waterloo Road*, wot was set rahnd ver back 'ere. Regimental boxing champion, y'know.'

Cynthia tells me Richard Attenborough was 'a bit podgy' for the part of Pinky in *Brighton Rock*, but apparently made the weight by training with the Chelsea football team: lucky for him lager and discotheques haven't yet been invented. Getting into the swing of the '40s, I trade Cynthia the story of when Dickie dropped into Dalton's record shop, at home in Leicester, just last year. Expecting to be given his selections free of charge, he called the manager and demanded the sales assistant – my mum – be given a public bollocking.

'*May name is Richard Attenborough,*' recounts the prosecution's star witness, given the least excuse. 'All of three-foot-six, he was.' The tosser. But isn't his brother David *smashing*?

Cynthia shows off interior shots of the palatial Finsbury Park Astoria, and the 4,000-seater Kilburn State. The Brixton Astoria is even grander, with stage and balconies swept away into a hacienda-style fantasyland for the masses. Looking into the future, Mr Williams thinks the Finsbury Astoria might one day be known as the Rainbow Theatre, before finding a use as 'some sort of Brazilian church'. Cynthia guesses the Brixton branch could, in fifty years' time, still function as a different kind of people's pleasure palace, known as the Academy.

'I was down there last Saturday,' she lets slip. 'All-night rave. But don't tell my character.'

By the time I'm let out of the back door of the Odeon, TV coverage has extended nationwide from its modest thirty-mile radius around the Alexander Palace. London nevertheless remains at the heart of TV production – home of the BBC's quivering Voice of Reason; the city where local, national and international news are synonymous, and a 'natural' doorstep location for the lion's share of early programming. *Dixon of Dock Green*. The Queen's Coronation and her annual Christmas Message to the Nation. *Saturday Night at the London Palladium*. The FA Cup Final. *Bill and Ben the Flowerpot Men*.

The Beveridge Report of 1951 concluded that 'television should be the Hyde Park of the air'. Nobody understood what it meant, but it sounded the business.

Only when the clips, the stills, the costumes, the TV annuals and board-games are laid out behind glass do London and Light Entertainment blur so plainly into a single, flickering entity. This single MOMI corridor recalls, even explains so much of my life, it's painful to admit to being so shallow. A TV kid. I watch the nine-screen array of forgotten adverts, and they're like old friends. Go Well Go Shell. For Mash Get Smash. Even If It Does Taste Like Wallpaper Paste. But it's the London bits I'm bound to be most affected by; was *always* bound to be most affected by: the blessed background crowd, bussed in to bop on *Top of the Pops*. The breaktime schemes and hometime scrapes of *Grange Hill*. *Randall and Hopkirk (Deceased)* – gimmick: one half of the private detective duo was a *ghost* . . .

If only they'd made *The Likely Lads* in London, the city could have claimed my whole set of influences, and I'd have *had* to ask Mum to pack me up a spotted hanky in the long summer holidays of '76.

It's a uniquely diminishing feeling, to be faced with the realisation that your strictly academic, ironic interest in gunplay and doing the Bump is quite so transparently based on a sincere adolescent fascination with gunplay and doing the Bump. It's a good job I'm a professionally disinterested, scientifically trained Londonologist, otherwise I could easily be mistaken for *something of a trainspotter*. Even the London programmes I only know as anachronistic repeats, or dimly remember as grown-ups' stuff – *Hancock's Half-Hour*, *Ready Steady Go*, *The Saint* – exert a certain spell: those we could have loved.

My only source of relative pride is having resisted *The Forsyte Saga*, then and now (rhyming slang refreshments not included).

No other British city has been glamorised to the irresistible degree of London, before or since the hard sell of the Moving Image. Liverpool? Manchester? Glasgow? They've all been used as a backdrop in a couple of long-running TV shows, plus the odd feature-film. Only Leicester gives London a serious run for its money, with its galaxy of home-grown stars and screen smashes. Even then, in the Londonised goggle-eyes of the average, impressionable TV viewer, the capital remains almost twice as beguiling as the unofficial Second City.

At MOMI, I can lie on a blue board tilted at 45 degrees, find myself superimposed on the River Thames, and finally realise my Tower Bridge-skimming documentary dream. *Doctor Who* travelled time and space in a converted London police box. At MOMI, it's possible to step inside a knobby armour shell and *talk like a dalek. Til Death Us Do Part*'s Alf Garnett was an insufferable cockney bigot: at MOMI, just press a button, watch his face appear on a screen mounted over a urinal, and hear what he has to say on a variety of sensitive issues. Charlie Chaplin's hat is here, too.

Apart from a wall-sized, dotty picture by the men's loos and a tape of the *Psycho* slashing music which creeps up when you're at your most vulnerable, I didn't catch any special MOMI exhibits devoted to Alfred Hitchcock. A 'BATES' MOTEL' dressing-gown on offer at £43.99 hardly seems the most apt tribute to London's greatest film-maker, no matter how deeply desirable the showerwear may be (to an inveterate trainspotter) (I imagine). Elsewhere on the bargain trail, £5.99 seems a bit steep for an A3 poster of a bunch of daleks crossing Westminster Bridge, even though the powerful image does serve as a reminder to us all of the precious *yet precarious* state of democracy. How about £19.99 for a disposable London Bus camera that takes 3D photos? How have I ever managed without one?

As I'm leaving the shop, a woman in a leather jacket stops me in my tracks. 'Hi, it's me . . .' And then Cynthia utters the words that every man dreams of one day hearing from a woman's lips: 'You didn't recognise me with my clothes on . . .'

The Royal Festival Hall was built as the centrepiece of the 1951 Festival of Britain, a centenary echo of the Great Exhibition, and a cue for the British people to cheer up and give themselves a pat on the back – or, as they put it at the time, as 'a challenge to the sloughs of the present and a shaft of confidence cast forth against the future'. Built on a bomb-site, Festival attractions included some wondrous Jet Age architecture and a state-of-the-art funfair in Battersea Park, which opened three weeks late thanks to delays and maladministration.

For one short summer, Festival-goers were invited to feast disbelieving eyes on the Skylon, a three-hundred-foot metal cigar supported upright in mid-air by wire rigging and the Wonders of Science; on banks of lights and fireworks and bands of young women selling oranges, dressed as Nell Gwyn. A lighthouse was constructed opposite the present-day site of the Festival Pier, allowing people not only to visit the Festival, but to *climb* it. Provision of a 'fantastic railway' meant they could *ride* it, too. According to pictures in my possession, a large triangular sheet of metal was bowed backward and secured to the ground, creating a mind-blowingly futuristic shape. A concrete pudding-basin was specially constructed in the Jubilee Gardens, and I'll bet they had some right old fun in there!

I don't know whether the Lighthouse and the Interesting Shape and the 'Dome of Discovery' were pulled down immediately or allowed to crumble and rust, but it wasn't until the '60s when the rest of the sprawling South Bank Centre began to be developed on the site. As for the Skylon, people are still growing their runner-beans up its precision-tooled girders in allotments all over south London: deemed too potent a symbol of the good times, it was disposed of with indecent haste by the incoming Conservative administration. Maybe our own new Labour government could consider arranging a Skylon amnesty week with local police stations, and piece it back together to generate some original, post-war victory Feelgood Factor.

The interior of the Festival Hall makes me feel like I'm back at school. Every school I ever attended, and every school I ever played football against, was built in the '60s to the Festival Hall pattern: tall windows, spacy white hall and foyer, always incorporating some quirky 'clever touch' that was out of date before the paint had dried. I spent years trailing in and out of hexagonal school halls, slopey-roofed school halls, and school halls featuring an out-of-bounds spiral staircase – and it's all because of the Festival Hall. In his *Penguin*

Guide to London, F.R. Banks calls the RFH 'one of the most successful examples of modern architecture in London', curiously forgetting the entirely new façade commissioned as a matter of emergency in the early '60s to lend some smoothness and sense to the original bodged job. Like the National Theatre which followed, the main lecture theatre – sorry, *auditorium* – is supremely functional, an acoustic marvel, and not much fun at all. After any performance, the audience filters out of the drab space into the secondary modern school foyer-cum-dinner-hall on its sloping underside. Pine floors and fab tubular-frame chairs complete the picture. Employ a waitressing team of pink-smocked dinner-ladies and this place could be *popular*.

Up six flights of open-plan stairs, I come across a pleasant, sunny-faced space under the eaves, like all of the convex façade an entertaining afterthought. Twelve flights of open-plan stairs later, I arrive back at my perch with the pint of fizzy lager I needed to complete my view across the river and the West End. The Savoy and Cleopatra's Needle. Nelson's Column, overgrown on all sides. The Post Office Tower, overgrown on none.

A train rumbles over Hungerford Bridge into Charing Cross. Oxo people nip to the corner shop. Beggars beg. A juggler juggles. Directly below, on the top shelf of the South Bank's futile dual-level patio, are the tea-time drinkers in the cheap seats. DO NOT PUT WINE GLASSES ON PARAPET, a polite notice asks on their behalf. The thought never crossed my mind.

Now all I've got to do is hang around for four hours to justify a mention of 'Waterloo Sunset'.

13 Park Life

Not a lot of people know that when Marble Arch was originally erected in the 1820s, it was the front gateway to Buckingham Palace. Just imagine the painstaking feat of architecture, when later they had to dismantle and rebuild the Palace on its present site, to prevent it blocking the rush-hour traffic coming up Oxford Street . . .

No, really, Marble Arch *did* once stand in front of Buck House, but they decommissioned it after twenty-odd years because it failed to meet two fairly basic specifications: first, it proved too narrow to admit George IV's state coach; then they found that the statue of the King on horseback, destined to teeter gloriously on top of the Arch, *didn't fit*. No kidding. A less wobbly perch for Georgy Porgy and Gluepot was subsequently found in Trafalgar Square; the Arch was removed bodily and relegated to the role of Hyde Park's north-east gate. Even by the early years of this century, the horse-drawn traffic along Park Lane was piling up at the Arch, which was decommissioned yet again and left to stand unemployed on a dusty island outside the park, in the midst of permanent jams.

Marble Arch may not have the most prestigious history of all London landmarks, but it does have one face-saving get-out clause: its gates, barring the way from a polluted desert island into the gutter of the busiest street in London (or vice versa) never open *except for royalty*.

Emerging from the ants'-nest of subways extending from Marble Arch Tube to the park, I have a quick look around the hallowed traffic island; but none of the privileged pass-holders appear to have come jogging across the park to form an orderly queue this morning.

Up around the top of the arch, small plexiglass windows betray the existence of London's most surreal police station, built to spy over this notorious trouble-spot. When the Tyburn gallows were finally removed, and public hangings transferred to Newgate Prison, rowdy crowds began to gather here at Speakers' Corner on Sunday mornings, to let off their social, political and religious steam . . . or just plain old hot air. If mass public insurrection was ever going to happen, it was most likely to start right here. Or so the Metropolitan

Police assumed. So they set up their pigeon-friendly lookout post and stocked up with a couple of extra truncheons and whistles.

This warm, airless Sunday morning, neither a gentle Irish socialist standing on an upturned bucket, nor an overheated African in full military camouflage gear are posing an imminent threat to the security of the state. There's no room for rowdiness in the lazy Sunday London morning being played out in the park, and little call for police marksmen with rifles and telephoto lenses. A docile crowd mills between the two speakers, smiling politely to themselves in judgement. A Zionist address has run into problems backstage, where one of the speakers has been sidetracked into some age-old argument with an Old Testament sandwich-man. The atmosphere is like a Sunday paper's letters page made flesh, with everyone's right to reasonable argument guaranteed, no matter how obscure or extreme their views.

A Texan evangelist in a straw stetson and a Stars and Stripes cowboy shirt stands up on his stepladder and starts making noise. JESUS IS LORD is spelled out down his trouser-leg.

'Since you Brits have rejected religion,' he shouts, '*thay-is* is what you all've become.' He takes a Union Jack hanky from his pocket and unwraps a plastic dog turd.

Oh, yes. Whatever you say, sir.

It's everyone's right to stand up here and spout at Speakers' Corner; but best not forget it's everyone else's right to tut, shake their heads and shuffle off for an ice-cream. In the case of the suddenly lonely Yankee preacher, you can tell even the sandwich-board sinner is thinking to himself, *Hallelujah*! What a *wanker* . . .

At the far end of the tarmac, the Nation of Islam is putting on the best value show. They've even brought their own portable pulpit. Six pairs of black shades stare out of six sculpted skulls into the sizeable crowd, an FBI-style bodyguard backed around their star orator, who is instantly likeable, although he probably wouldn't thank me for thinking so. After three minutes of home truths, snappy gags and fashion tips, I'm ready to sign up for a spot of this Black Supremacy. The proof of the argument is something to do with unlaced trainers, Liz Hurley's lip injections, fake tans and Frank Bruno. Oh, yes – and a healthy African influence on every decent record ever made (with Cat Stevens' hippy folk twittery the exception which proves the rule, I'm sure he meant to say).

'*This* is how to wear a bow-tie,' the speaker explains, 'neat and sharp like a little butterfly. I am *colour-co-ordinated* . . .' His pocket hanky and bow-tie are certainly both orange and green. '*This* is how to wear a suit,' he goes on. '*This* is how a suit is *supposed to be worn*. You gotta *learn* to wear a suit. You gotta learn to *move* in a suit. This is a suit that was *made* by a black man to be *worn* by a black man. Those crazy lil' suits you white guys wear, riding up all over the place . . .'

It comes as a relief to find there are at least a few politically minded Englishmen who don't dress like William Hague.

The Changing of the Guard takes place at 11.30 a.m. every day of the week, including Sunday, in the carpark at Buckingham Palace: I know this is the case because I've carefully cross-checked with all three of my London guides which were printed after 1980.

On Sundays, Pall Mall and Constitution Hill are both blissfully closed to traffic, so Pomp and Circumstance-spotters are safe to picnic and mill around with video-cameras suckered into their eye-sockets all over the desert of pink tarmac in front of the Palace gates. It's only twenty-past, and already Queen Victoria has been joined by hundreds of onlookers up on the dried-up fountains of her roundabout Monument. The crowd is pressed three or four deep at the railings, staring up at the large, fluted breeze-block beyond. No flag flying above the Palace means the Queen isn't in residence; but maybe she's just popped out for a paper, and will be back any minute. The crowd are clearly expecting some balcony action, even if it's only Prince Edward who's home.

Because I'm juggling a bagful of guidebooks, an American couple ask me why the guards are late. My *New Insider's Guide to London* doesn't exactly answer the question, but assures us we'll soon hear the band stomping up the Mall 'playing Broadway show tunes'. I explain that the guide is twenty-two years out of date, and the modern equivalent will most likely be 'S.H.O.P.P.I.N.G.' by the Pet Shop Boys. And while we're about it: 'England's 50p piece bears an uncanny resemblance to the 10p piece. The only difference? It has seven sides instead of being a circle, so feel your coins to avoid short-changing yourself.' The couple thank me, and hurry away.

In all, there are well over two thousand people waiting here: tourists from home and abroad, hot-dog and ice-cream sellers, and friendly London bobbies.

Then one of the bobbies shifts sideways to have a chat with his shoulder, and a shin-high noticeboard comes into view: NO GUARD CHANGING TODAY.

I ask his partner whether he knows the sign is standing there, and the terrible truth is confirmed – just when I was finally getting into the swing of this pageantry lark, and was looking forward to a grand, meaningless spectacle. 'Why don't you tell everybody?' I can't help wondering.

'It's not for *me* to tell everybody – "*sir*".'

Not him personally, maybe; but it wouldn't take much for someone to stick their neck out and break the bad news.

'We've put these notices out,' he says. 'And there are two more along there.'

Trouble is, the notices are inside the railings, and the railings are squashed with eager snappers who either can't read English, or are assuming the notices are wrong. They *must* be wrong. What are all these people doing here if the gig's cancelled?

I elbow my way forward and catch sight of a permanent noticeboard. SPRING – AUTUMN: GUARD CHANGES EVERY DAY, it says. Followed, in much smaller script, by an apparently casual clause: (*with rare exceptions . . .*).

The next board along makes a clear admission: NEXT CHANGING OF THE GUARD: TOMORROW 11.30 A.M. Aha! But that must be *yesterday's* notice. No – they must have changed it a few minutes *early*, so it'll be *right* the instant the Guards appear, body-popping down the Mall to the rhythm of 'West End Girls' . . .

I begin to feel like the bloke in *The Day of the Triffids*, wandering through the middle of London after it had been taken over by human-shaped vegetable imposters. I start checking the eyes of the crowd for the tell-tale cabbaged gaze. Results are disconcerting.

Is there another country in the world where you could witness such a scene? (I mean the Guards' no-show, not an alien invasion.) Where such official apathy would be proffered as an acceptable, by-the-book response? No, there isn't. Britain wasn't only the birthplace of free speech; we *gave the world* Sunday mornings, friendly policemen and timetables to ignore. We invented the megaphone, too; but consider its use rather Continental and uncivilised. The stapler: now there's a fine, reserved British invention. Cups of tea floating with soggy chunks of dunked biscuit. Ah, the lawnmower. What a *mighty* country this is. Britain didn't get where it is today by having its public servants answer questions that haven't even been asked. The changing of the guard at Buckingham Palace? It was never this disorganised when Christopher Robin went down with Alice.

A walk around St James's Park comes as scant compensation for the promised treat of breakdancing, synthesiser soldiers in scarlet – even if cutbacks have meant their breastplates are shiny plastic instead of steel, and their bearskins are soon to be replaced with a job-lot of nylon dalmatian fur from Brick Lane. The Queen Mum's Carlton House is painted a subtle shade of pink, just the same as her granny-flat in the grounds of Windsor Castle – 'Barbara Cartland', I think it's called on the colour charts. And I bet every single room inside is painted Barbara Cartland, too.

The little brick fort of St James's Palace was the residence of the monarchy from 1715 to 1837, when the newly overhauled and stone-clad Buckingham Palace welcomed young Queen Victoria. The mysterious machinations of Court life continue here today – minus the Regency rakes and sacrificial virgins of the bodice-ripping 'historical' novel, but not without a certain musty sniff of upper-class sexiness. Foreign ambassadors and royal barristers are still received into the Court of St James's, where, it can only be assumed, they eat legs of ox and waltz to sniffy chamber-music with the rich teenage girls whose families generously 'present' them to Court. 'Coming out balls', they're called. Intriguingly.

Prince Charles has lived at St James's since 1992, when he tossed into an Adidas bag the spare toothbrush he used to keep at Kensington Palace, and finally admitted his marriage to Diana had turned into the wrong kind of fairytale: grimm.

After the Restoration, Charles II installed his saucy mistress Nell Gwyn in a Pall Mall house overlooking St James's Park, handy in case he fancied a swift rubber of bowls (or *pelle-melle*). Nell's career began euphemistically as an 'orange-seller' to the ribald gents in the stalls of the King's Playhouse, whence she rose to become a much-loved comic actress, specialising in 'breeches parts', dressed as a man. There the similarities end between Charles's witty, vivacious 'people's hero' and Camilla Parker-Bowles.

St James's Park is London's favourite oasis of green, reaching all the way to within a minute's walk of Trafalgar Square. The awkward pelicans, flapping on their artificial rocks in the bright blue lake, present a curious sight set against weeping willows and the surprising minarets and turrets of Whitehall. The top of Big Ben looks almost close enough to touch. A gingerbread cottage and toy bridge span the short distance to Duck Island, which is all very Famous Five: the public are barred from the bird sanctuary, but Ministry moles seek out these shadiest corners of the park for their clandestine meetings with Bulgarians in furry hats, usually called Markov. St James's Park is Britain's busiest market for Official Secrets, and I don't just mean the acreage of gently roasting flesh exposed by office workers' swimsuits during summer lunch-hours.

Walking back past Buckingham Palace, I find the crowd outside the gates has actually grown over the last hour. News of the cancellation is spreading slowly by word-of-mouth, and people are trickling grudgingly away; but at least as many passers-by are joining the ruck at the railings or climbing Queen Vic to find out what everybody else is looking at. Stoical London list-tickers seem momentarily bemused by the shambles, but along the way they're getting the hang of the traditional local response: Oh well, mustn't grumble. Have another melted ice-cream. Luvverly jubbly.

The crowd at the railings are not, technically, videoing fresh air: there are two black-clad soldiers on guard over at the foot of the breeze-block. One stamps his foot, marches five paces to the right, swivels, and marches back. Then a pause. Then he repeats his trick. And again. This really is quite watchable. It's addictive. A green plastic bag blows slowly across the pink gravel-chip playground on the lightest of breezes. Wa-hey.

I'm using a brand-new second-hand guide to navigate about the parks today: Hunter Davies's *A Walk Round London's Parks* is recommended more for its rare large-scale maps than its in-depth interviews with gardeners, litter-collectors and dog-walkers; but there are some great useless facts in here, too. For example: how many parks measuring twenty acres or more would you guess there are in London? Answer: 387. Good *fact*, Hunter. And he's even found something interesting to say about Green Park, which isn't really very interesting at all. It's green. It's a park. All the trees are the same. And Queen Victoria survived three assassination attempts here, in 1840, 1842 and 1849 – every one by a certified lunatic! There must be something about pleasant green spaces with samey trees that triggers crazy gunmen. Think JFK; think grassy knoll . . .

As I'm strolling up Constitution Hill, it's impossible not to notice that the trees on the other side of Buckingham Palace's ten-foot, barbed-wired, rotating-spiky-topped wall are *not* all the same. In fact, they're all different. And I bet the grass is greener over there. Buckingham Palace Gardens are *better* than Green Park, and there won't be a soul out enjoying them. I'm struck with a sudden desire to peek in, and find out what the Queen's private gardens are like. Seeing as how they've failed to change the guard, I should *break* in, enjoy a billionaire's solitary laze, and report back my findings to a waiting world. Shame about that barbed wire. And they've even lopped all the lower branches off the trees near the wall, so you can't climb up for a nose, let alone inch out over the wall and drop in for a visit.

Annoyingly, even Hunter's city-park bible shows no detail other than the shape of the lake: a roundish stretch with a panhandle and two islands – one around the same size as Duck Island in St James's Park, the other no more than a cartoon desert island, minus the palm tree. *Nicholson's London Streetfinder* weighs in with a couple of bridges onto the main island: no KEEP OFF OR ELSE signs in *these* gardens. Come to think of it, all of my 'London from the Air' picture-books fight shy of a low pass over Buck House, probably scared off by lawsuits, or anti-aircraft buckshot emanating from Prince Philip's hide on the rather cramped but otherwise well-appointed Queen Camilla Island. Maybe when the Queen quits the Palace and moves to Windsor – as she's been threatening to do for some time – then the gardens will be thrown open, and the three-mile swathe of public green stretching all the way from Whitehall to Kensington and Notting Hill will be complete.

Failing that, there's always the remote possibility of being invited to one of the Queen's garden parties. I'm going to start brushing up on my curtsy and my tea-sipping little-finger etiquette the moment I get home, Your Majesty.

On the sloping northern bank of the Serpentine lake in Hyde Park, I join a large, scattered crowd for a Sunday afternoon laze, eschewing the green-and-white deck-chairs as a needless expense at 70p per four hours. Far better to save that 70p and spend it later on dry-cleaning my corduroy jeans, or else a quack herbal remedy for arthritis, contracted from the deceptively damp grass. All the ingredients for proper Sunday lazing are here: hexagonal tea-rooms; rollerbladers to watch skinning their knees for sport; a broadsheet newspaper and a rising breeze; a placid stretch of water the same colour as my trousers (goose-crap green). The sparkling lake is abob with pleasure-craft – pedalos, rowing-boats and larger family-sized vessels with fringed canopies and outboard motors. The dregs at the bottom of my bottle of Coke are flat and warm.

The sun disappears behind thick white cloud. Now everything is in its place.

Leafing instead of expending shoe-leather through *London's Parks*, I find a passage that makes me feel sick with a sense of missed opportunity. Waffling parkishly about the changing Hyde Park skyline, Hunter drops in a reference to the view into Buckingham Palace Gardens from the bar at the top of the Hilton. If only I'd thought of that when I was up there: a surreptitious spy in on those forbidden lawns could have pushed my Londonometer reading well into three figures. Somebody might have been *visible*.

When it comes to the view of the Post Office Tower from Hyde Park, Hunter hits the nail on the head: 'Buckingham Palace stays still but the GPO Tower is everywhere' – usually at least 60 degrees away from where you might have placed it yourself. 'I refuse to call it the Telecom Tower,' Hunter adds. And good on him. 'You catch sight of that familiar phallus in so many unexpected places, down narrow alleyways, through sudden windows . . . as if it has a life of its own and is wandering out and about the London streets in its seven league boot.'

I couldn't have put it half so well myself. And now there's no need.

On the southern side of the Serpentine, the lido is cut off from the yappy dogs and I'll Be Mothers of the pavilion patio by a coy bamboo fence. Compared to the fortified wall of the Palace Gardens, this is easy. On the other side of the fence is an area reserved for that curious breed of people who strip off at the drop of a hat, especially when the sun isn't out. Only army shorts, ankle socks and sandals distinguish them from the closely related breed of Naturists. The Serpentine Swimmers are all aged over seventy-five, despite their annual mass-suicide attempt, when they go for a bracing dip among the broken ice floes on Christmas Day. Today there are three nut-brown oldsters to be viewed in their natural habitat, picnicking on damp towels. One hardy devotee to the cult of Health and Efficiency is doggy-paddling about in the lido, which is neatly roped off with strings of buoys from the rest of the lake, so the ducks know where to aim. If he swallows so much as a mouthful of that water, I should think his Health will be severely impaired. That said, he's very Efficiently collecting up a string of slimy debris from the surface.

NO DIVING, says the sign on the end of the boardwalk, and with good reason: the Serpentine is three feet deep with water, under which lurks a good fifty years' worth of crawling, fermenting guano.

At a refreshments caravan further along the bank, I ask for a lovely steaming cuppa to combat the heavy, grey heat. The Italian hot-water operative gives me coffee and a damp muffin, but I don't like to cause a fuss.

As on every other public stretch of water *at this very minute*, one all-male crew of bored picnickers, having lost their frisbee in the lake, have discovered a new, age-old way to flex their competitive muscles. They've somehow managed to squeeze an illicit extra knot or two from their clapped-out fly-mo engine, and are conducting serious lake-long time-trials, making bobbing families and bikini'd teenage smokers squeal in their wake.

When the American religious crusader, Billy Graham, dropped into Hyde Park in the '60s, he was forced to shield his JESUS IS LORD loon-pants from the sight of the unselfconsciously entwined lovers snogging on the grass. 'It looked as though your parks had been turned into bedrooms, with people lying all over the place,' he complained at the time. And, lo! His vision has miraculously come truer than he ever imagined. A group of young clubbers with backpacks and sleeping-bags have just recently stirred after a night out on the town. Sitting up for their first smoke of the day, they've each chosen an area of grass to search for anything interesting. A twig . . . An Opal Fruit wrapper . . . A packet of Opal Fruits! I've picked up this much because they're only ten yards away, and they're giggling louder than they think.

'Cooyer, look! An *ant*.'

'Let's all look for animals.'

Someone else finds an ant: they're probably camping on a nest. But a girl in glasses can't find any animals.

'I was looking for rabbits,' she admits sheepishly.

John Peel admits to having taken mind-bending drugs just once in his life, and that was floating out on the Serpentine, with his best mate Marc Bolan along for the trip. It must have seemed like a good idea at the time – until animals and time-triallists entered the picture.

Walking under the Serpentine road-bridge, picturesque with the long needling spire of Bayswater Church on the skyline beyond, I pass insensibly into Kensington Gardens or, as it's more properly known, 'the posh end of Hyde Park'. A couple of hundred years ago, this was all the private back yard of Royal Kensington Palace. You can tell it's posh, because there are no pedalos out on this stretch of the Serpentine, but there is a scale-size fleet of radio-controlled Royal Yachts on the Round Pond. Rollerbladers say 'excuse me kindly' as they barge old ladies off the path at 50 m.p.h. Traditionally, there's *culture* to hoover up in Kensington Gardens, as distinct from Hyde Park's snack-food and cheap political jibes; but, alas, the Serpentine Gallery, marooned in the middle of the park, is closed for renovation and extension, and Henry Moore's 'Arse on Stilts' has been removed. I was once fortunate enough to catch a groundbreaking work by Damien Hirst at a Serpentine Gallery exhibition: a fishtank full of inky water with an old sack thrown over it, called something like 'Everything In The Past Is Deader Than Everything In The Present But I'm Still Looking Forward To The Future'. A work of blatant genius. Only when I saw the news on *London Tonight* did I find out there had been half a sheep floating in the tank, and its finishing touches of texture and symbolic inky essence were supplied by animal rights activists.

Peter Pan is one of the best-loved of all the city's statues. It's the Michael Jackson of statues; a statue that will never grow up, and one that doesn't look a day over its eighty-five years. The statue cuts a totally *London* image: the overall effect of an elfin figure in a pauper-chic mini-skirt is very Kate Moss, very Twiggy, very *Cosmo*. If those ravers ever tear themselves away from their square feet of grass and happen across Peter Pan, they'll probably make perfect sense of a brassy Art Nouveau supermodel posing atop a rabbit warren, crawling with fairies. A clue to the inspiration of the scene is the suspect 'ethnic' pipe Pan has to his lips – clearly of a sort available from the 'paraphernalia' stalls on Camden Market.

Even the dogs have more class in Kensington Gardens. In Hyde

Park I was stopped in my tracks by the six-foot limb of a tree being hauled around by a big black labrador. Here, there are dogs with shaved pom-pom legs and tartan jackets. Panting down the path is one pensionable Pekinese – a green tennis-ball wedged in, and totally obscuring, his flat face. He's pulling a trail of straw and twigs behind him, brushed up by his shaggy coat. Ahhhhhhhhhh.

One of my very favourite London guides is Nicholas Saunders' brilliantly hippy *Alternative London*: not so much a guide to the city, more a soap-dodging scrounger's guide to getting high, staying high, annoying rich people and smashing the capitalist state – all with the minimum of effort and expenditure, naturally. At the top of the suggested list of Fun Things To Do for 1972 is: 'See how the social élite are reared – being pushed around by smart nannies in Kensington Gardens.'

Just my luck – it's Sunday. Parents are on duty. It's Mary Poppins' day off. But no matter . . .

'There are millions of things you can do in London, like yelling at people in Speakers' Corner . . . climbing a tree in every park . . . flying kites just about anywhere, but it's best in the middle of Oxford Street or outside Buckingham Palace . . .'

In among tips on how to fiddle the dole, addresses of anarchist collectives and communes, there are useful shopping and eating sections: where to buy a short wig to cover long hair; works canteens where a square (pardon my language) meal can be rustled up for free – or 15½p. Sandwiched between pink-and-yellow op-art covers, some of this stuff almost makes sense today: see the second half of any play for free, simply by walking in at the interval; stock up on free drinks and have a laugh at the Beautiful People at art previews; drop in for a free debate when the light is on over Big Ben . . . 'Entrance is the arch by the carpark: you can leave your car where it says "Peers only" . . .'

Some of *Alternative London*'s attitudes and obsessions may now sound as anachronistic as the Tooting Popular Front, *Oz* and the *International Times*; but a surprising number of its dippy, way-out ideas have become absorbed into the modern mainstream. Nick Saunders' *Ecstasy and the Dance Culture* is a recent best-seller – this time he didn't have to go for a DIY print-job, and the book wasn't even distributed by hand. In 1972, anyone who visited an acupuncturist, declined to eat meat or used a word like 'ecology' would almost certainly own a starry cloak, live sprawled on a bean-bag and go under the name of 'Gandalf'. Now they're just as likely to be Prime Minister.

It's enough to make you wonder what the future holds for flying saucers, women's lib and free love.

Kensington Palace is the least prepossessing of the royal residences – chilly and foreboding, like a mental home tucked away in the middle of the countryside behind an unscaleable wall and tall gates. After the 'Glorious Revolution' of 1688, which brought about the removal of James II and a good measure of the powers of the crown, William and Mary were the first monarchs to live in the palace – purportedly making the move from the damp and smoggy Whitehall Palace because of the Dutch king's asthma, but more realistically to scale down the old royal grandeur and opulence, and avoid another nasty run-in with the hoi-polloi. Queen Anne lived here next. She gave birth seventeen times, but still died childless; as some small consolation, she did have some top-notch quality chairs named after her. The German King George I started the new Hanoverian line resident at Kensington Palace. Generally speaking, Georges I and II were nowhere near as mad as 'Mad' George III or 'Nearly as Mad' George IV – even if the adulterous number one did punish his wife for her extra-marital affair by locking her away in a German castle for thirty-two years.

Not until Queen Victoria was born did Kensington Palace achieve some semblance of iron royal decorum. For seventeen years before she acceded to the throne, she was hidden away in three second-floor rooms she described as 'large, lofty, fine and cheerful'; but I fancy 'cheerful' is a relative term, and I'm glad I never inherited her bed.

At the time of my trip, I couldn't help thinking this was an unlikely crashpad for Princess Diana – full of royal ghosts, of empty rooms and hollow, tiptoeing ritual. Who would want to live cooped up in their dodgy old ex's draughty family pile – let alone with his tragic Auntie Margaret as a housemate? As one of her sixty million expert amateur advisors, I was convinced Di would have been happier taking her kids away from this ramshackle royal relic and buying herself a smart modern flat. Even in the light of her death, I cling to my piece of useless advice as something that might have made a difference.

Back in the south of the park, I'm keen on finding the site of the

Great Exhibition of 1851, the very first 'World Fair'-style collection of newfangled wonders, which was housed in the spectacular Crystal Palace. Only a minimal amount of detective work is called for – 'Site of Great Exhibition', it says on Hunter's map – but I still muster a pleasantly eerie sensation finding and standing on the path opposite the Kensington Barracks skyscraper, in the long, narrow playing-field to the south of Rotten Row. If this were 1851, I'd be standing in the middle of a gigantic vaulted greenhouse, at 1,848 feet long (shame they couldn't stretch to another three feet) four times the length of St Paul's. The central transept was four hundred feet long and over a hundred feet high, not merely enclosing but *dwarfing* an avenue of elms, long since dead and gone. The whole exhibition was the brainchild of Prince Albert, Queen Victoria's Prince Consort, and it was they who opened the show, throned high beneath a vast velvet canopy, approximately where a young Indian batsman, possibly a Test player of the future, has just been controversially given out: bowled Dad, stumped Mum. They've obviously taken Norman Tebbit's 'patriotic' insult to heart, and are grooming junior to play for England.

Back on 1 May 1851, cannon were fired across the Serpentine, trumpets blared, a thousand-voice choir raised the roof with Handel's Hallelujah Chorus, then the National Anthem was played on four organs while V&A trundled around the nineteen-acre site . . . and, finally, the Great Exhibition of the Works and Industry of All Nations was declared open. The first of six million visitors, a third of the British population, rushed in to whoop and goggle at the breathtaking exhibits from forty-one countries, including all manner of state-of-the-art steam-driven contraptions (a locomotive, a threshing machine, a Goblin Teasmade) from Blighty! A Gothic sailor's chapel, fully seaworthy, from the U.S. of A!! A crystal fountain flowing with *eau-de-Cologne*!!!

I could go on. There were, after all, 100,000 displays to choose from.

The Koh-i-Noor diamond and an ivory throne from India! An alarm-clock which tipped its snoozing victim direct into an icy bathtub!! The 'Iron' Duke of Wellington, who regularly strolled in for a shufti from his Apsley House residence at 'Number 1, London', on Hyde Park Corner!!!

The tacit effect of showing off the ingenuity of the world in

London was to confirm the city's place at the centre of the world – at least locally. Other countries were acknowledged as a vital supporting cast to Britain's guiding star. All they needed was to be organised and given their chance to shine.

One final Trivia Stop: not a lot of people know that just one fragment of the Crystal Palace escaped its fate when the rebuilt cathedral of glass and iron caught fire and burned to the ground in south London in 1936: the clock adorning the front of King's Cross Station originally hung high over the central nave of the Great Exhibition.

A fast-growing percentage of London's cockney-come-lately population have never seen the Albert Memorial in all its glory, and may well think this outlandish monument to the certainties of the Victorian age is a 180-foot tower of corrugated plastic sheeting. A closer inspection reveals the tower to be surrounded with statues of camels, Red Indians and elephants; but they're only visible through peepholes in a mod-art security fence which keeps out camel activists and their bottles of Quink. The Memorial, in a dangerous state of disrepair, was sheathed away from view in 1990, but £14 million worth of restoration work is on target to be completed in time for the Millennium. At the foot of the building site is a portakabin exhibition about the monument, Prince Albert, and his Great Exhibition – including a mocked-up map of the Crystal Palace *in situ* in the park. So much for my detective work.

Completed some twenty-five years after the Great Exhibition, in honour of the Prince Consort, who had since died tragically young of typhoid, the monstrous pagoda shrine placed a fourteen-foot Albert at the centre of a microcosmic Victorian Empire and all its achievements. If you saw the scale model of the Memorial, you might think Albert was flicking through a bible or a giant greenhouse construction manual, but in fact it's a Great Exhibition catalogue. Surrounded by the continents and frozen life-size mock-ups of the industries and the more respectable professions, Albert sits amid a fantastic spangly shed of jewels, polished stones and glass, surmounted by four brightly coloured mosaics of the arts and a strangely familiar spire overrun with angels and bunnies, all topped off with a golden cross. It's as kitsch as anything I've ever clapped eyes on. It's so utterly irresistible, I chip in 47p toward the repair bill. That should sort out a fair thumbnail-sized chunk of those two hundred tons of crumbling ironwork.

Albert was a great king in all but name, turning around the British people's initial suspicion of the young German prince, to die as the nation's favourite adopted uncle. Never mind exhibitions, this is the man who gave us the *Christmas tree!* Nevertheless, to assist the early assimilation process, Albert changed his name and that of his ongoing dynasty from Saxe-Coburg-Gotha to 'Windsor' – the most English-sounding name he could think of. It's a good job William the Conqueror didn't settle on Leatherhead as a pretty spot for a castle.

Queen Victoria's lasting image as a grumpy old battleaxe dates exclusively from the period after Albert's death, when she retreated into her shell at the loss of her first love and guiding light. The couple had nine children. Prince Albert had drive, an unusual taste in jewellery, and a sense of humour: he was still alive when they started work on the Memorial, and resisted his statue being placed at its centre, knowing full well that it was just asking future generations to have a giggle at his expense. With the £200,000 profit made from the Exhibition, he built South Kensington for the people, a marvellously successful centre for the advancement of the arts, sciences and education, known to this day as 'Albertopolis'.

I cross the road in front of that superb cruiserweight hamburger, the Royal Albert Hall. I could stop and stare for hours at the creamy heroic friezes around this red-brick pleasuredome, but today there are too many Last Night of the Proms types milling about, and I'm already well behind schedule: it takes *hours* to walk five miles if you insist on punctuating your Sunday stroll with lazing breaks and damp muffins. Now I'm left with less than an hour and a half to take in the Victoria & Albert Museum, the Natural History Museum, the Science Museum and the Commonwealth Institute, Kensington's spiritual descendant of Albert's Imperial Institute, which was demolished in the 1930s.

Adding to my problems, I can never visit South Ken or even pass through the Tube station without starting to whistle or hum 'Sunny South Kensington' by His Cosmicness, the High Priest of Twitty Hippiness: *Donovan.* Donovan was even cooler than Cat Stevens: imagine *that.* And Donovan was the most Londocentric of his psychedelic '60s peers, even though he's actually Scottish. Don was suckered by the charms of the Maharishi and flew to India with the Beatles. 'Mellow Yellow' was banned on the understanding that it encouraged banana-smoking. Which is harmless. In 'Sunny South Kensington', Don invites his listeners to 'come loon soon' on the Cromwell Road, over wheezing electric organ *and* harpsichord. Mary Quant and Jean-Paul Belmondo are slandered – but groovily. Don rhymes 'trip out' with 'flip out' and 'skip out'. You get the picture. If I were to mention that Donovan also had a song called 'Sunny Goodge Street', you'd realise most of his lyrics were written by poking a finger at the Tube map, adding the all-important 'Sunny' prefix, and spouting colourful, if random, doggerel. But here's the rub: Don's a misunderstood genius. Don makes Syd Barrett's Pink Floyd sound like Dave Dee, Dozy, Beaky, Mick and Tich.

Interestingly, my mate Dave once gatecrashed a party on board Donovan's yacht in the South of France. My sister denies having a snog with him when she was fourteen. The Maharishi, too. My sister, I mean.

Now I've got an hour and twenty minutes to do South Ken.

The Commonwealth Institute collects together in one crumbling, clever-clever school hall (circular galleries; copper-peaked roof) all the economic and cultural glories of the former Empire, laying them out not as plundered goods but as a celebration of worldly diversity at the heart of its Capital. Canada is represented by a tatty stuffed porcupine; by spinning a magical perspex barrel, the dominion's innovations are revealed to include a paint roller, an ice-hockey mask and a faded carton of Magic Pantry Chicken. Bechuanaland, British Guiana and America look very jolly colonies. But, perhaps chauvinistically, I spend most time gazing at the cabinet devoted to all things hailing from the imperial outpost of Leicester. It's difficult to conceive of an Empire, an England or indeed a London divested of its Coritanian contribution. Historically, of course, Boadicea burnt London to the ground in AD64. Thomas Cook invented the holiday: where would we *be* without the *holiday*? And it was only an accident of time that prevented Showaddywaddy inventing *rock 'n' roll*. In the field of entertainment alone, we have Leicester to thank for Adrian Mole, prison-prone mini-rapper Mark 'The Mack' Morrison, and Joe Orton – the Fifth Beatle. Leicester was once home to Daniel Lambert, the fattest person ever. The roll of honour is virtually endless. Somewhere towards the nether end of the list lies Leicester's own Son of God, formerly known as sports reporter David Icke.

I spin the magic barrel and look in on a used packet of 'Gary

Lineker'-flavoured crisps.

The spirit of the Great Exhibition lives on in Sunny South Kensington.

At the Science Museum, I discover Britain didn't only give the world the timetable, but the railway, too. The sandwich. The toilet. The machine-gun. Anaesthetic.

At the V&A, there are sample-books of the world's first wallpaper. And lino. Direct from London, England.

At the Natural History I come face to face with some fossilised pond-scum which could lay claim to being the world's first cockneys.

It's impossible not to feel humbled.

14 Near to the Theatre

I must admit I had my reservations about visiting the London Transport Museum. I was worried I might be forced to consider the wheel arrangement of locomotives on the Metropolitan Line, and end up actually giving a toss. I was worried I might be drawn into conversation on the advantages of tram-travel (it was in the past), or a debate on the bus-routes running to the West India Docks (er, that'll be the 677 via Goswell Road and Dalston). Also, every day in August so far has been hot and humid, but today is positively tropical, and the Trainspot Museum just happens to be located in a greenhouse – one of the old flower market buildings around the edge of Covent Garden.

I take a deep breath, ditch my heavy flight-bag survival pack (guidebooks, compass, Kendal mintcake) in the cloakroom, and wade into the heat. Hell: there are children with clipboards. Men taking photos of buses from strange angles. I count eleven PLEASE DO NOT BOARD notices plastered over the AEC chassis London transport tower wagon No. 89Q, 1936 – the guidebook is depressingly detailed – and five schoolchildren crammed, bouncing, in its cab. The temperature is touching 100 degrees. Centigrade. Thinking ahead, I bought a large bottle of Lucozade, and left it in my bag.

I clamber on board a tram and take my turn holding the driver's rudder. Nothing happens. Something mustn't be plugged in.

Trolley-buses may have had twin back axles and been powered by the trams' old overhead electric cables, but inside they were remarkably similar to the Routemasters still in service today. Interestingly, the steps were slightly steeper.

Out of context, off the streets, these mothballed red double-deckers don't make a lot of sense – whether they were originally powered by plastic horses, by fume-belching diesel engines or jumbo extension-leads. Only when I slouch in a steaming puddle in front of an unpromising video console does the museum begin to creak into life: I find I'm watching over a driver's shoulder as he steers down the middle of a tram-packed Strand, devoid of motor traffic. Alive, the swaying tram clatters and clangs; workers in the street switch points and ease the car onto a new set of tracks with a giant pitchfork. The conductor fishes in the air for an electric line. People are hurrying everywhere, seemingly unaware of the subtle strangeness of their black-and-white universe. Landmarks slip past in unfamiliar surroundings, evolutionary survivors, while these museum rows of trams and open-top charabanc buses are the fossilised remains of the city of the past.

I wonder how many of these bustling monotone figures have bridged the chasm between then and now; between this irretrievable London and the city that has engulfed it.

The next tram I try for size seems appreciably more *human*, dating from this same inter-war era. Now I know what to do with the driver's handle: twirl it around, clacking madly, while shouting 'Scuse I, gel' from the open front window. The tram's strip of opening windows is still plastered with the adverts that spoke to those distant, scurrying Londoners in a language not far removed from English:

GOLLY IT'S GOOD!
ROBERTSON'S MINCEMEAT MAKES MANY
GOOD THINGS.

Like mince pies, for example.

HAYWARD'S MILITARY PICKLE
'BETTER THAN A SALAD'.

Better than being overcome with this infernal prickly heat. Better than dehydration. Disorientation. Dementia. Golly, I could just drink a jar now.

Backtracking to the wartime trolley-bus, the gas-masked cockney dummies are now no more convincing, but at least they stand for real people, in their drab macs, headsquares and cloth caps. I notice the smell of the seats and the feel of the hand-straps. I even have a fiddle with the blast netting tacked over my window, until I'm given a respectful dressing down by 'Billy Brown of London Town'. The cartoon Man from the Min. of Pub. Info. has been tipping his bowler and laying down the letter of the law ever since the Blitz, and he'll still be doing just the same another fifty years down the line.

On the museum walls, black-and-white Londoners huddle

together in their hundreds, sheltering from German bombs on an Underground platform. Armies of defluffers crawl between stations with brushes and dustpans in the middle of the night. Thousands of bus-drivers and conductors are recruited from the West Indies, answering a shortage in cheap labour, and forming the backbone of London's Caribbean communities. Dummies come fitted with a Mary Quant mini and a *Melody Maker*, but the adverts on board seem too stiff and old-fashioned for the '60s; the silver bell-pushes, the oddly dimpled rubber platform, and so many minor details seem all wrong, to me.

But this is the way it was: another world.

London was bombed and reborn; Londoners swayed along on trams, sung along to drown the sound of air-raid sirens, swung along to a soundtrack of calypso, ska and twitbeat . . . *and I wasn't there.*

In 1933, Frank Pick took his own hopelessly idealistic vision of London, and set about making it concrete. As head of the new London Transport Authority, responsible for the running of the Underground, the buses, trams and trains, Pick was soon setting new standards in line with his gospel of 'fitness for purpose'. The face of the city was changed as modern new stations sprang up, slick new trains were commissioned, and the system took on a unified image. The LT 'bullseye' roundel was adopted as a symbol; the beautifully clear Johnson typeface was put into service and, perhaps most famously of all, Henry Beck's entirely abstract Tube map was designed to leak information to the Tube-traveller on a strictly *need-to-know* basis. The map is a design classic; a paragon of clarity and user-friendliness, and a masterpiece of tactical misinformation, whose imaginative distortions affect our image of London to this day. If you're a hundred feet underground, bulleting between Bow and Bank, you don't *need to know* that you're actually half a mile south of the river, passing directly beneath the floorboards of your Bermondsey bachelor-pad.

The Tube map remains, nevertheless, the most honest and accurate summary of information to be found in the diary of anyone I know.

Apart from alerting Americans to avoid vats of boiling oil when in London, the single most startling contribution to my *Let's Go: London* guide is a map of the Tube with the lines superimposed on real-life

London. The Jubilee Line forms an ugly, zig-zagging slash through the middle of town. The river is shown bending at ridiculous angles other than 45 and 90 degrees. The Circle Line isn't even a regular oblong. Bloody Americans! A child of five could design an underground system more logical than this unholy mess.

The new stations of the '30s were boldly futuristic creations, garnished with curves and conning towers, which still stand out in the suburbs; but it was Pick's ongoing public information programme that most changed the image and outlook of London. Ever since 1908, when he was first appointed Publicity Officer of the Underground Group, he had been applying subtly positive pressures on the public's perception of the capital as a place to explore and enjoy. Now he was given absolute power. Avant-garde artists were plucked from the galleries to produce posters for platforms and ticket-halls, promoting eye-opening travel opportunities about a city whose promise and very portrayal bordered on the mystical. As a transport chief, Frank Pick was wildly overstepping his remit, but every part of his plan was carried out with the people at heart – and the people loved it. The pleasures of living in the new suburbs were graphically depicted by Pick's team of cubists and futurists, their clean lines suggesting efficiency and dynamism, with no mention of tea, toast or slippers in the oven. GREET THE SUN: healthy trips out of the smogbound city were promoted with just as much suggestive skill as its mind-expanding museums and institutions. I aim to be spending most of next summer in the unspoiled London countryside of Dorking, Staines and Hampton Wick, closely following London Transport's irresistible treasure-map, *School Picnics and Pleasure Parties*. No need to set foot outside London to explore all THE WEALTH AND BEAUTY OF THE EMPIRE, at Harrods, The Commonwealth Institute, the British Museum . . .

See BRIGHTEST LONDON, and Home by Underground.

By the time he retired, Frank Pick's vision of a modern, vibrant, enlightened London was still to a large extent a figment of his imagination; but what an imagination.

Just as I'm piloting a computer mock-up of the Metropolitan Railway's 4-4-0 steam locomotive no. 23 into Baker Street – expertly tooting and easing off the dead-man's handle as the station looms out of the iron-ribbed tunnel – I sense I may well be enjoying myself a little too much, and give way to a grown man with a jotter and school jumper, who has formed an orderly, though restless, queue at my side. He's completed his re-enactment of a 1937 commuter's oak-panelled ride in from Metroland, and now he's looking for a little light relief before taking on more vital work in the simulated signal-box. Goodness gracious, that slovenly young schoolma'am's army of sweaty charges are climbing all over the fog-repeater, and don't seem to know their semaphores from their coffee-pots. And that will never do.

In the museum shop, I find a quintessential London accessory priced very reasonably at £2.99. It's a two-tone Tube whistle, and it Sounds Like The Real Thing. If The Trainspotter happens across it, he'll most likely buy two – one to file away under 'W' in his LT-related Lever Arch File, and one with which to torture relatively sane passengers from the end of the platform.

My favourite accessory for advanced transportologists is the *Connection Guide*, a pocket-sized booklet which tells you where to catch your Oxo-cube. You might think a normal Tube map does the job quite nicely, thank you; but these specialist time-saving guides for the committed commuter go further, indicating not only which platform to head for, but how far along you should stand for the ultimate and optimal trip across London. The idea is, you make use of time you would normally waste to barge to a position, say, three-quarters of the way along the platform, ready for car number three: then, when you arrive at your destination, you'll be bang opposite your exit, or the burrow leading to your District Line connection.

Just imagine the pudgy, Brylcreemed Trainspotter, who chooses not to get on just *any* carriage of the first train to Wembley Park, oh no. He takes up his optimal position on the platform, and waits five minutes for another service. But when he does finally alight at Wembley, he'll save fully 23 seconds, and beat the crowd to the ultimate spot to catch his connection home to Chalfont & Latimer.

It might not be a bad idea for someone to produce a *Connection Guide* that includes some genuinely useful information for Tube-travellers: 'Tottenham Court Road Centre Point subway: public toilets closed years ago, but just go ahead and unzip anyway'; 'Covent Garden passageway to lifts: avoid gaze of psychotic busker who only knows the chorus to "Streets of London" . . .'

I settle for a set of London Transport's *double entendre* postcards – Hold tight; Mind the gap; Penalty for improper use £50 – and only then start worrying whether they're meant to be *double entendres*, or whether it's just me. I reclaim my bag, and make the desperate discovery that hot Lucozade tastes quite a lot like Earl Grey tea, with six sugars.

Covent Garden is a spelling mistake. The first of London's planned squares, it was built on the site of a *convent* garden in the 1630s, some one hundred years after Henry VIII dissolved the monasteries and gifted the land to his chum, the first Earl of Bedford. As London expanded north and west, the piazza was to prove an irresistibly trendy template: Leicester Square was developed next, followed by Bloomsbury, Soho, Berkeley, and so on, until London became a city of squares. The Beautiful People clamoured for an address in the fourth Earl's smart new Covent Garden neighbourhood, designed Italian-style by Inigo Jones. The Theatre Royal soon established the area's thespian connection, and it became known as a fashionable place to stroll and gossip . . . until the fifth Earl rather short-sightedly allowed a fruit and vegetable market to become a fixture in his back garden.

For some reason, the growth of the noisy, stinking market and an influx of less than impeccably mannered traders, thugs and thieves saw the toffs moving away in droves – although the gentlemen were soon tempted back to 'the Great Square of Venus' to visit the staggering number of coffee-houses, gambling dens and 'Turkish baths' which grew up to fill the vacuum. At least, that's what they told their wives.

The atmosphere of the area in the mid-eighteenth century seeps out of scenes from the artist William Hogarth's most popular satirical engravings: *The Rake's Progress* details The Rake making appreciable progress ('whoopee') with one of the playful strumpets at the Rose Tavern in Russell Street. The grotesque cast of *Gin Lane* are captured not raising hell, but living in it. The hovels and stews of Seven Dials, just north of Covent Garden, made up one the city's filthiest, most dangerous rookeries. A baby slips from the breast to the cobbles as its mother takes a swig of gin from the bottle.

Covent Garden's modern-day reputation as a centre of entertainment is still based around the popularity of the 'theatres' which flooded into the area in Hogarth's era, even if the main attraction on offer has changed with the times, and now rarely involves anything more risqué than watching a play. The centrepiece of the piazza is the covered halls erected by the eleventh Earl in the 1830s, in a final, vain attempt to curb the chaos of the marketplace. A ghostly sigh of relief must have sounded around the market in 1974, when the fruit and veg merchants were finally shunted south of the river; but the breakout of peace didn't last long. For once, plans to bury a sizeable slice of prime London real estate under office blocks were opposed and shelved, and shops, stalls and pavement cafés were beckoned in. The street entertainers invited themselves, adding yet more colour and noise to London's most popular outdoor tourist traffic-jam.

Oh, well. One mustn't grumble. Or, as the Bedfords' motto had it, 'Che Sera Sera' – still to be found emblazoned resignedly above the portals of the market building. Familial stoicism aside, I bet the old fifth Earl doesn't half wish he'd sent his butler to see off those oikish cabbage-floggers with a large stick.

Ever since the mid-nineteenth century the Royal Opera House has been struggling to elevate the tone of the area, on the face of it not a difficult task. Patrons of 'The Garden' long had to tread a careful path between piles of rotten fruit, discarded boxes, rickety stalls and denizens of the square's downmarket attractions. Today, the Royal Opera House is undergoing a major renovation and extension, reducing the entire north-east corner of the square to a building site. The cost of the work is currently trumpeted as £213 million – £78 million of which came from Lottery funds. The taxpayer's keenness to subsidise the project was just as finely judged by the government of the day as our respectful longing to chip in for a new royal yacht. Personally, I'd be happier seeing my own annual opera handout of 63p going towards the bill for the Queen Mother's unfortunate gin-ciggies-curtains accident at Windsor Castle. But it's a close call.

The legendary hustle of the early-morning fruit and veg market is today echoed by Covent Garden's army of jugglers, strummers and out-and-out chancers. The quality of entertainment varies greatly: some of these modern-day marketeers smilingly serve up a short weight of pigswill from their pitch in the gutter, while yet fresher characters press upon passers-by a cornucopia of deceptively slim pickings. The tables set out beneath umbrellas across the north of the piazza are all circled with holidaymakers in that priceless London mood which can override any consideration of value or taste; and anyhow, isn't it a fine old English tradition to launch your loose change at a shuffling tap-dancer – maybe even slip in a 50p if he only has one leg? It's too glorious a day to quibble. The pubs are overflowing. The bagsnatcher police are out in their shirt-sleeves. Even the winos have peeled off their outer layers of clothing to sun themselves along the kerbside, and are close to collecting the price of a shared refreshment.

I'm painfully aware that my weak entertainment-as-fruit-and-veg metaphor ran out of juice quite some time ago. However, at the end of Floral Street, I come across the inevitable robotic mime-artist, whose still-life attractions could only possibly be likened to those of a pippy satsuma twenty years past its sell-by date. This bloke really is taking the pith. He's painted himself silver, and he's standing stock-still in a tinfoil suit in the baking sun. Yes, he can rotate his hand *just like an android*, and has scribbled a cheeky sign to inform his fluid audience of thirty or forty that he's 'coin-operated'. But get this. He's added a note asking anyone taking pictures to make a contribution. And people are playing along. As if they'll be able to tell he's standing *still* in a *photo* . . .

In the piazza, a clown-faced drummer has set up a full kit: in response to the cash gifts flowing in from his bemused audience, he oh-so-skilfully speeds up and slows down. In the cooler air of the market-cum-craft fair, a team of slapstick students are doing battle with a string quartet. Outside the Theatre Museum, housed in another of the old flower market buildings, another major new talent is busy hurling a heavy projectile shaped like an apple core twenty feet into the air, and catching it on a piece of string between two sticks. His small space in the middle of a crowd is growing larger by the second. He manages a thirty-foot launch, bolts to his left and just catches the spinning weight. His next throw is easily a record, soaring – *woo!* – over four storeys high. But now the hefty object is plummeting toward the ground . . . and crash-landing in the midst of a crowded pavement. I swallow. The spotty hurler swallows. The crowd holds its breath. Someone is going to *die*.

A suave black kid crossing the road nonchalantly plucks the missile out of the air above his head, and carries on walking without breaking pace or looking around. The hurler doesn't know whether to laugh or cry. Our superhero turns and bowls the projectile back to the virtuoso, who catches it expertly on his string, takes his 17p and resigns while he's on top. A crowd of fifteen applauds wildly, but the star of the show has already melted back into the crowd.

There aren't many turns in Theatreland who'd want to have to follow an impro performance like that. Even Andrew Lloyd Webber would baulk at the challenge, and most of his shows are every bit as attractive as a lead weight lodged in the cranium. The good news (at least for that mad, lonely typist from Ashby-de-la-Zouche who's seen *Phantom* 570 times) is: our one-man West End musical industry is bang on target to have a production on at *every* London theatre by the year 2015!

So tell me, Andy: what, exactly, is *Cats* all about?

I was planning on dropping into the Theatre Museum to see if I could find a poster or a programme relating to my own début London theatre experience, when my parents took me along to see Bruce Forsyth at the Palladium. As it turns out, the immediate prospect of another sauna is none too enticing. Also, to this day, I'm plagued by the memory of one of Brucie's side-splitting jokes, which went along the lines of 'I'm going on holiday to Mexico, blah blah . . . amusing pronunciation, blah blah . . . I don't know whether to go in *Hune* or *Huly!?!*' Boom-boom.

Stupidly, I memorised that gag in the hope that I might one day understand it. Likewise, the bunnyish, grimacing charms of the Young Generation Dance Troupe who, at the time, exercised the mysterious ability of strapping older girls in big pants to make me blush to the very bottom of my Clark's Commandos. I now realise, of course, my reaction was something to do with boys-only gym classes, and Sandie Shaw on *Top of the Pops*.

Even by the tender age of nine I was a veteran of four or five star-studded variety bills. We're talking Mike and Bernie Winters. Ken Dodd and his Diddymen. So far as I recall, ex-New Seeker Lyn Paul was second on the bill to Forsyth, not my first rock 'n' roll gig – that was Gerry out of Gerry and the Pacemakers – but my first on solid land. It felt so much *safer* clapping along to a cravated four-piece big-band's version of yesterday's hits in a smart London theatre, rather than suspended over a choppy summer sea on the end of a Victorian pier. Harry Corbett's Sooty and Sweep puppet show was my long-standing favourite gig, with the sultry Soo providing the blushes. For a panda, she was a *fox*.

You might say the roar of the greasepaint and the smell of the crowd courses thicker than water through the veins of my family.

Crap band, baldiefish joke and passing acquaintance with the Rank gong-banger's nephew aside, my dad's cousin is Eddie Izzard's dad! – which makes Eddie my third cousin twice removed, and me the step-aunt-in-law of someone who's been on the telly.

Scrubbing the Theatre Museum off my itinerary – there might have been actors dressed up in period gear, pretending to like music hall – I do the sensible thing and *rehydrate*. As any serious London-trekker will tell you, it's important to replace the fluids lost in tropical tram-sheds with a pint of icy, excessively carbonated Forsyte – as served up with some alacrity at the Punch and Judy. This miniature pub, set up in the gables of the Covent Garden market halls, is one of the very busiest in the West End. I don't put this down to the the pub's blaring techno jukebox, or its particularly fine selection of different-coloured alcopops. The Punch and Judy's balcony looks down over the cobbles of the western end of the piazza, taking in the one remaining stretch of terrace, and the street entertainers' main stage, beneath the portico of St Paul's Church. When I re-emerge into the afternoon sun on this lowly first step to heaven, there's a beefy black American thrilling a crowd of some two hundred children and grown-ups with a finely honed act. He can dance to some extent. He can pull a kid out of the crowd, and watch *them* dance to some extent. Aha, he can do a handstand! But his main talent seems to be keeping a large crowd looking in his direction on the assumption that this is all leading somewhere – while his assistants do the rounds with the hat. And so to the *real* glory of the Punch and Judy: no one up here is going to be obliged to give the bugger a penny.

Down on the steps under the thick, smooth columns of the church-front is where Rex Harrison (Doctor Doolittle) came across the hopeless cockernee case of Eliza Doolittle (Audrey Hepburn) in *My Fair Lady*. She couldn't talk proppah, so the good doctor took her under his wing to mould her into a social butterfly. In the Hollywood stage-set version, they glossed over the closeness of the couple's relationship – even before they met. The portico of St Paul's has never been used as an entrance; it's just a big, friendly space that has always been a favourite meeting place from the time Inigo Jones set the original model in his smart piazza, through the market years right up until today. In 1662, Britain's first-ever Punch and Judy show took place on this time-honoured, makeshift stage, as witnessed by the diarist Samuel Pepys. St Paul's is known as 'the actors' church', and I would go in to pay my respects to Boris Karloff, only a roped-off building site is blocking the way.

There's something about the smell of a glass of beer, drunk outside in the sun, that simply insists, 'stay and have another'. Although the weather isn't letting on, it's getting late in August now – and how many more times will it be possible to laze in the sun this summer, especially with pressing chunks of London still to be done? I order another half, catch myself stifling a laugh at the street hoofer, and wave away the worry that swathes of the city could easily go the way of Doc Johnson's 'sausage', at this rate.

The Theatre Royal Drury Lane isn't on Drury Lane at all, but on Catherine Street. 'Theatre Royal Catherine Street': no, it just doesn't have the same ring to it. Although the original theatre was marked as the place where Charles II first clapped eyes on Nell Gwyn, it enjoyed its most impressive royal action in the Georgian period: attempts were made here on the lives of first George I, and then George II. Failing to take the hint that this was not a happy spot for kings called George, George III then had a public slanging match in the lobby with the future George IV – hence not one but two royal boxes at the theatre. In the '50s and '60s, *My Fair Lady* played here 2,281 times, and every one cheered on by that wretched typist from Ashby-de-la-Zouche.

Miss Saigon is on at the moment, having barely embarked on its nine-hundred-year run. I always assumed *Miss Saigon* was a Lloyd Webber production, mainly because it's a musical, and it's on in London. *Time Out* calls it 'a massive spectacle complete with floor shows, dream sequences and a helicopter'. No cats, face-masks or human chess pieces – that was *Aspects* – but it's clearly deep in Andy territory.

Can I be the only cockney tourist in London who wouldn't walk next door to see Webber's musical version of *Sunset Boulevard*? The only one who'd snap their curtains shut on Sarah Brightman roller-skating at the end of the garden?

Yes, I thought so.

OLD CURIOSITY SHOP, someone once daubed in authenticke Olde Worlde letteringe across the front of the Old Curiosity Shop. IMMORTALISED BY CHARLES DICKENS, it says. Even though

Dickens' O.C.S. was at the bottom of Charing Cross Road. BUILT 1567, it says. It's really too hot and humid to argue the toss, especially now someone could make the addition, CLOSED DOWN 1997. Dickens' shop or not, this junk emporium stood here for 430 years before I pencilled it into my agenda, when it promptly went out of business.

Just around the corner, by Lincoln's Inn Fields, an unmistakable cacophony drifting over the park promises one of the many final, missing pieces in my London jigsaw: a dodgy, jolly cockney funfair! – with young David Essex riding on the back of your dodgem, claiming all the loose change he's found on your seat, even though it hasn't yet jiggled out of your pocket! Disappointingly, the barrel-organ music proves not to be emanating from a rickety waltzer, and there are no shooting galleries with bent rifle sights or coconuts nailed to posts. The barrel-organ music is being pumped wildly from the bellows of a barrel-organ. LIST' AND I WILL ENCHANT THINE EAR, it boasts; but up close it's deafening. Bass-drum, cymbal and machine-gun snare are all crashing away on their runaway auto-setting. The high notes on the pipe organ are painful, and something that sounds suspiciously like kazoo accompaniment is, by definition, sheer torture. The front of the organ is a mess of mirrors, musical scrolls and Union Jacks, the whole shebang of MUSIC, MIRTH AND MERRIMENT seemingly in the maniacal control of a miniature Hammer-horror conductor, jiggling eerily on his shelf. Luckily, the watchful owner looks nothing at all like Boris Karloff.

I decline the offer of his organ cassette – this music is a bit like disco, fine and dandy in its place, but you wouldn't want to be caught playing it at home – even though my eye is drawn to the organ's selection of well-known machine-gun kazoo selections from *My Fair Lady*: 'I Could Ov Darnced Orl Night', 'I'm Gettin' Cut and Carried in ver Mornin', 'Oops! Upside Your Crust of Bread' . . .

Giving in once again to the sun, I buy an ice-cream and flop on the grass, joining a smattering of people doing what comes naturally in London: lazing, and playing tennis badly in unsuitable weather conditions. The lawns and trees are still green, but the first dead leaves of summer are collecting along the edges of the paths. Reading up on Charles Dickens' house, I find he only lived there for two years, during which time his most important written output was notes for the milkman. That isn't strictly true, but he didn't reach the height of his fame until he lived for *twelve* years in Devonshire Terrace, off Regent's Park – which was bulldozed in the '50s. And so, Dickens is effortlessly yet more-or-less justifiably sliced from my schedule. As I laze, I atone in part by doing my best to picture a really interesting writing desk and pen, undoubtedly two of the star attractions of all Bloomsbury. Already today I've flagrantly ignored Bow Street, east of Covent Garden, and this despite the pivotal importance of its Magistrates Court and eponymous Runners in the history of British law enforcement.

Having exposed my solar-powered Londonometer to a control reading of lager and crisps, policemen and judges scored a combined must-see funability score of just under 0.7 whoops per century.

Doubling back west to the '90s fashion and shopping epicentre of Neal Street, I find it's too hot and sticky to shop. At the Pop Boutique, a banner suggests DON'T FOLLOW FASHION, BUY SOMETHING THAT'S ALREADY OUT OF DATE. But it's too late. I've got untouched wardrobes full of that stuff. All the people who are supposed to be shopping for clothes are instead discarding the ones they've already got on, and cramming into the sunny brick-and-ivy courtyard of Neal's Yard. They're busily replacing sweaty fluids with unnervingly healthy ones. Coffee without coffee. Fruit-juice without a mixer. Holistic guarana punch. Bread is baked on the premises, chock-full of vitamin E and wood chippings. Homoeopathic remedies, walk-in back-rubs and therapy rooms beckon. No, really.

Neal's Yard was set up in the early '70s, on the initiative of none other than Nicholas Saunders – bringing to life the radically herbal love-in vision of *Alternative London*. And to think Nick's mates said cheesecloth rebellion was just a passing phase.

It may be too hot to shop till you drop, but it's never too hot for a spot of light celebrity-spotting. Covent Garden and the Neal Street area enjoy a reputation as the best spotting spots in London, awash with people in sunglasses, which they'll casually remove if heads don't start turning. The best part of spotting a celebrity is subsequently ignoring them: this is *London*, for God's sake, not somewhere squealy and touchy (or cold and superior) like New York or Paris. In London, it's good form to let a celebrity pass at least twenty yards down the street before blurting out, '*Woh!* Him out of *On the Buses!*' On a busy Saturday, it's well worth pepping up your window-shopping by placing a small wager on which star shopper you'll bump into and be struck how short/tall they are in real life. The last time I was Covent Gardening with Lesley Wallace, we followed our hunches and each risked a 10p flutter on Paula Yates (10-to-1) and Ron 'Chopper' Harris (50,000-to-1). Just our luck – we spotted Cliff Richard. He was 20,000-to-1, as well. But, ooh, he's ever so tall and good-looking in real life. Another time, we spotted the not-so-famous one off the Carling Black Label ads (2,000,000-to-1) trailing in his wake whole crowds of shoppers making scrambled cockpit noises, at that all-important respectful distance.

Crossing back through Covent Garden, I notice an all-new shift of street entertainers has taken the place of the old favourites. On the android's bench at the end of Floral Street are squatted three fresh-faced tribal drummers, all the way from exotic Amersham, plus a strawberry-faced down-and-out accompanying the trio on an empty Tennent's Super can.

When Covent Garden was first developed, The Strand had not long been more than a bandit-ridden cart-track linking the City of London with the Abbey and royal palaces at Westminster. The last time I saw it, it was crawling with trams, and indeed the Savoy Hotel, Simpson's and the Shell-Mex Building survive from the 1930s, along with the few smaller theatres pointing the way to the Garden. I love the art deco golden knight riding high over the Savoy's riveted stainless canopy. Above the level of the plastic shopfronts, stretches of the Strand have hardly changed in the last sixty years.

Not so Zimbabwe (formerly Rhodesia) House, on the corner of Agar Street, whose first-storey statuary offers a fascinating insight into the character of those black-and-white Londoners skipping between the trams. After a long battle of morals between public opinion, good sense and right-wing press baron Lord Rothermere, Jacob Epstein's beautiful series of figures, representing the Ages of Woman, were officially vandalised, smashed to smithereens to rid them of their offensive breasts and buttocks. When the statues first went on display, people would crowd over to the windows on the top deck of the trams for a glimpse of stony T&A. Having treated himself to a weekly tram-pass to study the offensive bodily parts at his leisure, the proprietor of the *Evening Standard* decided he was SHOCKED, APPALLED, OUTRAGED. Sadly, the MORALISING

CAVEMAN pulled too much power for the rest of humanity to tell him to mind his own business. Rothermere's dismembered women remain here to this day, providing a shocking warning of the dangers of listening to people who know what's good for you.

Around the same time, Epstein's statues of *Night* and *Day* were *un*officially vandalised at Frank Pick's London Transport HQ, at 55 Broadway. *Night*'s crime: more of that depraved nakedness business. As we all now know, the Lord would never have given us wobbly bits if he'd meant them to be gazed upon by reactionary dopes.

To the south of the Strand, on the slope down to the Embankment, are two adjoining clusters of magnificently immodest street names. First up are Adam Street, Robert Street, and John Adam Street, which mark the site of the Adelphi (Greek for 'brothers') housing development, built in the 1770s by – you guessed – the Adam brothers, John and Robert. Although the Adelphi was the Ideal Home showcase of its day, the houses sold slowly, and despite patronage from the likes of Thomas Hardy, George Bernard Shaw (author of *Pygmalion*, later rewritten as *My Fair Lady*) and David Garrick (actor and manager of the Theatre Royal, where he successfully revolutionised the art, if not the behaviour of its audiences). Adelphi Terrace still stands overlooking the river from the height of three storeys, built out from the street-level of the Strand. Only two of the original houses now survive, the best being at number 3 Robert Street, at the old corner of the development, which retains the subtle honeysuckle-patterned pilasters on its blackened brickwork. Most amazingly, a winding subterranean road leads into the foundations of the Adelphi from the adjoining street, York Terrace: each of the residential roads was built with a service road beneath, leading from the Embankment up to the Strand – and Lower Robert Street has somehow survived.

York Terrace, in turn, is built on the site of York House, the earlier, seventeenth-century residence of George Villiers, Duke of Buckingham. At the foot of Buckingham Street stands a weathered stone watergate which led from York House down to the Thames mudbanks – only now the river is *150 yards away*, on the other side of Embankment Gardens.

Reclaiming acres of land along four miles of the river may have saved London from flooding and cholera, lending it a trunk sewer, an Embankment highway, Tube line and promenade; but it left the poor old Adelphi and its neighbours high and dry.

Going back to George Villiers, he swanned sexily into London from sunny Leicestershire in the early 1600s, and quickly became the Court favourite of King James VI and I. It's now widely assumed there was a gay element to their relationship: a canny short-cut to having a whole corner of London named after you. But, as ever, there was a price to pay. When the old charmer later gained the ear – if nothing else – of James's son, Charles I, his influence in Court grew out of hand, and he was horribly murdered. In the immediate vicinity of Buckingham Street once lay George Street, Villiers Street, Duke Street and the absurd Of Alley . . . Of these, Duke Street has long gone missing in action, a George Court survives, but most scandalously, some LCC penpusher was allowed to standardise the unique Of Alley to York Place.

Today, just down the incline of Villiers Street from 'Formerly Of Alley', an ice-cube truck is making its deliveries to the pre-theatre special menu restaurants, watched longingly by a couple of overheated chefs hanging out of a window in the brick bluff flank of Charing Cross Station. Ducking into the cool of the vaulted brick tunnel which passes right underneath the station, I find concealed in one arch the entrance to the minute Players' Theatre, best known for its run of *The Boy Friend*, which catapulted Julie Andrews to stardom, and emerged in 1971 as a Ken Russell film, starring not an actress, but Twiggy.

Just as *Miss Saigon*, the Royal Opera and Ballet were overshadowed by a flying apple core, so the English National Opera, plus the six or seven Webber pantos being staged within spitting distance of St Martin's Lane, are trumped by Stringfellow's Cabaret of Angels – an entertainment which manages to be at once reassuringly expensive and deliciously cheap. On Friday, Saturday and Sunday nights, Stringfellow's reverts to a 'classic club', with a restaurant, cocktail bar and optional smooching alongside suspiciously hyperactive soap-stars from the recent past. During the week, those same old men are given the chance to pay beautiful young women to fawn and spill over them. Proudly displayed in the club's window are paparazzi-style snaps of London's foremost movers and shakers, surrounded with jammy-faced movers and shakers, sloshing over the front of their basques. Terry Major-Ball is here. Richard Branson. Michael Barrymore, looking lost. Assorted EastEnders. Sundry British boxers, apparently keen to snap up their one-way tickets to Palookaville. And right in the middle of his collage of stockings and suspenders, it's London's own King of the Middle-Aged Reprobates: Peter Stringfellow. If only I could rustle up a tux and a feather-cut wig with a ponytail, I could pay one of Benny Hill's real-life seaside-postcard Page Three luvverlies to pretend to fancy *me*.

Blimey, I wonder if it's St Trinian's or Lingerie Night, tonight?

The back room of The Salisbury pub on St Martin's Lane was the preferred '60s drinking-den of a group of actors that included Peter O'Toole, Richard Harris, Terence Stamp and Albert Finney, who used to let Stamp's bit-part flatmate Michael Caine come, too. It's an ideal room for actors to meet in, being mirrored across all four walls. Nowhere else in all Theatreland can surpass The Salisbury's sensationally overplayed glitz and glamour. A stagy crowd is still drawn to the gilt-and-jewelled limelight, but the days are sadly past when actors would deign to appear amongst their public, to be so studiously, so luvvingly ignored. The sparkling fussiness of the interior – all brass fittings, cut-glass mirrors and Art Nouveau lamps – held less happy memories for closet gay barrister Dirk Bogarde, cool on the trail of a homosexual-hounding blackmailer in *Victim*.

Cutting onto Charing Cross Road through Great Newport Street, I pass the high arched doorway of what used to be the Pickwick Club at number 16 – very much the Stringfellow's of its day, except it was wildly happening, and dead with-it. The members' list included Noel Coward, Roger Moore, Burt Bacharach and Brigitte Bardot; but, strangely, no Terry Major-Ball. Stamp and Caine were regulars, but they used to sit at the bar to save cash. Tables cost money, and as for food, best not eat on an empty stomach, eh? When I finally make it into the restaurant at the top of the Post Office Tower, remind me to sit at the bar, instead of some velvety revolving alcove, because that's how Bond-producer Cubby Broccoli discovered Caine at the Pickwick: he was looking for some scruffy, downbeat no-hoper to play the part of Harry Palmer in *The Ipcress Files*, liked the look of what he saw, and the rest, as they say, is an apocryphal showbiz slice of after-dinner history.

Like so many stories involving London, or any top-drawer London superstar, I think the Caine-at-the-Pickwick myth might actually be devalued if it were proven to be true. Here are a few similar corkers, lifted direct from a primary source of almost-certainly-verifiable

London facts: Caine's own 'Almanac of Amazing Information', *Not Many People Know That!*

- 'The Duke of Wellington suggested that the Houses of Parliament be built on the banks of the River Thames, so that it could never be surrounded by an angry mob.' Not a lot of people know that! Primarily because it's not true.
- 'Karl Marx disapproved of Engels' mistress because she was *too common*'!
- 'The door to 10 Downing Street only opens from the inside'!
- 'William Shakespeare had *eleven* different ways of spelling his surname'!
- 'The Niagara Falls are switched off at night'!

Nothing to do with London, this last one – it's just one of those gobbets of information that makes you wonder how you ever managed to get by before you found it out.

In the subterranean bar beneath the Phoenix Theatre, I meet up with Lesley Wallace, Niall and Maria. I'm also pleased to make the acquaintance of Marcia and Edson, from Brazil: they're living, breathing proof of my theory of London as a mythmaking, golden-paved panacea; 'The City Where All Sorts Of Good Stuff Might Happen'.

It's a fledgling theory, okay?

Earlier this year, Marcia and Edson decided the spark had gone out of their relationship, so they booked a holiday. They knew everything would work out *if only they came to London* . . .

The Phoenix is the most atmospheric of all the West End theatre bars. Playbills are strewn over its walls, only the diffuse orange light glowing down from the gold-tiled ceiling makes it difficult to see any further than those enclosed in your own private partition. Decades' worth of old wine bottles and absurd theatrical relics are cluttered above eye-level – a pith helmet, a bust of Ye Barde, a biscuit-tin crown – but this is *collected* kibble, not a skipload of rubbish brought in by developers. Best of all are the painted screens and the strange DIY oil-paintings hanging unstrategically around the place: reclining nudes, lumpily out of perspective, and possibly the most startling nativity scene in art history, set some time circa 1961. As usual, the dungeon bar is buzzingly busy, but not with theatre-goers, who tend to head for the brighter lights above ground.

At the back of the bar is a curtained-off table in a candle-lit cubby-hole of its own. Ever since it was drawn to their attention, Edson and Marcia have had their eyes on 'The Bunker'. It's that old London magic, weaving its spell.

'*Si*,' says Marcia, 'we theenk eef our love can survive ze cold wezzer and ze traffic and ze 'ostility of ze beeg ceety, our love she weel leeve forever.'

Agatha Christie's *The Mousetrap* opened at the Ambassador's Theatre in 1952, moved down the road to the St Martin's Theatre in 1972, and just *keeps on running*. It's a world record run. It'll run forever. It's a quintessential London Theatre Experience if ever there was one – not a thriller at all, but a camped-up farce in the finest English tradition. I always wanted to see a play set in a drawing-room, with a stage-centre sofa and a French window. In the bar at half-time, we don't recognise a single name on any of the 11,000 playbills plastered over the walls. That said, tonight's cast boasts prestigious past credits in *Wife Begins at Forty* and *Up Pompeii!*, as well as the usual refugee from *The Bill*. Every London production is bound to employ, albeit usually some way down the cast-list, at least one actor who's been in *The Bill*. It's probably something to do with Equity, and a policy of positive discrimination. If you don't believe me, go ahead and check the cast-lists for yourself.

At the end of the panto, an important announcement unfurls down the safety curtain: so that *The Mousetrap* might run for another forty-seven years, and to avoid spoiling the enjoyment of any friends who might come along in the future . . .

WE ASK YOU TO PLEDGE SILENCE
AND NEVER REVEAL
IT WAS THE BUTLER WOT DUNNIT . . .

15 Old Father Thames,
Old Father Time, Inc.

Bing-bong bing-bong, bing-bong bing-bong.
Bing-bong bing-bong, bing-bong bing-bong . . .

Then that awkward, overlong pause when everyone looks at their watch; has time to wonder if there's a German spy gumming up the works; opens their mouth to . . .

Bong.

Big Ben chimes the hour.

It's one o'clock.

Obviously.

Time creaks back into motion. For'ard on the bridge, the skipper revs his foc'sle, splices his mainbrace, lets out the clutch, and we're off. We're floating. Reliving our nautical heritage.

Her Majesty's Pleasure Craft the *Royal Princess* is a long, handsome single-decker sloop. Only the most determined landlubber could mistake her for a barge on a booze cruise.

The captain is quick to set our minds at rest with a tannoy announcement about safety procedures – just in case a bridge jumps out in front of him, or he hits an iceberg. 'I don't wish to *alarm* any passenger,' he intones, 'but if any passenger *is* alarmed, may I draw their attention to the fully stocked bar to aft. That is, to the *rear* of the vessel . . .' His accent isn't yer typical cockernee oojimiflip; it's pure Officious Londoner, as performed by ex-Household Cavalry commissionaires and our very friendliest London Bobbies. The captain doesn't actually say, 'We shall be *pro*-ceeding in an easterly direction . . .', but you can tell he's sucking in his gut and wiggling his moustache.

Within seconds of setting sail, the skipper has scuppered my ideas about the Thames dredgers up ahead: he tells us they're putting a new roof on the Jubilee Line under the river. Fortunately, he doesn't start explaining *how*.

As I was hurrying along the gangplank at 12.59 p.m., the *Royal Princess*'s chief petty officer and bo'sun – a barmaid wearing a sailor's shirt – pressed into my hand a free glossy leaflet called *The Royal River Thames*. And jolly good it is, too – comprising a map of the river with numbered points of interest along the banks, and text in five languages, including English. The Mudlark and Scuffle Hunters Ferry Co. of Westminster Pier actually seems to *care*. I recognise some beautiful images of the cluttered, working river taken from the Museum of London, with literally hundreds of sailboats, ferries and galleons jostling for space on the city's first highway. The empty Thames is a wholly modern sight: only in the last thirty years has the closure of the docks left the open river almost entirely to pleasure boats, police launches and the odd floating skip. Dan Farson, who turns out to be a river-spotter as well as a Sohoite and Ripper-trapper, wrote of tugs pulling long, snaking strings of the London Docks' five thousand barges; of East European liners and French coasters; the royal yacht *Britannia*; of submarines, freighters, houseboats, hovercraft and home-made boats floating by. Nautically speaking, there has only been one small step forward to set against withering of river trade and river life: now around 95 per cent of boats on the river are licensed.

It's great to be out here in the middle of the sweet-smelling, muddy river, hanging out of the sunny window to watch the bridges go by, drinking in the sight of London from the one perspective that will never change. London is only *here* because of the river. Old buildings and new crowd shoulder to shoulder, others teeter on tiptoe for a river view in the stacked slope backing up from the sheer Embankment wall. In nine out of ten guides, it says you can 'only *really* see London from the river' – which isn't true, but it's just the sort of thing you want to read when you've just shelled out the best part of an Ayrton Senna on a 'Voyage Through History'. For full effect, they also say, London should only ever be approached by river. It's too late for that, but I'm hopeful the same goes for puttering out to Greenwich. I've never been out on the Thames before, but it immediately seems the most natural place to be. I hardly feel sick at all.

I don't know if it's anything to do with our glorious naval past, but there's something about water that still stirs the British blood. We paddle. We build piers. We fill our parks with boating lakes, and take our vestigial oarsmanship pretty bloody seriously. Personally, I've even been known to walk down to the river to watch the Boat

Race go by: a two-horse race between college kids, where the favourite always wins, and the losers only sink once every twenty years. What *is* it with us about water? About boats in the bath, and messing about on the river?

For the Queen's 1977 Silver Jubilee knees-up, she was driven in her diamond-encrusted state coach along the Strand to St Paul's; but later in the week she made an even more special symbolic splash with her triumphal passage down the river. The same principle was applied last year by the Queen's distant relative, Michael Jackson – the Prince of Pop – when he arranged for a thirty-foot effigy of himself to be hauled up the river by tugboat. The banks of the river were solid with fans in awe of the image, pointing and laughing. Best of all was when Jacko subsequently demanded the press respect his right to privacy and a normal life.

The Thames bore the funeral processions of Elizabeth I, Nelson and Churchill. But it isn't only royalty who are free to tap into the power of the river. One of the most disturbing evenings in London's recent history came on Jubilee night 1977, just two days before the Queen's regal float-past, when the Sex Pistols hired the *Queen Elizabeth* pleasure-cruiser from Charing Cross pier, festooned it with Union Jack bunting, and proceeded to shoot off a twin-guitar, sneering salvo midstream. Police intervened. Harsh lessons were administered.

Meanwhile, the Pistols' 'God Save the Queen' single was ready for release. The Jubilee edition of the *People* had already carried a picture of Jamie Reid's safety-pinned Queenie cover, with the caption 'Punk Rock's own *nasty* little bit of Jubilee fun'. An angry spokesman for the Silver Jubilee Appeal said, 'Every citizen must be hopping mad.' PUNISH THE PUNKS, the *Sunday Mirror* chipped in. The BBC banned the offensive disc – so, predictably, it rose to number one by the end of Jubilee week. Only the swift action of the British Market Research Bureau averted a national crisis: they took it upon themselves to juggle the chart and pretend Rod 'the Mod' Stewart's smashingly wholesome 'I Don't Wanna Talk About It' was top of the pops. A constitutional crisis was narrowly averted.

No thanks to that darn river.

Out on the river, you're subject to different, ancient laws: there are no petty rules about keeping left or keeping right. There are no speed limits. The captain will be keeping his eyes open for dead bodies: he can claim seven shillings and sixpence if he fishes out a corpse on the south side of the river, sixpence on the north. Needless to say on which bank the captain will be depositing any unfortunate floater today. Meanwhile, he can keep his eyes off any choice rafts of driftwood, which rightfully belong to the Queen.

While it's true to say I don't know the difference between flotsam and jetsam, and have never before chugged up the middle of the river, I have bobbed about a bit in the shallows off Charing Cross Pier. In fact, on board the pub-boat *Tattershall Castle*, I once experienced a defining London Moment that was almost on a personal par with the Sex Pistols' boat trip. Three years ago, shortly after stand-up comedy and just before poncho-crocheting, poetry was mistakenly hailed as 'the new rock 'n' roll'. And so, for a little over twenty seconds, I became a 'new rock 'n' roll' poet. London's contagious Wannabe Fever again held me briefly in its grip. In the disco-hold of the *Tattershall Castle*, I read out a rib-tickling ode about the probable contents of the audience's pockets. All six were unimpressed and I was forced into early retirement. I still believe my career might have taken off if only I'd thought of a rhyme – if only there *were* a rhyme – for 'Durex Arousers', at the end of the second line.

When the cycle of 'new rock 'n' roll' fashions once again swishes past bad poetry in a couple of years time, a single moment's inspiration could still provide grounds enough for a pointless and humiliating comeback.

The skipper, it transpires, is quite a joker: 'We are now passing under Waterloo Bridge, constructed during the war years by female labour. That's why Londoners call it "the Ladies' Bridge" . . . *although they do say there was a man in charge.*' And, not content with rubbing my nose in the dredger mud, he's now doing his best to unravel my image of the South Bank. A month after I paid my last respects, there's no denying that Bankside Power Station is still standing. How embarrassing. Apparently, they're leaving the monstrous chimney-stack more-or-less untouched, and are only demolishing sections of the front wall. The power station's innards are still undergoing their agonising surgical removal – not to create the world's biggest bedsit but, the skipper informs us, a new extension of the Tate Gallery.

Having left behind Westminster for the City, we soon pass the point destined to be spanned by London's first new bridge in living memory: the Millennium Bridge. The idea is to create a direct footway linking St Paul's with the Globe Theatre on the Bankside, saving tourists the pain of having to walk through Borough Market, past my dilapidated warehouses and the Brothelkeeper of Winchester's forgotten rose window, and being forced to look at any part of the city that is neither freshly steam-scoured nor featured on one of the top five best-selling London bum-bags.

London Bridge itself always comes as something of a letdown – it's just a plain concrete plank thrown down lovelessly between the two banks. But if we're talking disappointments, consider for one minute the good citizens of Lake Havasu City, Nevada, USA, on whose behalf the fast-sinking, Georgian London Bridge was snapped up in the '60s for a cool £2.4 million – on the assumption that they were getting Tower Bridge.

You mean there's, like, a *difference*?

Ever since Roman times a bridge has crossed the Thames at this point, the first stone-arched span of 1176 lasting a good deal longer than any of its wooden predecessors – right up until 1831. The river guidebook includes a famous Dutch-school painting of London from before the Great Fire, in which the bridge's twenty tight arches can be seen inching across a row of paddle-shaped piers. Rickety wooden shops, houses and taverns grew up along the sides of the bridge, overhanging the stream at the rear, where they were supported by struts. After a couple of hundred years, successive extensions up and out from the buildings' original frontages virtually enclosed sections of the bridge. Also visible in the painting is the northern gate-tower, on which severed heads from the Tower, first boiled and dipped in tar, are spiked as a deterrent against crime – and probably appetite, too.

In order to support the weight, the bridge's nineteen stepping-stones were built too close together, so steering any boat between the piers was akin to shooting white-water rapids, and totally dependent on the tide. It was common for passengers who valued their lives to disembark on the bank, walk around London Bridge and catch another boat on the other side. No such problems today. We hope. And little chance this winter of a Frost Fair on the frozen surface of the river, once a regular treat – if once per lifetime can be called 'regular' – due to the damming effect of the medieval bridge. Whole streets of market stalls and amusements were dragged out onto the ice, with icebound bull-baiting and horse-racing always a draw. A printing press was set up midriver in 1693. In 1716 an ox was roasted whole, and somehow failed to disappear down a large, steaming hole in the ice. The last time the Thames froze, in the winter of 1813–14, a quick thaw saw icebergs floating away with stalls, swings and ice-football players still on board. The referee was forced to abandon the game.

As the first solid obstacle on the river, London Bridge has long dictated the reach of seagoing ships into the city. Historically, the few legal quays were found on the northern shore of the Pool of London, between the Bridge and the Tower. With the larger ships regularly taking three or four weeks to be unloaded on the eighteenth-century river, the opening of new docks east of the Tower came as a great relief to the shipping companies and the log-jammed river. Which left only the Thames watermen, the lighter-men, the City porters, and the proprietors of the private wharves cursing the loss of their cushy monopolies, and their free first pick from the cargoes.

The battleship HMS *Belfast* proves a much more fearsome sight when viewed from the deck of a boat that barely comes up to its waterline. I'm glad it isn't angry today. Anchored midstream, alongside the *Belfast*, is the *Minerva*, registered in Nassau, which a maritime expert would call a cargo ship in the Very Big class. Enjoying a crafty fag-break out on the fire-escape hanging thirty feet – halfway – up the ship's hull, are a posse of oriental crewmen. We exchange happy waves, like sailors do.

It's a shame there's no need for the drawbridge bastules to be wound phallically upright when the *Royal Princess* passes under Tower Bridge: we're denied the chance of seeing John 'Brannigan' Wayne shooting over the chasm in his cop-car, cornering the villains, saving the girl and ensuring the future of little old England. But now we've entered East End waters – where the history of law enforcement leaves even The Duke looking like some wimpy pinko advocate of talking first and lynching later. Near the dead-end entrance to the original London Docks in Wapping is the headquarters of the Thames river police, descendants of the forma-tive force charged with the task of saving some proportion of the West India Company's booty from acquisitive locals, using cutlasses and blunderbusses.

'They soon fought back against the smugglers, the thieves and river pirates,' says the skipper. 'There are only a few of us left now. Only joking!'

From out on the river, it's possible to see the white tablet marked 'E' for Execution Dock, on the gable-end of a Georgian wharf. As well as getting the full hanging and triple tide-washing treatment, the body of the notorious pirate-catcher-turned-pirate, Captain Kidd, was left dangling here in an iron cage in 1701. Quite a deterrent, you might think; yet thousands more would share his fate on this shallow beach by the Town of Ramsgate pub.

In the middle of last century there were no less than thirty-six waterfront taverns on Wapping High Street and Wapping Wall alone. Now there are three or four. River pubs used to be ten a penny. Yet, if folk history is to believed, every surviving pub between here and Southend was once Charles Dickens' extra-special local, chalking up a cunningly disguised mention in *Zebediah Spunkthrift* – plus perm any three from the following four celebrity clients: Sam Pepys, Jonathan Swift, Dr Dictionary, and gangland boss Bob Hoskins getting blown to Kingdom Come in *The Long Good Friday*. On second thoughts, maybe that last one only applies to The Angel, Rotherhithe, over on the south bank.

Also on the crest of Rotherhithe's southern mudbank sits The Mayflower pub. 'If there are any *Americans* on board,' the skipper recites, 'you might like to *pay attention* at this point. This is *part of your heritage* . . .' Before the *Mayflower* set sail for Plymouth and America from London, the crew wisely spent their final week esconced in the snug-bar here, topping up for the dread months they had to spend in the company of a group of finger-wagging teetotallers.

Now the river widens, and disused wharves become commonplace among the freshly spruced balconies and window-boxes which enjoy a river view, but no more intimate relationship with the fast-flowing Thames. Any picture of the working river wouldn't be complete without the squat framework silhouettes of the cranes lining the busiest docks in the world; without the Chinese sailors crowding to Fu Manchu's opium and gambling dens in Limehouse; without the chilling boom of foghorns and mobile phone jingles echoing over the surface of the water.

As the tallest building in Britain at eight hundred feet, it's odd how Canary Wharf rarely fails to underwhelm. Its proportions are all wrong: it's too fat to be a proper tall building. The impact of more successful show-off skyscapers lies not just in their height but in their ability to soar; to appear wonderfully unstable, balancing precariously on one stiletto-tip. People yearn to lean over the edge of the Post Office Tower's viewing rail and feel the thrill of standing in space on the end of a giant pencil. Tall buildings should be terrifying. If the Post Office Tower were ever hit by an earthquake, it would snap near the bottom and crash spectacularly across Bloomsbury. Canary Wharf would merely *crumple* – propped in place by its claque of lesser unimportant office blocks.

As we putter around the U-bend of the river, the theme-tune from *EastEnders* pops magically into the mind of everyone looking at the map in the guidebook. Because we seem to be making no ground in relation to Canary Wharf, centred in the 'U' of the Isle of Dogs, it's as if time has gone into a nightmarish loop. The seventeenth time the tune draws to a close with a patter of imaginary syn-drums, I realise that it's *true*. Anita Dobson was *right*. Anyone *can* fall in love – see?

Never mind Donovan in Sunny South Kensington *trip out flip out* – I haven't faced a knee-jerk whistling problem like this since my first trip to Madame Tussaud's and the dreaded 'Baker Stree*aaaaaaaaaaaaaaaaaaaa* . . .'

It's the ultimate London soundtrack medley.

While we've been going round in circles, I've worked out my primary objection to Canary Wharf City. It isn't just the airport quality of the place, which makes it an unlikely place to visit and an even less likely place to linger: see the workers flow out of their distorted cubes and straight onto their toy railway for a sherbet in a *real* bar. It isn't the awful absence of diversity: I'd never have believed offices and tie shops could make you long for the sight of a brick or a bakery, let alone a patch of mud, or a *church*. I shouldn't think it's too rewarding, either, living on the Isle of Dogs, working as a security guard or a cleaner in the new city, while your windows are overshadowed by high-lifers' hexagonal heli-pads. No – personally, I can't stand Canary Wharf because it fails the King Kong Test. If they ever remade *King Kong* using London instead of New York, they wouldn't want to shoot the climax on this soulless totem – it's too fat and smooth for the big boy to get a proper grip. No one would care if he trashed the place. Capped off with the conceit of an inane neon pyramid, Canary Wharf means so very little to man or man-in-gorilla-suit.

The West India Docks, cut in the 1800s, made a real island out of the Isle of Dogs, protecting the safety of the rum, bananas and sugar flooding into the docks. Over the river at the Greenland Docks, they didn't bother making an artificial island, assuming guards would notice any light-fingered docker sidling out of the main gate with a whale under his tightish tunic. This western side of the Isle of Dogs was famous for its shipyards, the most ambitious project ever undertaken being Isambard Kingdom Brunel's ill-fated *Great Eastern*, at seven hundred feet four times the length of any other steamship afloat when it was launched in the 1850s. Unfortunately, it was so huge it had to be launched sideways down a slipway that is still visible at low tide, and it stuck fast in the Thames mud. A year later they tried again, more successfully, but the ship only ever made twenty trips to America. At the end of its fated life, when the 23,000 tons of metal were broken up for scrap, skeletons of Millwall shipyard workers were found trapped behind the thick plates – riveters who had painted themselves into the ultimate corner, so to speak.

Just short of Deptford, the Royal Docks were the home of Henry VIII's navy. Elizabeth I knighted Francis Drake on board his *Golden Hind*, for the part he played against the Spanish Armada, and as the first Englishman to circumnavigate the globe. Captain Cook set out on his voyages of discovery from these very docks. It almost makes you feel like saluting, or signing up for the Queen's sixpence. But, just in time, it's land ahoy!

Up ahead is Greenwich, its riverfront dominated by the columns and domes of Wren's Royal Naval College, by the naked rigging of the *Cutty Sark*, and the messy wooden pier strung between the two, dipping a speculative toe into the briny from the safety of the bank. Behind the town is the green and gold-tinted backdrop of Greenwich Park, capped by the follyish dome and bright red time-ball atop the Royal Observatory. Because it's past one o'clock, the red ball has already made its sloth-like daily journey to the top of its pole, and has fallen to signal standard time to the riverful of waiting ships' captains.

Our own skipper hopes we've enjoyed our time on board the *Royal Princess* – and explains that he'd *hate* to *deprive* us of an *opportunity* to *show appreciation* for his tannoy performance. 'Welcome to Greenwich,' he signs off, '. . . where all time starts and finishes in the western world.'

Better have a look at that, then.

In its day, the *Cutty Sark* was the fastest ship on the seven seas, although it has been forced to slow down in recent years, being marooned in a dry dock by the domed entrance to Greenwich Foot Tunnel. Over seventy years, up until 1938, it shifted 1.3 million pounds of tea on its successive four-month return trips to China. Because there are flights of concrete steps leading down into the deep dock, I go down for a poke about, come over all claustrophobic, and return to ground level in three-step bounds. It's scary down there under the overhang of the smirking topless figurehead on the prow, and the ballooning, aquadynamic copper hull sweeping up from the knife-edge bow. What if the dock had sprung a leak? What, then? And I didn't even stop to think about rats . . . Scarier still, the other boat on the Greenwich front is the *Gipsy Moth IV*, a yacht the size of a milk-bottle, sailed singlehandedly around the world by Sir Francis Chichester – aged sixty-six. It's not for the faint-hearted, this maritime lark.

Far safer than anything capable of floating either now or in the distant past is Greenwich town centre. Large tracts of land are under development, heralding the extension south of the river of the Docklands Light Railway, but Greenwich still looks like Noddyland compared to vertical London. Posters everywhere proclaim THE MILLENNIUM STARTS HERE. There's going to be a killing to be made, soon. Building-sites, dodgy slogans and rocketing local business rates are the first signs of the imminent arrival of the big three zeros. Opposite the Millennium Café is the kind of gift-shop I find irresistible: Here's London is stocked up in good time with Millennium-brand Greenwich tea, with London bus BEST OF BRITISH moneyboxes and red telephone-box teapots. They're not so big on displaying prices at Here's London, but the BEER LONDON ALE L.E. bar-towel props are £2.25 each. A model of the Houses of Parliament – or rather what some spectacularly misguided Taiwanese infant *imagines* the Houses of Parliament might look like – plus an indeterminate bridge cut off in space, all encapsulated in a half-pint snowstorm – may well see some change from a dickie diver. There are no cash-in Princess Diana souvenirs on sale. I don't know if that's because they've been removed from display, or because they're all sold out.

Greenwich's cobbled covered market of 1831 (oh, *no* – it's not Georgian and it's not Victorian!) harbours not only a tempting, shady pub, but a bargain CD shop and a bookshop well stocked with Londoniana in a narrow, adjoining alley. One bookshop leads to another in a small town like Greenwich. And when I'm sidetracked for the fourth and final time, I'm repaid handsome dividends. I can hardly believe my luck when I see the lurid lime-green spine blinking from the shelves, and when I pull out *The Sordid Side of London Town*, I know I'm onto a winner. I'm holding the key to my wildest afternoon's day-tripping this summer. Ask Norman Nash.

The cover features a basic line drawing of a bloke in a V-neck jumper and tie, holding a sherry glass – ONE SIDE RESERVED AND STEEPED IN TRADITION – while, squirming in the background, belly-down and bottom-up, on a pink-and-yellow leopardskin Brick Lane rug is *a girl wearing pants* – THE OTHER A CARNIVAL FOR THE DEBAUCHED AND CORRUPT . . .

I snap up another rare copy of *Nairn's London*, too, because it's only two pounds, and I'm sure I'll be able to find it a happy home.

From the top of the hill, there's a famous view of hazy London over the National Maritime Museum and the Queen's House, the Royal Naval College and the river. Canary Wharf squats in the middle-distance, too.

'It's not so high, is it?' one middle-aged tripper comments to me, presumably because his wife gave up listening years ago. 'No need for oxygen masks – it's only two or three hundred feet.'

Stretching to the right, away behind the disused power station, the gasometers and industrial debris of former-docklands, lies North Greenwich peninsula, the contaminated waste site designated for reclamation, redevelopment and world celebrity as home of the Millennium Exhibition.

'It looks better from a distance, this view,' says the tripper. Irrefutably.

Everyone up on the hill today has had their photo taken standing astride the prime meridian line, which extends from the front of the Observatory and through the centre of its courtyard, then – more importantly for the army of videoers and snappers – through the outer wall, over a sloping path with *free* access, and away around the world (from up here, you can confirm it gets as far as Chingford). The idea is, you have to stand with one foot in the western hemisphere and one foot in the eastern, preferably with the large red papier-mâché time-signal in the background, and the next person in the patient queue lurking very nearly out of shot.

According to an atomic clock showing ten-billionths of a second, it's *approximately* 978 days till the final second of 1999 comes storming across the North Sea, with everyone in Britain waiting for it to pass over this worn bronze strip set in the tarmac.

The Royal Observatory, designed by Christopher Wren on his half-day off, was first manned by John Flamsteed in 1675. His twin tasks were to map the stars and to solve the longitude problem, a navigational nightmare which had plagued ship's captains ever since the first one was swept away over the edge of the earth. By using a sextant and plotting against the stars, it was always possible to tell how far from the equator you were sailing; but no east-west, lateral co-ordinate existed to help tell the difference between, say, the Bering Straits and the Serpentine boating-lake. A prize fund of £20,000 was established for anyone who could unravel the problem; but only after ninety years of feverish, often farcical, failure was it claimed by John Harrison, a Derby watchmaker.

A series of push-button displays and antique timepieces makes the concept easy to understand, and it's marginally more fun than the mock-up of Flamsteed's living-room. Listen. When it's twelve o'clock midday in London, it's twelve o'clock midnight on the other side of the world. It's something to do with time-zones: if you know what time it is in London, and you can work out what time it is in the Indian Ocean, then you can work out how far around the world you've travelled. I don't *quite* understand how it's done; but I'm more than willing to accept that it's possible. They wouldn't have just given away that prize-money, willy-nilly – £20,000 was a lot of lolly in 1763. But a small price to pay for global naval supremacy.

Thanks to Harrison's accurate seagoing clock and the standardisation of Greenwich mean-time, Britannia was able to set sail and really Rule those Waves – largely by dint of knowing exactly *which* waves she was bossing and bullying.

But hold on. I think they've gone and told us *too much* . . .

Now Greenwich's millennium catchphrase has begun to seep into public consciousness, it seems almost churlish to note that at the moment THE MILLENNIUM STARTS HERE, it will already have been 2000 for twelve hours on the other side of the earth, in New Zealand. Didn't Greenwich turn down its chance to be 'where time starts and finishes' a long, long time ago, choosing not to be the first and last place on the planet, but slap bang at its centre? Now it's changed its mind to fit the bill, hoping no one will notice.

More likely no one will care: the millennium party at Greenwich will still involve a big clock, an even bigger dome, and a monumental hangover.

As much as I enjoy climbing through the Observatory for a peek at the brass telescope set up in the dome, my favourite few minutes are spent at what is little more than a sideshow in the great millennial theme-park. The camera obscura is housed in a separate brick block at the front of the Observatory compound, overlooking the steep drop down the hill and the criss-crossed, sloping paths of Greenwich Park. When I first brush aside the thick black curtains and step into the dark, it feels as dangerous as a palm-reading at some Dickensian fairground. In the centre of the small room is a round table, onto which is being beamed from above a perfect image of Greenwich and the serene park. After thirty seconds of groping and whispering apologies, I realise I'm alone. At first glance, the gently panning image seems to be tracking across a large still photograph; but down on the slopes a sunbather stirs. A car pulls up in front of the Maritime Museum. A man in a suit gets out and sets his alarm, hitching up his trousers, triple-checking his locks. He isn't one inch tall, on the camera obscura table, but I've got my eye on him. In reality, he must be half a mile away. He has *no idea*. I don't want to start sounding like 'Petronius', but this long-range prying is addictive – it's so much more satisfying, spying from this insulated den, than standing outside a length of iron railings and watching someone fiddling about in their trousers-pockets from ten yards. The mirrors and lenses up on the roof track automatically across the town, then back along the river as far as the millennium gasworks. Other Peeping Toms stumble in and out, but only the weird ones stay and point and giggle.

Luckily, ten of the National Maritime Museum's twelve galleries are closed for refurbishment, leaving the time I'd allotted for the whole shebang – the half-hour before closing time – to linger over Twentieth-Century Sea-Power and Nelson. As it happens, I get lost up a back staircase, find a short-cut direct to Nelson and miss out entirely on Twentieth-Century Sea-Power. Nelson's pretty good value, though.

From the time I stood in Trafalgar Square wondering what such a little man was doing up such a large column, I've happened across Nelson's tomb at St Paul's, his funeral effigy at Westminster Abbey, and his deathbed letter to Lady Hamilton at the British Museum. Now I get the chance to catch up with his bloody stockings and breeches, his waistcoat and jacket, complete with musket-hole drilled neatly beneath the right epaulette. It's the first time I've ever actually thought of Nelson as a person. So then what does he do? He only goes and dies on me.

> *Dear Emma,*
> *Appear to have stopped a slug, old girl.*
> *Should still be home in time for*

Just when his fleet was on the verge of beating the combined Spanish and French forces eighteen-nil, saving Britain from certain invasion, the fatal musket-wound was added to Nelson's already impressive long-term injury-list, and he died in his first mate's arms. It's a great human story, a tale that will bear retelling in another two hundred years; but it's no insult to say its relevance has waned somewhat ever since the navy stopped cruising all over to plunder, annexe and deal deserved spankings to ungrateful, godless foreigners – ever since modern Britons started taking out our world-beating frustrations on the snooker table, and on Tamagochi cyber-pets.

On the other hand . . . there's a computer animation of Nelson's *Victory* sidling up to the flagship of the Continental fleet and giving it a broadside blast; but the right-thinking Admiral didn't want to risk missing, and wasting cannonballs in the briny – so when the opposing gun-crews simultaneously lit the blue touch-paper and stood well back, they were literally just feet apart. It's a terrific image of courage and the desperation of war, even if it doesn't tell young boys much about getting in touch with their feminine side.

Ironically, perhaps, old Nelson has been least well served by the staunchest supporters of the Old British values. While it was just about understandable for First World War generals to wheel out the Nelson image while their men were drowning in the mud of the trenches, the shining example of 1815 sat less comfortably against the chilly mutual slaughter of the Falklands. As for the fleet paddling about the Gulf, lobbing Cruise Missiles into a chemical desert sand-storm . . . no.

In keeping with a new national mood, isn't it time Nelson was humanised instead of being left untouchable up his pole, gathering layers of historical pigeon-crap? Even the Maritime Museum manages to deal with Nelson, War and Power in a surprisingly caring-sharing way. As a counterbalance to marvelling at the PERSONAL BRAVERY and RESOLUTION AGAINST THE ODDS of ENGLAND'S PRIDE AND GLORY, isn't it refreshing, a *relief*, to acknowledge the littlest-known of Michael Caine's little-known facts: Nelson never did get over his seasickness.

I take a detour along by the pier to walk the riverside footpath in front of the black Naval College railings. Up until the '70s, the Five-Foot Walk was completely covered at high tide, which must have been great fun for the Jolly Jack Tars, who presumably didn't share my petty, irrational fear of being drowned. The great, colonnaded blocks of the College, squaring up to each other over wide lawns, open to the river, were originally designed as a spare palace for Charles II, but found a more practical use as a naval hospital. This was Nelson's last-but-one resting-place when his body was brought back from Trafalgar, and for years his crewmen filled the hospital. Up until recently, the navy's top brass were still trained here, although they, too, have now decamped to Dartmouth along with all the press-ganged conscripts, leaving the building's future uncertain. My mate Niall assures me there's an ancient nuclear reactor underneath the College, hampering its redevelopment – a secret relic from the Cold War. It might make a telling addition to Greenwich's millennium sightseeing rounds.

One night, after Niall had overindulged himself at one of the Trafalgar Tavern's Dickens-retro whitebait suppers, he found the Five-Foot Walk closed by roadworks, so he did the smart thing: he climbed the workmen's barriers and took a short-cut home through the Naval College grounds. Where he was held up by paramilitary guards with machine-guns. Or maybe it was pistols. And maybe it was a nuclear bunker. But, anyway, there's still a tangible whiff of old-style military order and overriding might about these severe classical façades.

Incidentally, only by chance did Wren's ranks of stone columns come face to face across the lawns: the original design was scrapped when Charles II demanded that there be a view of the river from the Queen's House. Built in 1616 by Inigo Jones, the Queen's House was a milestone in British architecture – our first classical structure, and the first to resemble a block of Wall's Viennetta ice-cream. It was the only part saved when the Tudor Palace of Placentia was torn down to make way for the new. Henry VIII and both his daughters, Mary and Elizabeth, were born at Greenwich. Right here. Where Walter Raleigh later earned a knighthood for throwing his cloak over a puddle for the grown-up Queen Lizzie.

Past the Trafalgar, past the Yacht Inn and the flag-fluttering rowing club, I push on along the Thames Path. The river slops thickly around the concrete supports of the power station pier, while its empty brick walls and severed chimneys await a prettifying fate. On Ballast Quay, I stop off for a pint at the Cutty Sark Tavern which, my *Alka-Seltzer Pub Guide* informs me, is furnished like the interior of a ship. Morris dancers appear here occasionally. Usually on Saturday mornings. Forewarned is forearmed. Built in 1795, there's really no need to log the fact that Charles Dickens is counted on the client-list: his last novel, *Our Mutual Friend*, was set around all of his favourite places in Greenwich, and he certainly didn't shirk his research when it came to alighting on a favourite pub. How cool of him then to transpose the names of all the places he inserted in his fiction, giving virtually every pub in London grounds for a claim to be the original Six Jolly Fellowship Porters.

Inside, the Cutty Sark is a *bit* like a ship, with black wooden beams patched across walls, a haphazardly flagged floor and exposed brickends. The chairs cut out of old oak barrels are suitably piratical. The upstairs bar is built on so many levels, the brickies and chippies must have been working from different plans; but they did get the delicate bow windows pointing out over the river.

Across the cobbled street, I sit out at one of the riverside tables. Looking up the northward meander of the river, there are rusty tubs and seagulls bobbing off the shored-up banks of industrial wasteland. Inland, there are warehouses and piles of cement, an empty gasometer and a chemical plant whose silver cooling pipes and chimneys are coiled and twisted like a euphonium. There's no sign of construction starting on the Millennium Dome, even though I read the first hundred-yard-long mast was all set to be piledriven into place this week. Alone along Lovell's Wharf, past the old

Harbourmaster's Office, the *Seacombe Trader* – registered in Belize, although Seacombe might be more realistic – is being loaded by crane, so every minute or so an echoing clanking ruptures the quiet. Then we're joined on the waterfront by a mixed group of a dozen student drinkers who bunch tightly around the two remaining tables, watching the blinding pink sun fall over the river, while they talk in low voices. About Princess Diana.

Since her tragic death, Diana has made the quantum leap from candidature for the crown of Miss London to the brink of acceptance as a new, modern national symbol. The basic requirements are strikingly similar for each; all you need is a supernatural ability to mean all things to all people. Suddenly, finally, Nelson and Churchill and a musclebound, salivating dog seem oddly irrelevant.

Given little choice, an investigative excuse and a nosey urge to listen in, I hear Lady Di described in hushed tones as a single mother, a wronged woman, a tortured bulimic, and the first royal to date a non-WASP. Naturally enough, such human, glowing references draw dissenters into the conversation. Personally, I'm just bursting to lean over and add 'style consultant to the first prince in a backwards baseball cap' – purely to give a bit of balance, you understand. The following minute's dialogue is noisier and higher pitched, concluding tetchily that Diana was a moderniser working in an antique profession. The royals' last hope and republicans' dream come true. She was hounded. She was a carer, a dabbler; a shy, manipulative innocent.

With a CV full of such extremes, it seems ingenuous to say Di's greatest ability was to appear bizarrely average. There's something in there for everyone to relate to, for whatever reason: the ideal, all-inclusive figurehead. Even the slow boys with big ideas have their emotional needs fulfilled; but when one of them unfolds a copy of *The Sun* from his back pocket, I switch off. I'm already bang up to date with the latest attempts to update the story, to patch together *what if*, and *why* . . .

While it's still light, I can't resist a dip into *The Sordid Side of London Town*. Just like the Lady Di conspiracy theorists' Secret Service supremacist drug-ring paparazzi hit-squads, there isn't exactly a surfeit of detail behind the sexy sound of the words themselves.

Of such is the stuff of mythology made.

In 1967, Norman Nash went in search of Swinging London, failed abjectly to find it, and proceeded to dash off a lurid exposé aimed squarely at the American traveller's market. Norman is almost certainly somewhere propping up a snug-bar at this very minute, offering insights into the saintly life and mysterious death of the Princess of Wales, whom he knew as if she were a close personal friend.

WANT A LITTLE ZIP IN YOUR TRIP? Norman nudge-nudge, wink-winks. 'It's easy if you know the "right" people who swing in the "wrong" places.' They'll take you to see:

A strip-tease club for homosexuals . . .

Blue films . . .

A secluded chapel complete with organ music, incense — and wild orgies!

None of which is especially debauched or corrupt, once you've taken into account the blurb-writer's licence for the bit he made up about the orgies. In truth, the closest Norman comes to a Conquest is when he drops in to check up on the teenage daughter of a friend. Her room-mate says one of them will probably end up sleeping on the sofa tonight. Norman thinks he's scored. But the room-mate was only hinting at the sordid and scandalous prospect of dragging her boyf home for a snog. And, even then, she was only saying it to wind up the prurient Mr Nash.

Norman writes a book which accidentally undermines the myths of Swinging London and a reserved, traditional Britain. A leopardskin rug is badly drawn on the cover — and both myths are propagated.

Believe what you want: ideas and expectations are everything. The Coolest City in the World. Millennium City. Cool Britannia. The DianaDome . . .

A few miles downriver at Woolwich, there's a park where Michelangelo Antonioni shot *Blow Up!* – one of the films that put Hip Young London on the map. David Hemmings plays a sexy young photographer (*not* David Bailey) in white jeans and an open-top sports car. He's rich, successful, irresistible to women, and rather confused.

He knows what he's seen, but he can't be sure.

Wanting to heighten the greenness of the park, Antonioni set on an army of volunteers to paint the trees, the grass and railings *hyper-green*. And even today, flakes of Antonioni's green paint can still be found on the park railings.

One day, I'll go and see it for myself.

I take the Greenwich Foot Tunnel, an eerie Victorian-tiled pipe under the Thames, to the Isle of Dogs. Clocking up Wren's own favourite view of his handiwork is easy: now for that first sighting of the Millennium Dome, and the future. Turning east, I follow the northward curve of the river past the Newcastle Drawdock, a long, slippery slope into the water right opposite Ballast Wharf and the Cutty Sark terrace.

The pub commanding the reverse view is the Waterman's Arms, which briefly came under the media spotlight in the '60s when Ripper-riverman Dan Farson – him again – attracted names like Shirley Bassey and Tom Jones to sing here, first alerting waves of squealing West End outsiders to the possibilities of the East. The pub was soon hailed as an 'in' place, where celebrity slummers, dressed down in jeans and headsquares, could be found 'relaxing' with dockers around the old joanna. It's Clint! Judy!! Groucho!!!

'POW!' shouted one *Sunday Mirror* centrespread. 'So this is what really goes on in our great FUSED capital.'

It's Mary Quant! Alan Bates!! Brian Epstein – the Fifth Beatle!!! The place was such an incredible star draw, a series of TV cabaret shows was shot on its stage, and at the bar.

It isn't only the Waterman's Arms whose stock has since deteriorated. Once again, I have to report the untimely death of one of London's irreplaceable characters no more than a month or two after I crossed his trail. Daniel Farson joins his old friend Jeffrey Bernard, unwell no longer, in a smart new drinking-den with attractively eternal opening hours.

For over a mile, new riverside developments afford only rare views of the river, then the road swings back to the open riverside at the drawbridge entrance to West India Docks. The water in the expanse of the dock is calm and empty, heading into jungle of office-space. I can't see anything that looks like a DianaDome strut on the peninsula over the river, although one day soon there will have risen a giant inverted saucer with a ring of hedgehog spikes. The design is by Richard Rogers, the man who turned the Lloyd's Building inside-out. Possibly the greatest living British architect. And it's going to be built to last – for an estimated twenty-five years. It's the modern equivalent of what Wren called 'building for eternity'.

Controversy is already raging about the projected contents of The Dome. Like the 1851 Great Exhibition and the 1951 Festival of Britain, the theme will have to be global love and neighbourly potential – with Britain coming out of it looking pretty darned chuffed with itself. The £800 million exhibition will need to have one eye on the past and one on the future. Hopefully, there'll be more on offer than a straight vote between *A Clockwork Orange*, *Things To Come* and *1984*. Personally, I'd be disappointed if there wasn't at least one model of SuperLondon City, with the Thames paved over and Hyde Park converted into a hexagonal spaceport: *forewarned is forearmed*. That's why only a fool would discount that awful, haunting MOMI image of the daleks trundling across Westminster Bridge.

THE GUN, it says on the fairing running along the front of the pub's flat roof. Ramshackle, stucco peeling in the ravages of the brackish river winds, it stands on its own at the end of Coldharbour. One side of the street is currently being rebuilt with new flats, although the southern terrace is still in place. On the poop-deck above the quartermaster's bulkhead (it could just be the toilet block) Union and Welsh flags are tugging at their mast. The dusk is grainy enough for the bar to glow pale orange through the open door.

The ceiling of the bar is covered with naval ships' flags, all signed and sagging from their drawing-pins. There's a piano on a tiny corner stage, with 10 x 8 publicity photos of the singers who have performed here. Five or six locals are in for an early pint. There's a toddler playing with beermats under the dartboard. So much for that flag being a tribute to the Princess of Wales: the landlord is Welsh.

I take my pint of Nelson and flick through the *Standard*, then have a browse at *Nairn's London* to add up everything I've missed and everything that's gone missing on the Isle of Dogs. And, shiver me timbers, The Gun itself warrants a mention! I know it doesn't sound like much, but it means more to me than missing the boat back to Westminster; more, even, than a fabulous sunset over Canary Wharf, which was far too corny to mention. Nairn reckons you've really mastered the topography of the East End if you ever manage to find your way to this backwater. He doesn't say if it counts if you're just wandering around, thinking of *King Kong* and *Flash Gordon*, and you just bump into it.

Through the back room, on the concrete patio overhanging the gunmetal river, the landlord proudly shows me the cranes that have started work on the Dome.

16 Fantastic London

All summer long I've been yearning to scale the Post Office Tower and revolve above London as my birthright. The possibility of substituting the NatWest Tower or Canary Wharf offered neither compensation nor consolation: they're just tall buildings. They don't have moving parts. They're the kind of buildings where, if you asked the right person politely enough, having dreamt up a far-fetched reason why you really needed to make it to the top, they'd probably, eventually, say yes.

The BT Stupid Enquiries Helpline is womanned by Debbie in Milton Keynes. Debbie sounds fresh and cheerful, saying she'll contact Special Events Group and ask them to give me a call; but not before she's let slip a line about quite fancying a trip up the Tower herself: 'Ooh yes, it's open to staff, family and friends . . .'

A week later, Special Events Group still haven't been in touch, so I ring Debbie again. Her freshness noticeably wavering at the awful capacity of man to cause disappointment, she gives me the SEG number to call myself.

SEG give me the number of the Press Office.

But the Press Office is merely concerned with leaking news of BT's good works and seamless efficiency to the business world. 'Sorry,' says PR Bloke, 'we only deal with British Telecom customers . . . Yes, I'm sure you *are* a British Telecom customer, but . . .'

Some weeks later, the Special Events Group categorically deny a policy of allowing staff, family or friends up the Tower for a celebratory corporate spin: 'Who told you that?'

Back at the Press Office, Uppity Paul says, 'Yeah, and anyway, the Tower was bombed, y'know. That's why we had to close it to the public.'

Early in the morning of 31 October 1971, a bomb exploded in the false ceiling of the gents on the thirty-first floor of the Post Office Tower. No one ever claimed responsibility. No one was injured. No major structural damage was caused, and two years later, restoration work was complete. The Tower-top restaurant – part of the Butlin's Group, no less – reopened and remained open to the public until 1980.

'Yeah, and *actually* it's called the *Telecom* Tower now,' Uppity Paul reminds me. 'It's been renamed.' Here is a man who has dedicated his life to keeping people away from the Post Office Tower. 'Look, it's a commercial building now. A *working* building. We've turned away a lot of people from here. We've said no to some *pretty big* film crews.'

Time to try the other number pressed into my hand as an afterthought by the Tower's subterranean security guard. The scribbled note, on a TV charity's 'Interesting Calls Sheet', simply says 'Mark Moth – Security'. The number is unavailable. So I ring the Stupid Enquiries Helpdesk and ask for Mr Moth's new number; but they refuse to give it to me as a matter of policy. So I wait thirty seconds, ring again, and get through to another operator, who gives me the number.

Mark Moth remains unavailable, but the Telecom Security department have let a potential troublemaker through their net: Dav is friendly and helpful. He says he'll check wiv upstairs and get back.

Thirty minutes later, it's 'Bad news for you, I'm afraid, Derek. *Ver Stick*, as we call it – vat's part of Customer Services, and as such is out of our jurisdiction, I'm sorry to say. Vere's no one allowed up in Ver Stick. It's being used all ver time fer fanctions, so vey can't 'ave people getting in ver way.'

Dav can't give me the number for Customer Services' Special Events Group, because it's an internal number 'and vey'd be snahed andah – sorry again, Del.' But he does take my address and post me off a Post Office Tower visitor's pack, bless his heart.

Earlier this year, Tony Benn MP turned up at the non-entrance at the foot of The Stick, and asked if he could drop in for old time's sake. 'No' was the essence of the security guard's reply – but spotting the BBC *Watchdog* camera-crew a couple of paces behind the erstwhile Member, his suspicions were aroused:

''Ere, you're that – wotsisname?'

Benn explained that, as Minister of Tall Buildings, it had been his pleasure to *open* the building *to the public* back in 1965. Tony Benn really is very good at irony. Stage-managed to stress the unfairness and inequality of the Post Office Tower's colonisation, it was a cheap political point, all right; but aren't they always the best kind? The security guard double-checked the pointless rigidity of his instructions on his mobile phone. Unfortunately, he probably got through to Uppity Paul's department, and was reminded of his prime directive to turn away anyone and everyone. *Especially* pretty big camera-crews.

I rang Tony Benn's office at the House of Commons, and spoke to his secretary, Sheila, who confirmed the splendid cheapness of the TV prank, and the unforgiveable crime being perpetrated against the past, when a privatised company was handed the rights to the grooviest view of London – and then they go and claim the *moral* high ground, too. As it turns out, a few days after the programme was broadcast, Benn received the expected cordial invitation to a corporate hospitality photo-opportunity with a bunch of BT executives in the 'Presentation Suite'. Perhaps understandably, he had better things to do.

And, no, Sheila didn't think the invitation was transferrable.

So I sent a letter saying I'd like to hire the business end of The Stick for a private function, just so I could say I'd got a snotty letter on PO Tower notepaper. I put all my mates with proper jobs on alert, hoping that the Undeserving Guardians of the Stick would be duty-bound to do their corporate clients one little favour to keep the wheels of industry oiled . . . And I sent a final, fawning letter to Ted Graham, BT's Chief of Press. And he didn't even have the courtesy to order Uppity Paul to stick a stamp on one of their standard reply-forms: 'Thank you for your enquiry, blah blah, now kindly piss off.'

The view from the top of the Tower is fantastic, and I'm not even talking about the one out of the window. I can't tear my eyes away from the scene set out a step or two below me, across the seething sunken dancefloor toward the central core of the circular, studded velvet bar. The BritPop bossa nova b.p.m. bad-boys in blazers and cravats. The red spotlights and mirror-ball sparkles. Iridescent cocktails. Strange bottled lagers. The sloshing formaldehyde tanks of Modern Art could almost have been deliberately commissioned to make the Hilton's upside-down slashes of green and mauve acrylic look distinctly cheap – even passé. It reminds me of a scene from the remade *Avengers* – played dead straight. It's like the final, missing scene from Gary Oldman's *Nil By Mouth*, where Kathy Burke and Ray Winstone kiss and make up. This is how Antonia Bird's *Face* – at last, another gangland picture with *slaaaags* and slappings and shooters – could have turned out, if the rogues had got away with the loot.

PLASTIC CATSUIT ALERT!?! My table-mounted Londonometer is tapping out party-streamers of ticker-tape.

NOEL, TONY AND CHERIE!?! it flashes. RON 'CHOPPER' HARRIS!?! DANGEROUS REALISM!?!

Showing a reading of 125, it fizzes and pops – IT-GIRL ALERT!?! – before blowing a transistor and dying with its final message on screen:

WHATEVER ONE OF THEM IS.

Up on the revolving three-yard rim of the dancefloor, diners are feasting on a set menu prepared with lavish love and gentleness by those chiefs of complementary cuisine from the Angus Steak House. Or should that be the *Aberdeen* Steak House? I knew the steak chains had premises at all the prime corners of London, but an outpost up The Stick was beyond my strangest dreams.

Through the flashing reflections in the three-inch-thick glass, I notice long, ragged spaces in the regular carpet-pattern of white lights below. From the top of London's light-sabre, perspective has flattened Regent's Park and Primrose Hill to black holes. By the time I refocus, I can see the dumpy white stud of Canary Wharf on the horizon, closely followed by the haphazardly lit tangle of the City.

Below our feet, The Stick is comprised of sixteen floors of transmitting apparatus and an eighteen-foot-per-second turbo-lift, still Europe's fastest method of descending six hundred feet without making a mess on the pavement. The next six floors of kettle-drum aerials and dishes are sucking up and spitting out signals belonging to all the domestic TV companies, terrestrial and extra-terrestrial, bouncing them from transmitters to satellites, rooftop aerials and artfully bent coathangers across Britain. We are at the hub, in the fattest part of The Stick. Around our heads, fifty TV channels, thousands of phone messages and screenfuls of computer data shoot off into the night on a microwave.

You could almost cook a steak in the sparking electricity. Maybe that's the reason not all of the Stick Club guests seem to have much of an appetite.

I was mostly right about the prawn cocktail, which is served not in a little metal dish, but New York-style, on a king-size divan of lettuce. The starter sees us safely past the searchlight-strafed beacons of St Paul's dome and Tower Bridge. My medium-rare rump is succulent, with mushrooms and more salad tossed in *gratis*, and peas and onion rings at a very reasonable increment. The Stick's house wine is Mateus rosé – yet further proof of London's Euro-transatlantic-global melting-pot culture, with British ingenuity even finding an earth-friendly use for the empty bottles, as candlesticks. The West End: every alleyway and square from which you've ever caught a glimpse of the sky-blue Tower is now picked out in streetlights below. Buckingham Palace, shadowy at the brink of its dark Gardens, and Hyde Park. The whole of north London, panned slowly by camera obscura. Red and white stripes of traffic. Thousands of electric-blue windows in every nameless skyscaper.

Only Lesley Wallace manages to battle through to the sweet tray, and a chocolate mountain of Black Forest gâteau. The river. Buckingham Palace. Canary Wharf. Coffee and After Eight mints.

Londonography

Martin Amis, *London Fields* (Jonathan Cape, 1989; Penguin, 1990)
David Backhouse, *Walks in Central London* (Brown-Eyed Sheep, 1997)
F.R. Banks, *Penguin Guide to London* (1971)
Josie Barnard, *London: the Woman's Travel Guide* (Virago Press, 1994)
Isobel Barnet and Ronald Searle, *Exploring London* (Ebury Press, 1965)
John Betjeman, Pennie Denton, ed., *Betjeman's London* (John Murray, 1988)
Roy Berkeley, *A Spy's London* (Leo Cooper, 1994)
Michael Caine, *Not Many People Know That!* (Robson Books, 1984)
Harold P. Clunn, *The Face of London* (Spring Books, 1970)
Katy Carter, *London and the Famous* (Frederick Muller Limited, 1982)
Sir Arthur Conan-Doyle, *The Penguin Complete Adventures of Sherlock Holmes*
    (1985)
Julie E. Cooper, ed., *Let's Go: London* (St Martin's Press, New York, 1995)
Robin Cross, *The Silver Lining: Britain in Colour 1945–1952* (Sidgwick and
    Jackson, 1985)
Robin Cross, *Curious London* (Pan, 1996)
Hunter Davies, *The Other Half* (William Heinemann, 1966; Panther, 1968)
Hunter Davies, *A Walk Round London's Parks* (Hamish Hamilton Ltd, 1983)
Hunter Davies, ed., *The New London Spy: a Discreet Guide to the City's Pleasures*
    (Anthony Blond Ltd, 1966)
Len Deighton, *The Ipcress File* (Hodder and Stoughton, 1964; Panther, 1974)
Len Deighton, *London Dossier* (Penguin, 1967)
Charles Dickens, *Oliver Twist* (Everyman, 1996)
Adam Diment, *The Dolly Dolly Spy* (Michael Joseph Ltd, 1967; Pan, 1968)
Anita Dobson, *My East End* (Pavilion Books, 1987)
James Dowsing, *TV London* (Sunrise Press, n. d.)
James Dowsing, *Showbiz London* (Sunrise Press, n. d.)
Nell Dunn, *Up the Junction* (MacGibbon & Kee, 1963; Pan, 1966)
Daniel Farson, *Limehouse Days* (Michael Joseph, 1991)
William J. Fishman, *The Streets of East London* (Duckworth, 1979)
Ian Fleming, *Moonraker* (Jonathan Cape 1955; Pan Books, 1961)
Geoffrey Fletcher, *The London Nobody Knows* (Hutchinson, 1962; Penguin, 1965)
Geoffrey Fletcher, *Geoffrey Fletcher's London* (Hutchinson, 1968; Penguin, 1970)
Gillian Freeman, *The Leather Boys* (Anthony Blond Ltd, 1961; NEL, 1973)
Arthur Frommer, *Europe on $10 a Day* (Arthur Frommer Inc., 1977)
Jonathon Green, *Days in the Life* (William Heinemann Ltd, 1988; Minerva, 1989)
Leon Griffiths, *Arthur Daley's Guide to Doing It Right* (Willow Books, 1985)
Fran Hazelton, *London's American Past* (Papermac, 1991)
Rob Humphreys, *London: The Rough Guide* (Rough Guides Ltd, 1997)
Harold F. Hutchinson, *Visitor's London* (London Transport, 1966)

Betty James, *London on £1 a Day* (Batsford Books, 1965)

Richard Jobson, *The Virgin Insider's Guide to London* (Virgin Books, 1993)

John Lahr, *Prick Up Your Ears* (Allen Lane, 1978; Penguin, 1980)

Colin MacInnes, *Absolute Beginners* (1959; Allison & Busby, 1980)

Joyce Marlow, *Kings and Queens of Britain* (St Michael, 1977)

Ian Nairn, *Nairn's London* (Penguin, 1967)

Norman Nash, *The Sordid Side of London Town* (Macfadden-Bartell, New York, 1967)

Bill Naughton, *Alfie* (MacGibbon & Kee, 1966; Panther, 1966)

Ian Norrie, *A Celebration of London* (Deutsch, 1984)

Loiuse Nicholson, *London: Louise Nicholson's Definitive Guide* (The Bodley Head, 1988)

George Orwell, *Down and Out in Paris and London* (Gollancz, 1933; Penguin, 1982)

D.C. Perkins, *Cockney Rhyming Slang* (Domino, 1995)

'Petronius', *London Unexpurgated* (New English Library, 1969)

David Piper, *The Companion Guide to London* (HarperCollins, 1992)

Michael Parkinson, *Best: An Intimate Biography* (Arrow, 1975)

Ted Polhemus, *Streetstyle* (Thames and Hudson, 1994)

H.E. Popham, *The Guide to London Taverns* (Claude Stacey Ltd, 1927)

V.S. Pritchett, *London Perceived* (Harvest Books, New York, 1962)

Jonathan Romney, and Adrian Wootton, eds., *Celluloid Jukebox: Popular Music and the Movies Since the '50s* (BFI, 1995)

Donald Rumbelow, *The Complete Jack the Ripper* (W.H. Allen, 1987; Penguin, 1988)

Nicholas Saunders, *Alternative London* (Nicholas Saunders, 1970, 1971, 1973)

Jon Savage, *England's Dreaming: Sex Pistols and Punk Rock* (Faber and Faber, 1991)

B. Webster Smith, ed., *The Wonderful Story of London* (Odhams, 1956)

R.M. Smith, ed., *Alka-Seltzer Guide to the Pubs of London* (Bayard, 1976)

Colin Sorenson, *London on Film: 100 Years of Filmmaking* (Museum of London, 1996)

Terry Venables and Gordon Williams, *Hazell and the Three-Card Trick* (Macmillan, 1975; Penguin, 1977)

Evelyn Waugh, *Scoop!* (Chapman & Hall, 1938; Penguin, 1988)

Virginia Woolf, *The London Scene* (Hogarth Press, n. d.)

Peter York, *Style Wars* (Sidgwick and Jackson, 1980)

AA Illustrated Guide to Britain (Drive Publications, 1971)

London A–Z (Geographers' A–Z Map Co. Ltd, 1995)

The New Insider's Guide to London (Macdonald and Jane's, 1975)

Nicholson London Streetfinder 1993